BATMAN
THE BLACK GLOVE

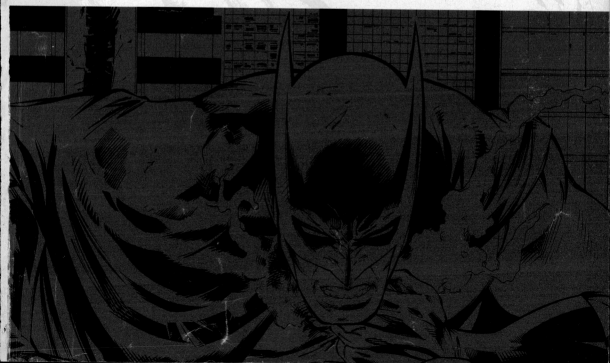

Dan DiDio Senior VP-Executive Editor **Mike Marts** Editor-original series **Jeanine Schaefer** Associate editor-original series **Bob Harras** Editor-collected edition

Robbin Brosterman Senior Art Director **Paul Levitz** President & Publisher **Georg Brewer** VP-Design & DC Direct Creative

Richard Bruning Senior VP-Creative Director **Patrick Caldon** Executive VP-Finance & Operations **Chris Caramalis** VP-Finance **John Cunningham** VP-Marketing

Terri Cunningham VP-Managing Editor **Alison Gill** VP-Manufacturing **David Hyde** VP-Publicity **Hank Kanalz** VP-General Manager, WildStorm **Jim Lee** Editorial Director-WildStorm

Paula Lowitt Senior VP-Business & Legal Affairs **MaryEllen McLaughlin** VP-Advertising & Custom Publishing **John Nee** Senior VP-Business Development

Gregory Noveck Senior VP-Creative Affairs **Sue Pohja** VP-Book Trade Sales **Steve Rotterdam** Senior VP-Sales & Marketing **Cheryl Rubin** Senior VP-Brand Management

Jeff Trojan VP-Business Development, DC Direct **Bob Wayne** VP-Sales

Cover by J.H. Williams III   Publication design by Amelia Grohman

BATMAN: THE BLACK GLOVE

BATMAN
THE BLACK GLOVE

GRANT MORRISON WRITER

J.H. WILLIAMS III   TONY S. DANIEL   RYAN BENJAMIN PENCILLERS

J.H. WILLIAMS III   TONY S. DANIEL   JONATHAN GLAPION   MARK IRWIN
SANDU FLOREA   SALEEM CRAWFORD INKERS

DAVE STEWART   GUY MAJOR COLORISTS

KEN LOPEZ   JOHN J. HILL   ROB LEIGH   RANDY GENTILE   STEVE WANDS   TRAVIS LANHAM   SAL CIPRIANO LETTERERS

BATMAN created by **Bob Kane**

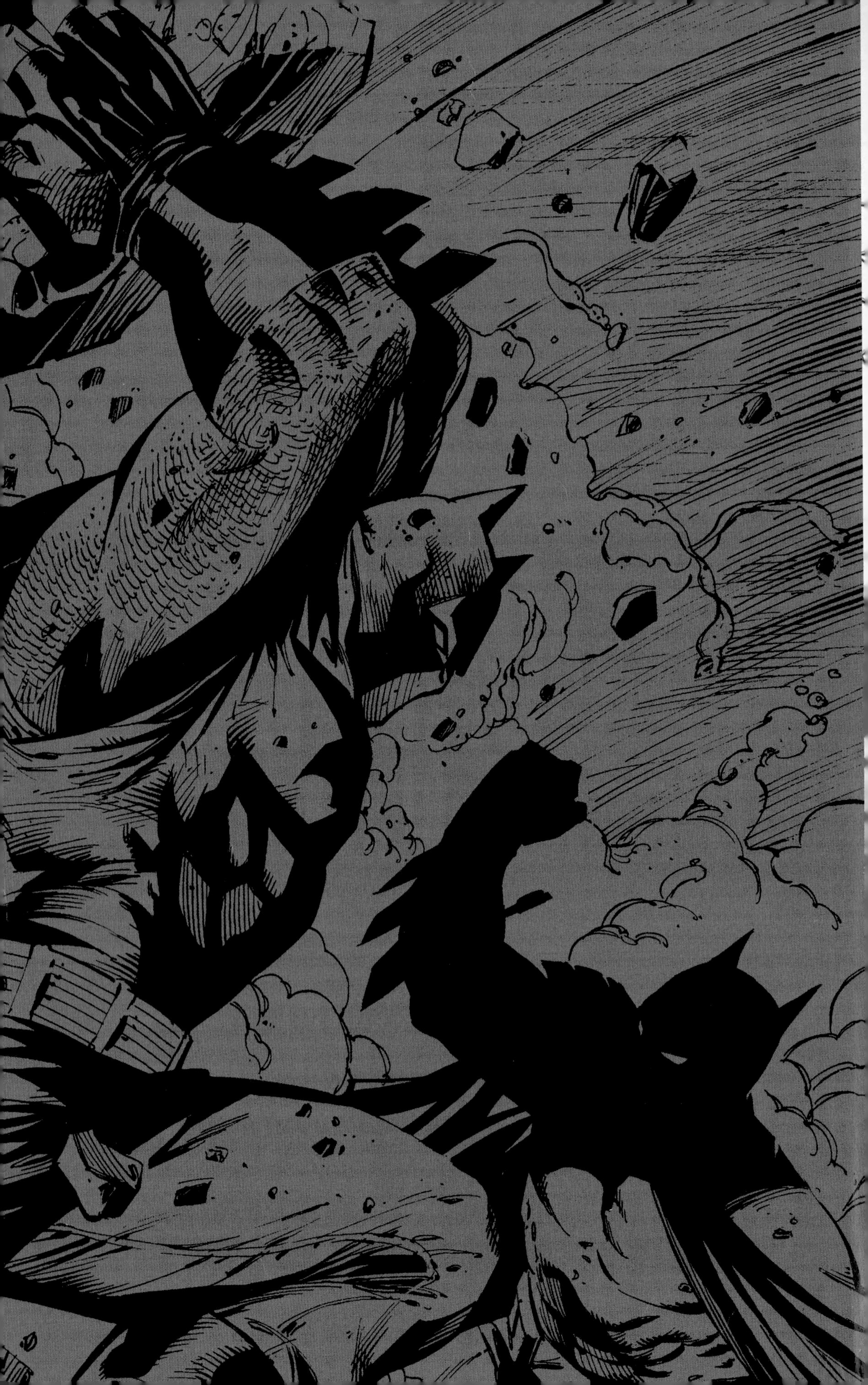

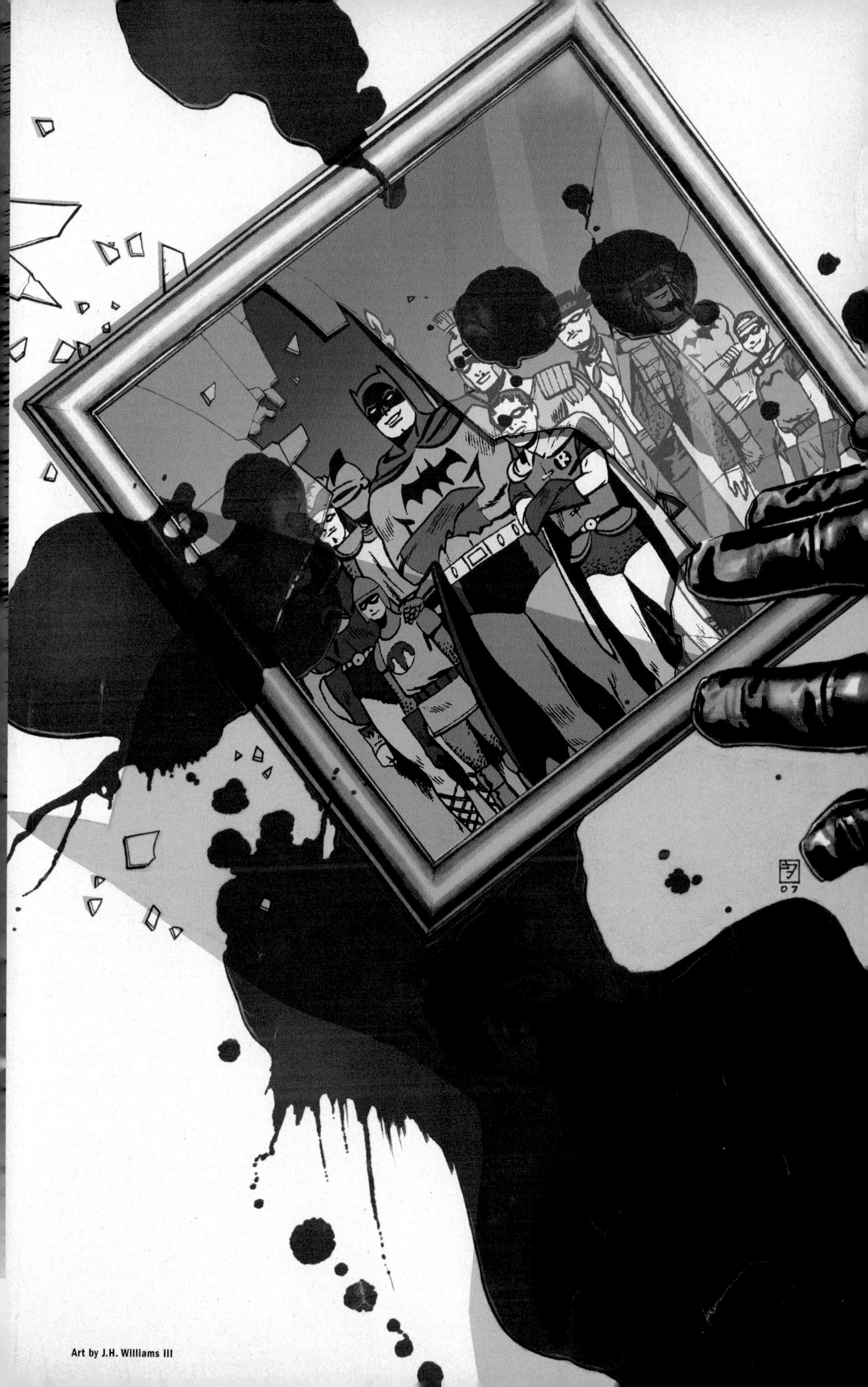

Art by J.H. Williams III

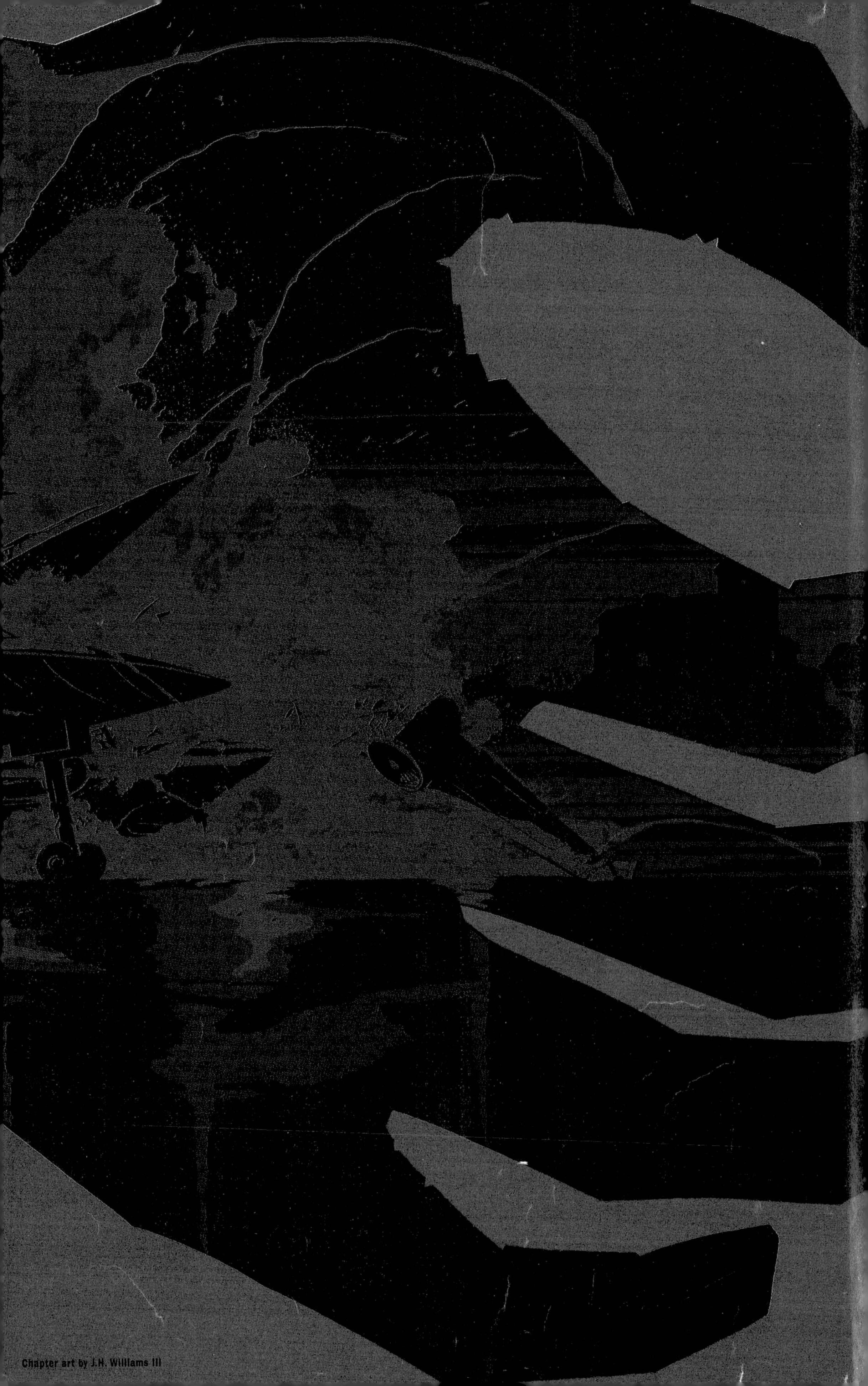

Chapter art by J.H. Williams III

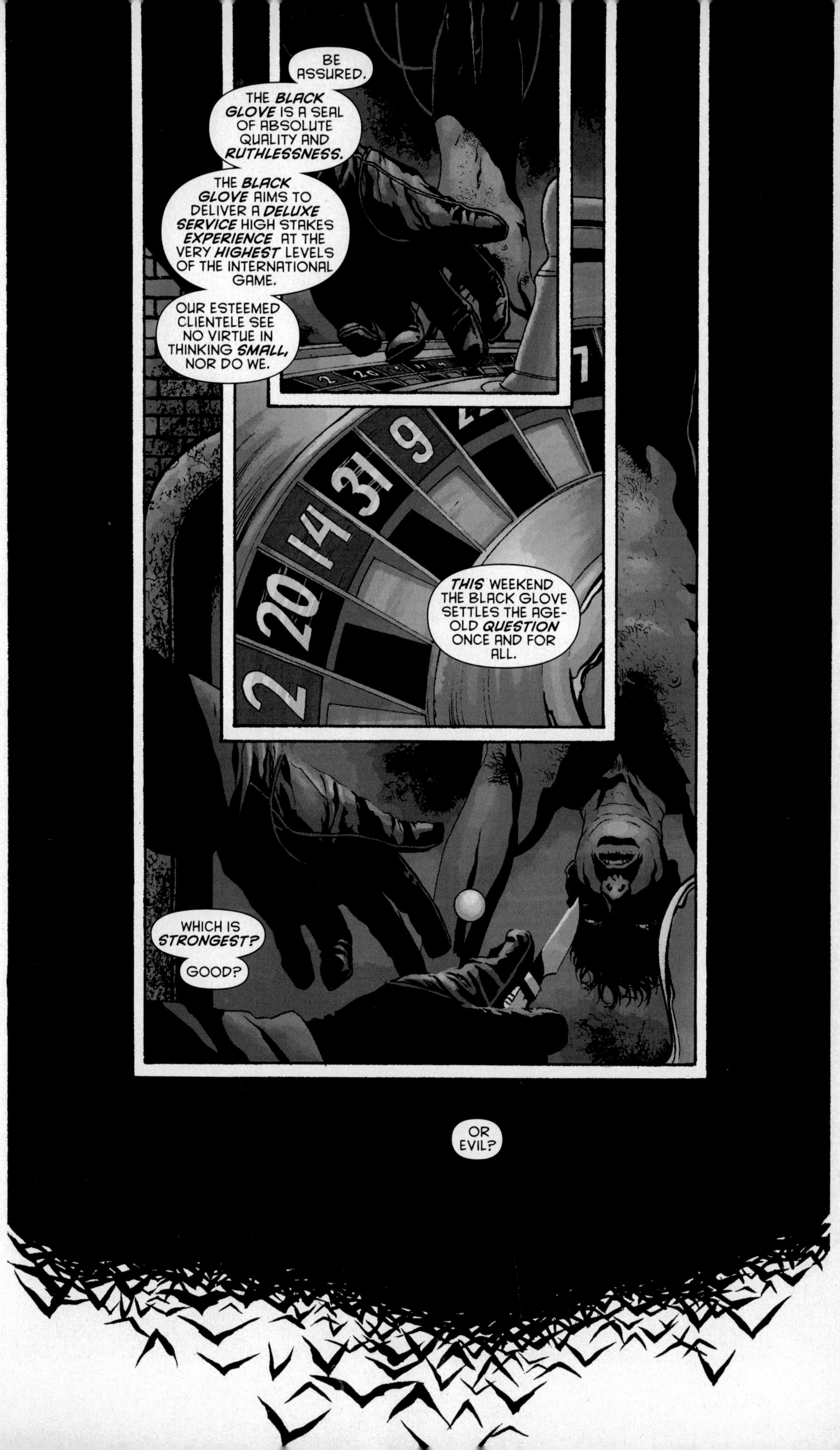
BE ASSURED.
THE BLACK GLOVE IS A SEAL OF ABSOLUTE QUALITY AND RUTHLESSNESS.
THE BLACK GLOVE AIMS TO DELIVER A DELUXE SERVICE HIGH STAKES EXPERIENCE AT THE VERY HIGHEST LEVELS OF THE INTERNATIONAL GAME.
OUR ESTEEMED CLIENTELE SEE NO VIRTUE IN THINKING SMALL, NOR DO WE.
THIS WEEKEND THE BLACK GLOVE SETTLES THE AGE-OLD QUESTION ONCE AND FOR ALL.
WHICH IS STRONGEST?
GOOD?
OR EVIL?

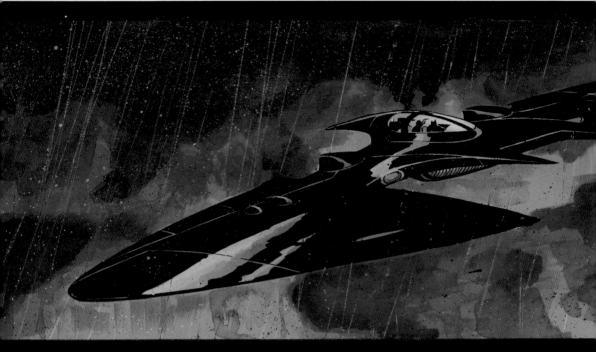

THE ISLAND OF

YOU *OKAY* WITH THIS?

I ONLY DISLOCATED MY ARM. WHY ARE *YOU* HERE?

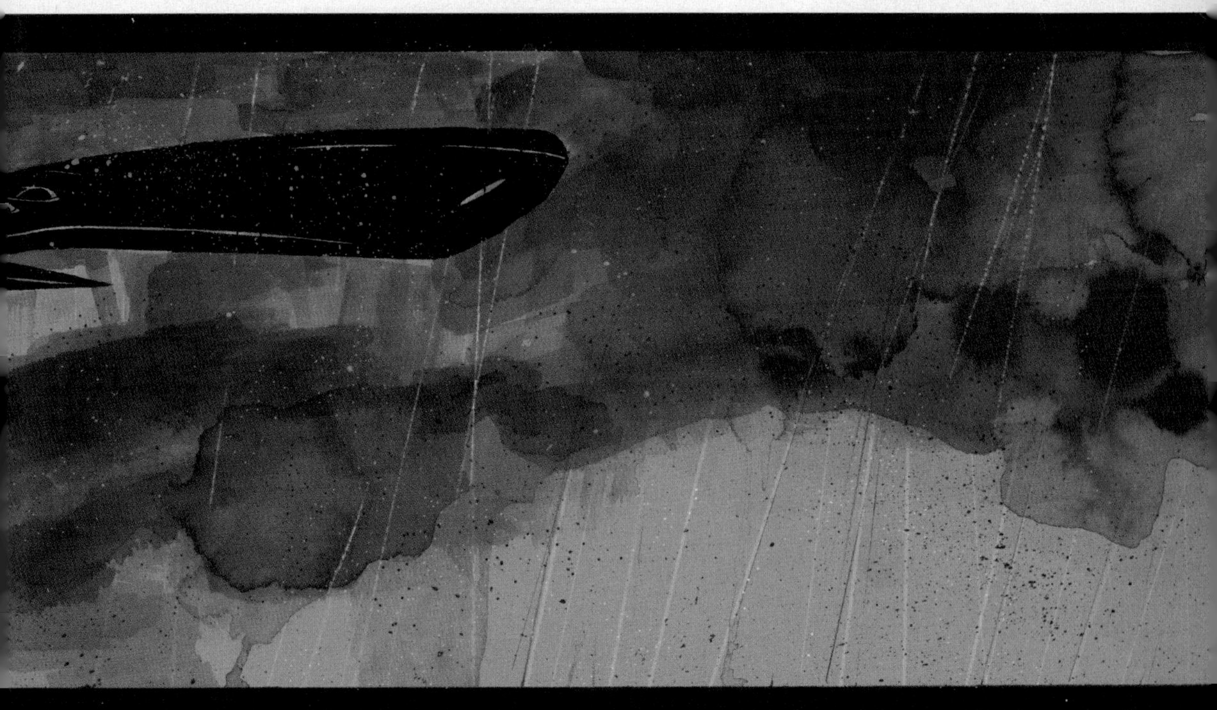

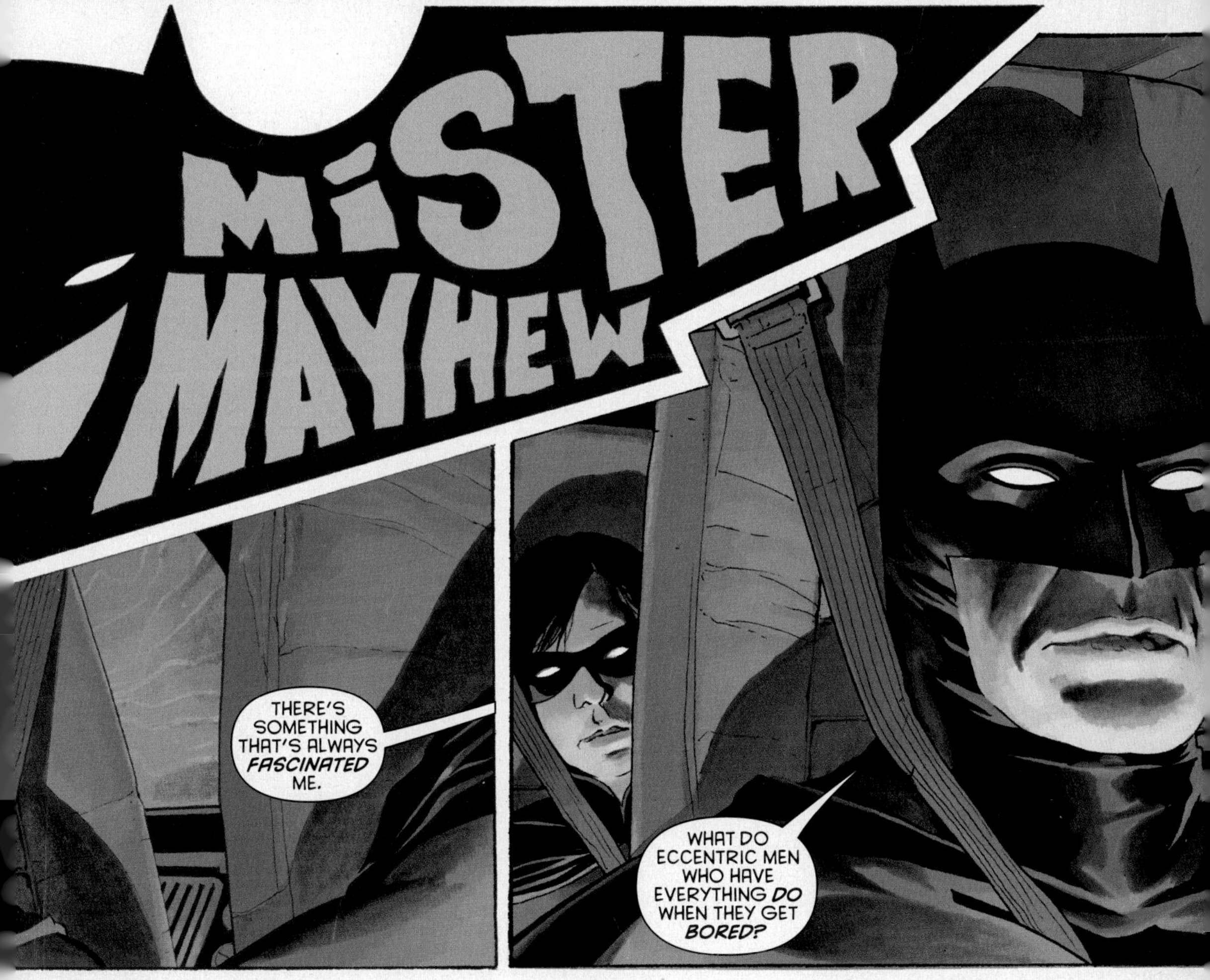
MISTER MAYHEW
THERE'S SOMETHING THAT'S ALWAYS *FASCINATED* ME.
WHAT DO ECCENTRIC MEN WHO HAVE EVERYTHING *DO* WHEN THEY GET *BORED?*

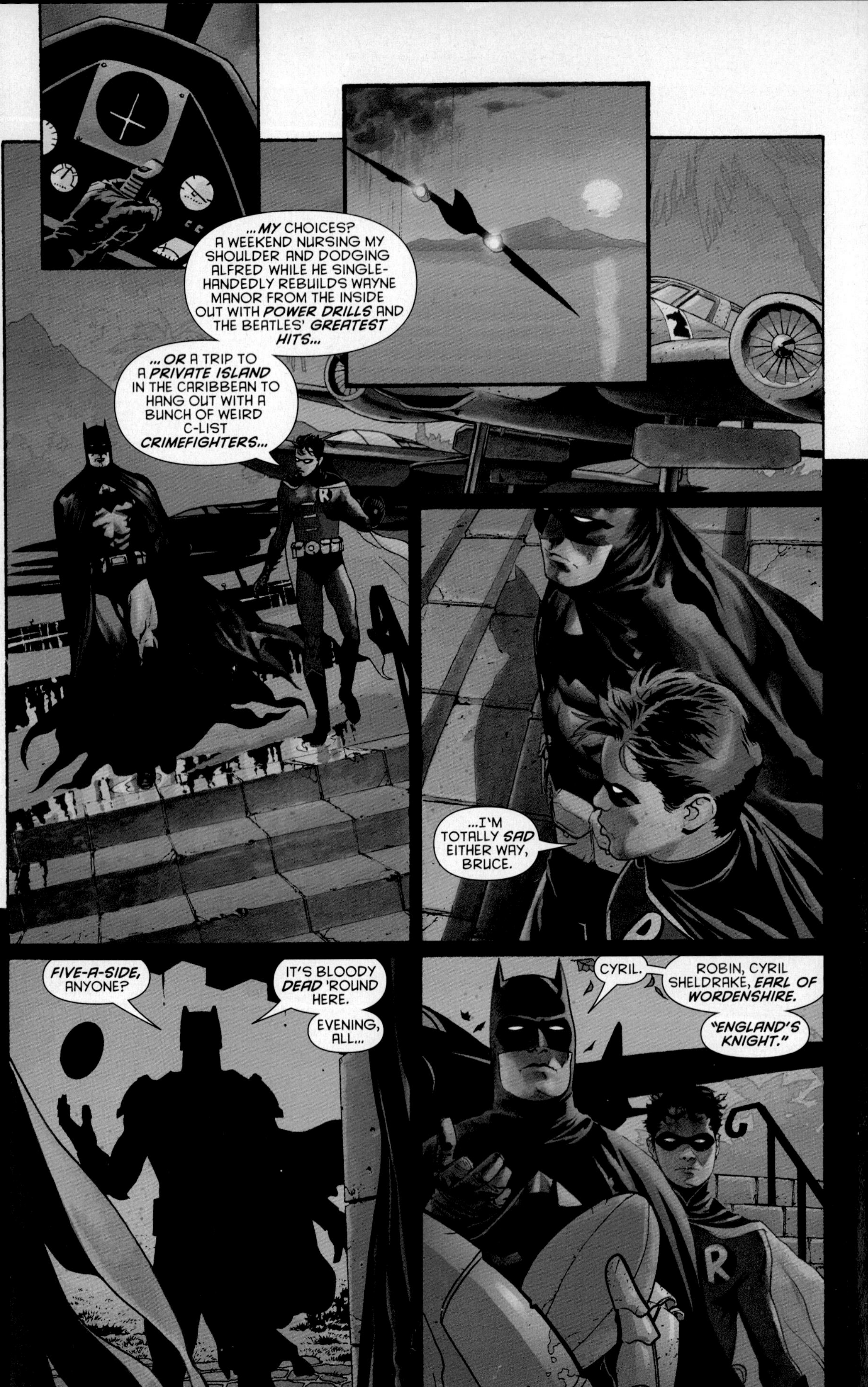
...MY CHOICES? A WEEKEND NURSING MY SHOULDER AND DODGING ALFRED WHILE HE SINGLE-HANDEDLY REBUILDS WAYNE MANOR FROM THE INSIDE OUT WITH POWER DRILLS AND THE BEATLES' GREATEST HITS...
...OR A TRIP TO A PRIVATE ISLAND IN THE CARIBBEAN TO HANG OUT WITH A BUNCH OF WEIRD C-LIST CRIMEFIGHTERS...
...I'M TOTALLY SAD EITHER WAY, BRUCE.
FIVE-A-SIDE, ANYONE?
IT'S BLOODY DEAD 'ROUND HERE.
EVENING, ALL...
CYRIL.
ROBIN, CYRIL SHELDRAKE, EARL OF WORDENSHIRE.
"ENGLAND'S KNIGHT."

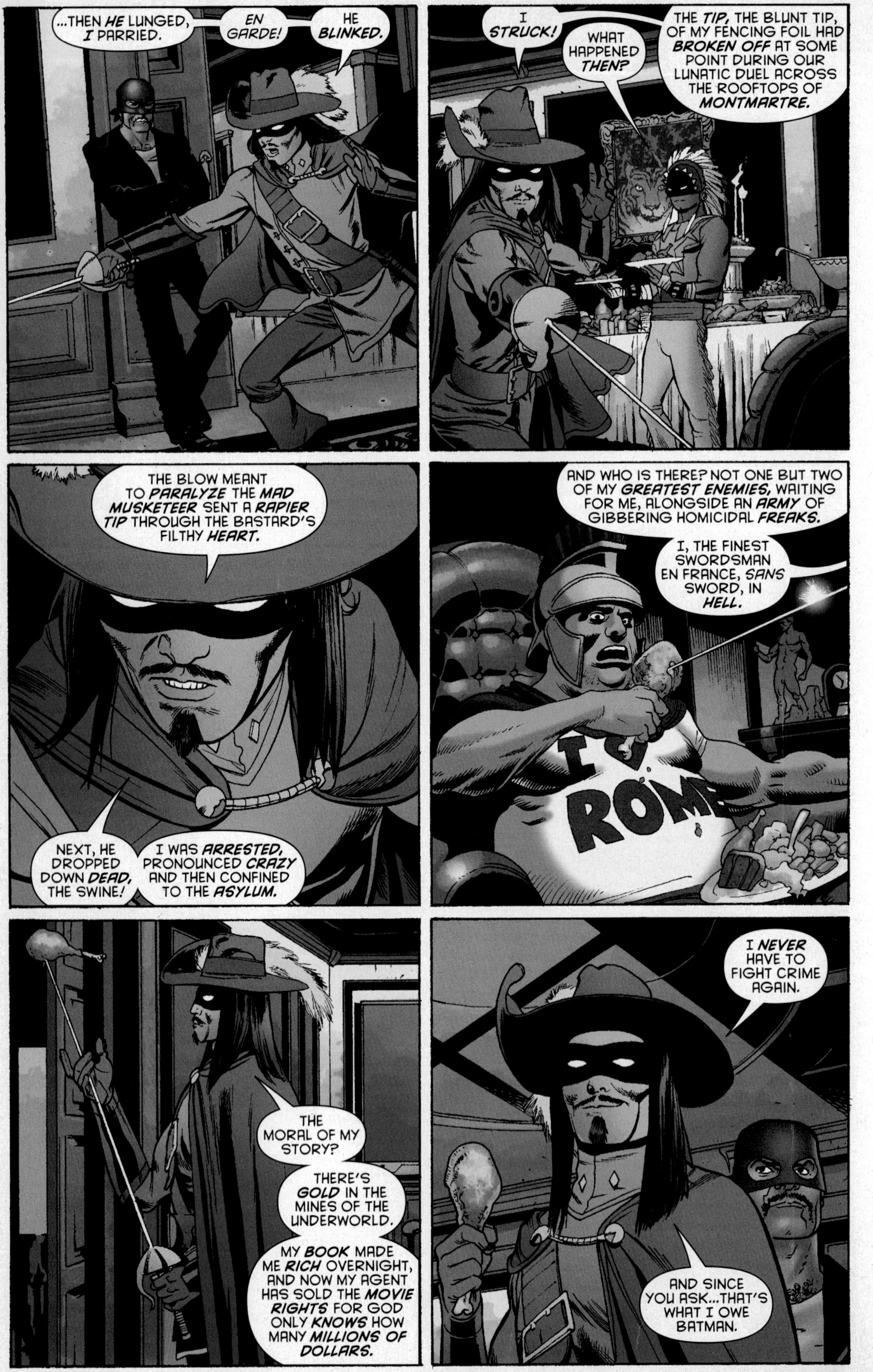
...THEN HE LUNGED, I PARRIED.
EN GARDE!
HE BLINKED.
I STRUCK!
WHAT HAPPENED THEN?
THE TIP, THE BLUNT TIP, OF MY FENCING FOIL HAD BROKEN OFF AT SOME POINT DURING OUR LUNATIC DUEL ACROSS THE ROOFTOPS OF MONTMARTRE.
THE BLOW MEANT TO PARALYZE THE MAD MUSKETEER SENT A RAPIER TIP THROUGH THE BASTARD'S FILTHY HEART.
NEXT, HE DROPPED DOWN DEAD, THE SWINE!
I WAS ARRESTED, PRONOUNCED CRAZY AND THEN CONFINED TO THE ASYLUM.
AND WHO IS THERE? NOT ONE BUT TWO OF MY GREATEST ENEMIES, WAITING FOR ME, ALONGSIDE AN ARMY OF GIBBERING HOMICIDAL FREAKS.
I, THE FINEST SWORDSMAN EN FRANCE, SANS SWORD, IN HELL.
I ♥ ROME
THE MORAL OF MY STORY?
THERE'S GOLD IN THE MINES OF THE UNDERWORLD.
MY BOOK MADE ME RICH OVERNIGHT, AND NOW MY AGENT HAS SOLD THE MOVIE RIGHTS FOR GOD ONLY KNOWS HOW MANY MILLIONS OF DOLLARS.
I NEVER HAVE TO FIGHT CRIME AGAIN.
AND SINCE YOU ASK...THAT'S WHAT I OWE BATMAN.

JONATHAN *MAYHEW*, MEGA-RICH DAREDEVIL FROM THE OLD SCHOOL.

The Black Glove.

SHARK FISHING, AIRCRAFT DESIGN, ROUND-THE-WORLD BALLOONING, DIRECTING MOVIES: HE MADE A FORTUNE IN HIS 20s, TRIED HIS HAND AT *EVERYTHING* THEN WOUND UP LIVING LIKE A *RECLUSE* ON HIS OWN PRIVATE ISLAND, SO THE STORY GOES.

Starring ... and ... in a John Mayhew Film. Mangrove Pierce ... Marsha Lamarr

AND LET'S NOT FORGET THE *SIX WIVES.*

MAYBE *THAT* EXPLAINS WHY HE NEVER BECAME A CRIMEBUSTER *HIMSELF...*

TOO MUCH LIKE BLOODY HARD WORK ON THE PARALLEL BARS.

THIS IS THE MAN WHO TRIED TO *BUY* HIS OWN SUPER-TEAM, LET'S FACE IT.

HANDED US OUR OWN SWANKY 20 BILLION-DOLLAR *HEADQUARTERS* IN MIDTOWN *METROPOLIS* AND TOLD US TO GET *ON* WITH IT...

WE HARDLY *KNEW* ONE ANOTHER, AND EVERYBODY WAS IN AWE OF *BATMAN.*

NO WONDER IT LASTED ALL OF HALF AN HOUR.

THE INTERNATIONAL CLUB OF HEROES

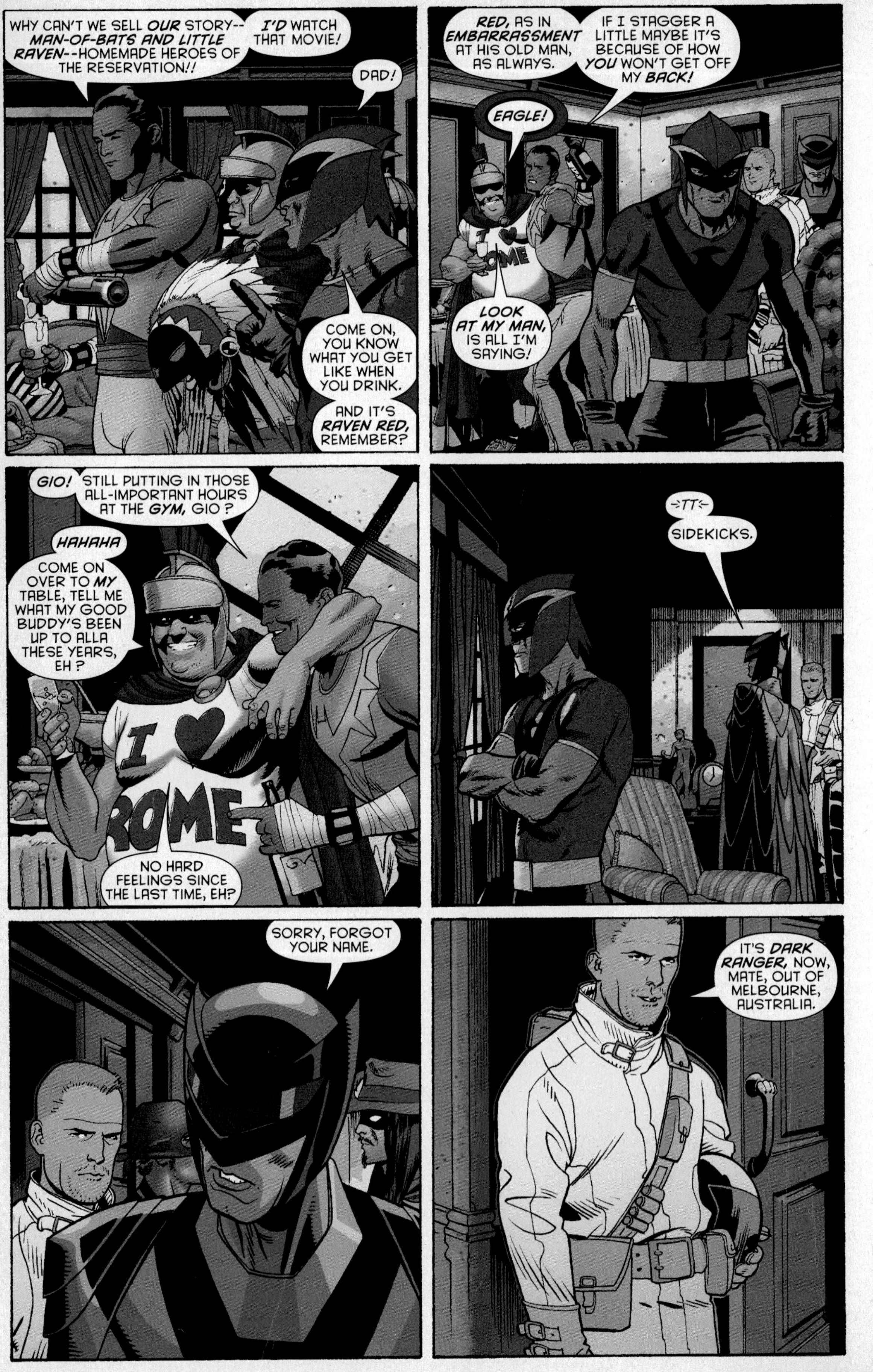

WHY CAN'T WE SELL *OUR* STORY-- *MAN-OF-BATS AND LITTLE RAVEN*--HOMEMADE HEROES OF THE RESERVATION!!
I'D WATCH THAT MOVIE!
DAD!
COME ON, YOU KNOW WHAT YOU GET LIKE WHEN YOU DRINK.
AND IT'S *RAVEN RED*, REMEMBER?
RED, AS IN *EMBARRASSMENT* AT HIS OLD MAN, AS ALWAYS.
IF I STAGGER A LITTLE MAYBE IT'S BECAUSE OF HOW *YOU* WON'T GET OFF MY *BACK!*
EAGLE!
LOOK AT MY MAN, IS ALL I'M SAYING!
GIO!
STILL PUTTING IN THOSE ALL-IMPORTANT HOURS AT THE *GYM*, GIO?
HAHAHA
COME ON OVER TO *MY* TABLE, TELL ME WHAT MY GOOD BUDDY'S BEEN UP TO ALLA THESE YEARS, EH?
NO HARD FEELINGS SINCE THE LAST TIME, EH?
TT
SIDEKICKS.
SORRY, FORGOT YOUR NAME.
IT'S *DARK RANGER*, NOW, MATE, OUT OF MELBOURNE, AUSTRALIA.

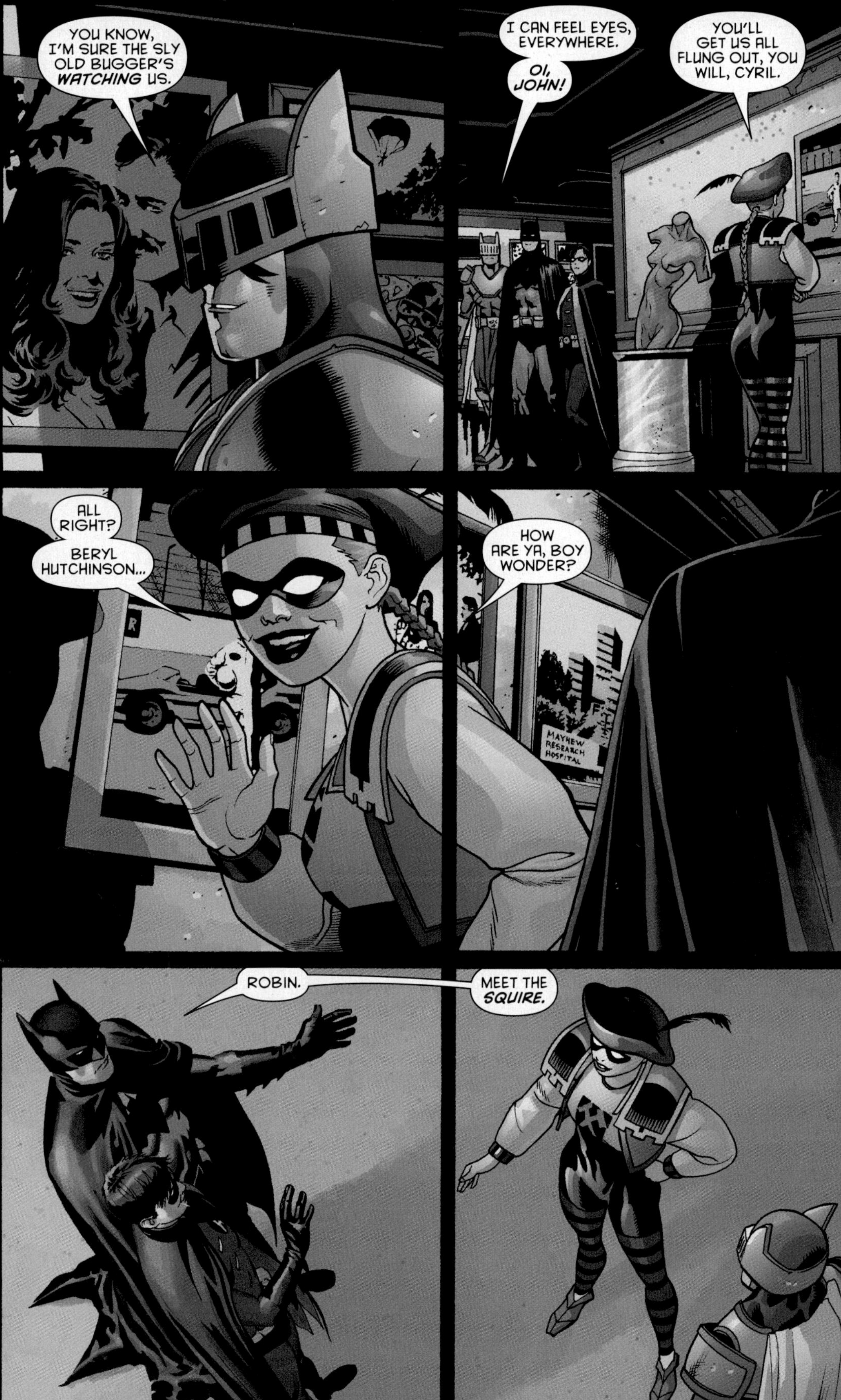
YOU KNOW, I'M SURE THE SLY OLD BUGGER'S WATCHING US.
I CAN FEEL EYES, EVERYWHERE.
OI, JOHN!
YOU'LL GET US ALL FLUNG OUT, YOU WILL, CYRIL.
ALL RIGHT?
BERYL HUTCHINSON...
HOW ARE YA, BOY WONDER?
MAYHEW RESEARCH HOSPITAL
ROBIN.
MEET THE SQUIRE.

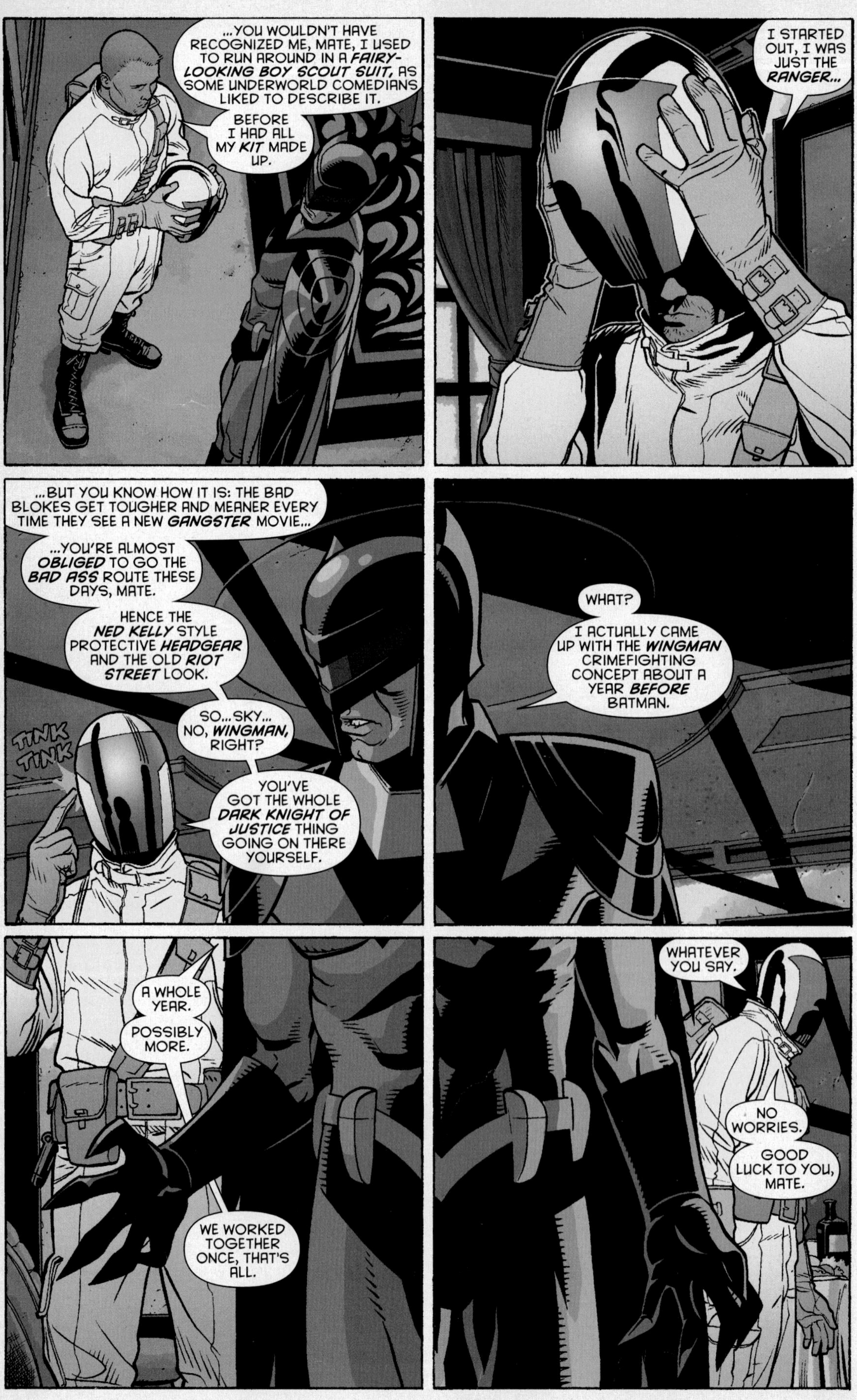
...YOU WOULDN'T HAVE RECOGNIZED ME, MATE, I USED TO RUN AROUND IN A FAIRY-LOOKING BOY SCOUT SUIT, AS SOME UNDERWORLD COMEDIANS LIKED TO DESCRIBE IT.
BEFORE I HAD ALL MY KIT MADE UP.
I STARTED OUT, I WAS JUST THE RANGER...
...BUT YOU KNOW HOW IT IS: THE BAD BLOKES GET TOUGHER AND MEANER EVERY TIME THEY SEE A NEW GANGSTER MOVIE...
...YOU'RE ALMOST OBLIGED TO GO THE BAD ASS ROUTE THESE DAYS, MATE.
HENCE THE NED KELLY STYLE PROTECTIVE HEADGEAR AND THE OLD RIOT STREET LOOK.
TINK TINK
SO... SKY... NO, WINGMAN, RIGHT?
YOU'VE GOT THE WHOLE DARK KNIGHT OF JUSTICE THING GOING ON THERE YOURSELF.
WHAT?
I ACTUALLY CAME UP WITH THE WINGMAN CRIMEFIGHTING CONCEPT ABOUT A YEAR BEFORE BATMAN.
A WHOLE YEAR.
POSSIBLY MORE.
WE WORKED TOGETHER ONCE, THAT'S ALL.
WHATEVER YOU SAY.
NO WORRIES.
GOOD LUCK TO YOU, MATE.

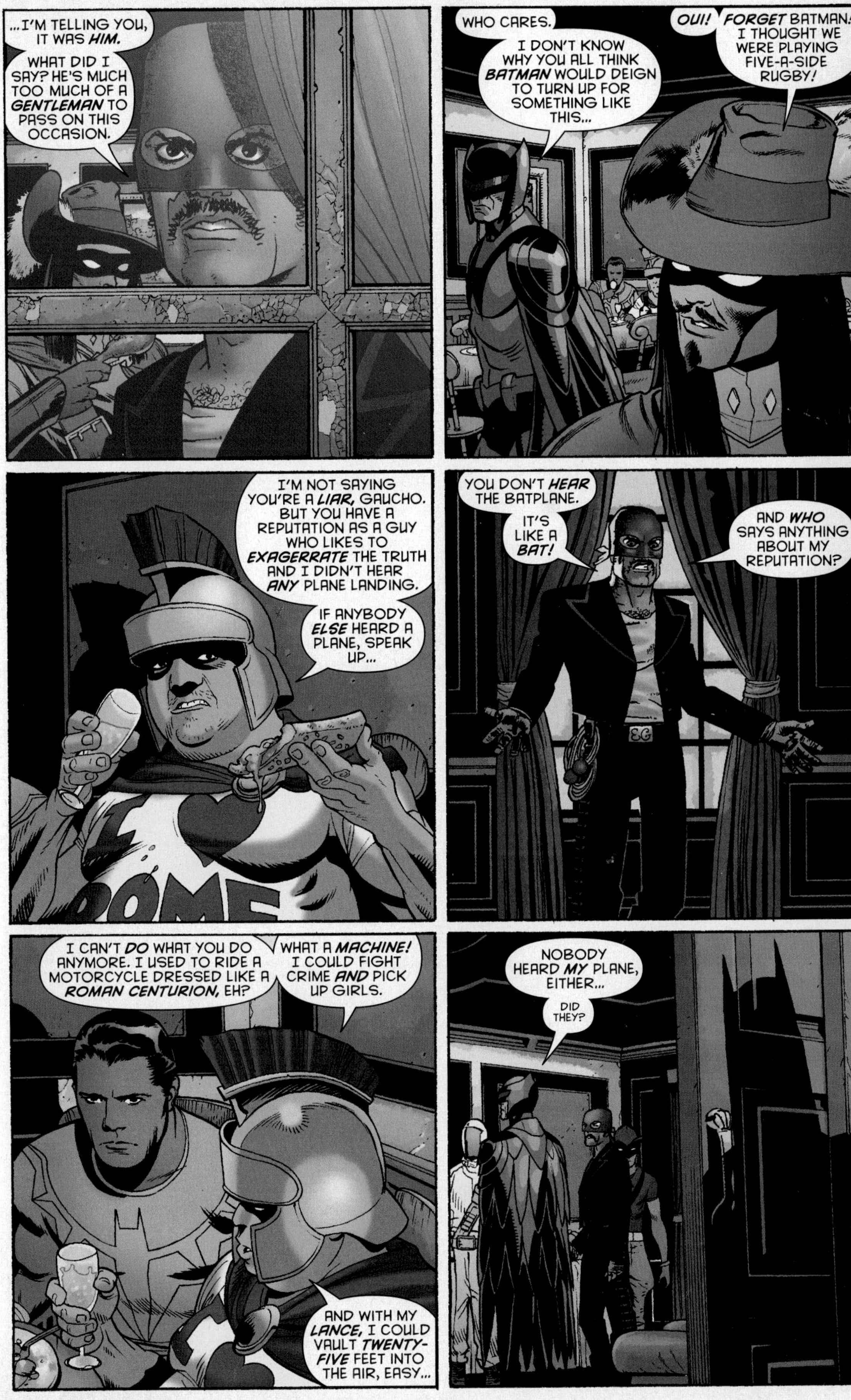
...I'M TELLING YOU, IT WAS HIM.
WHAT DID I SAY? HE'S MUCH TOO MUCH OF A GENTLEMAN TO PASS ON THIS OCCASION.
WHO CARES.
I DON'T KNOW WHY YOU ALL THINK BATMAN WOULD DEIGN TO TURN UP FOR SOMETHING LIKE THIS...
OUI!
FORGET BATMAN! I THOUGHT WE WERE PLAYING FIVE-A-SIDE RUGBY!
I'M NOT SAYING YOU'RE A LIAR, GAUCHO. BUT YOU HAVE A REPUTATION AS A GUY WHO LIKES TO EXAGERRATE THE TRUTH AND I DIDN'T HEAR ANY PLANE LANDING.
IF ANYBODY ELSE HEARD A PLANE, SPEAK UP...
YOU DON'T HEAR THE BATPLANE.
IT'S LIKE A BAT!
AND WHO SAYS ANYTHING ABOUT MY REPUTATION?
I CAN'T DO WHAT YOU DO ANYMORE. I USED TO RIDE A MOTORCYCLE DRESSED LIKE A ROMAN CENTURION, EH?
WHAT A MACHINE! I COULD FIGHT CRIME AND PICK UP GIRLS.
AND WITH MY LANCE, I COULD VAULT TWENTY-FIVE FEET INTO THE AIR, EASY...
NOBODY HEARD MY PLANE, EITHER...
DID THEY?

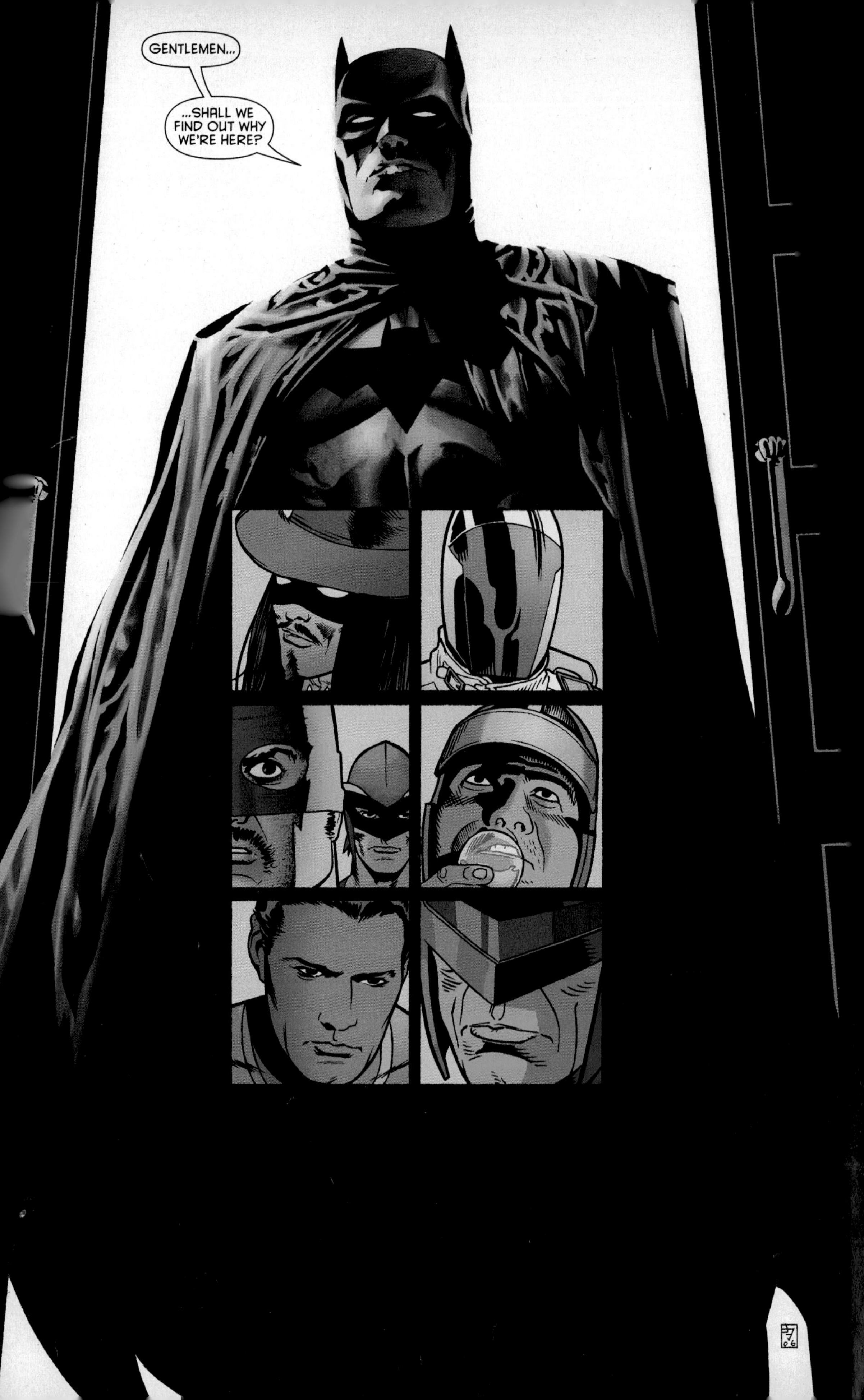
GENTLEMEN...
...SHALL WE FIND OUT WHY WE'RE HERE?

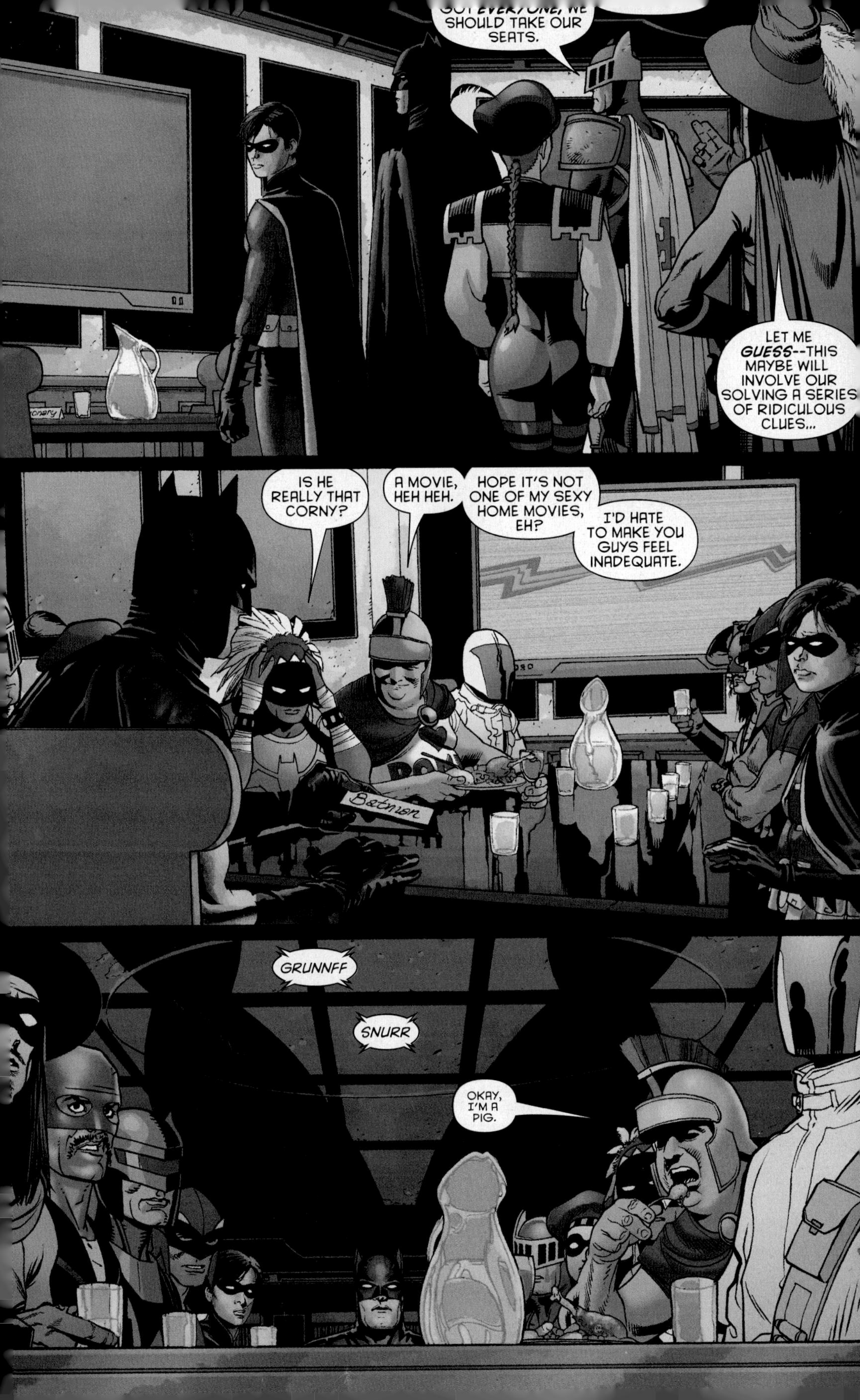
SHOULD TAKE OUR SEATS.
LET ME GUESS--THIS MAYBE WILL INVOLVE OUR SOLVING A SERIES OF RIDICULOUS CLUES...
IS HE REALLY THAT CORNY?
A MOVIE, HEH HEH.
HOPE IT'S NOT ONE OF MY SEXY HOME MOVIES, EH?
I'D HATE TO MAKE YOU GUYS FEEL INADEQUATE.
Batman
GRUNNFF
SNURR
OKAY, I'M A PIG.

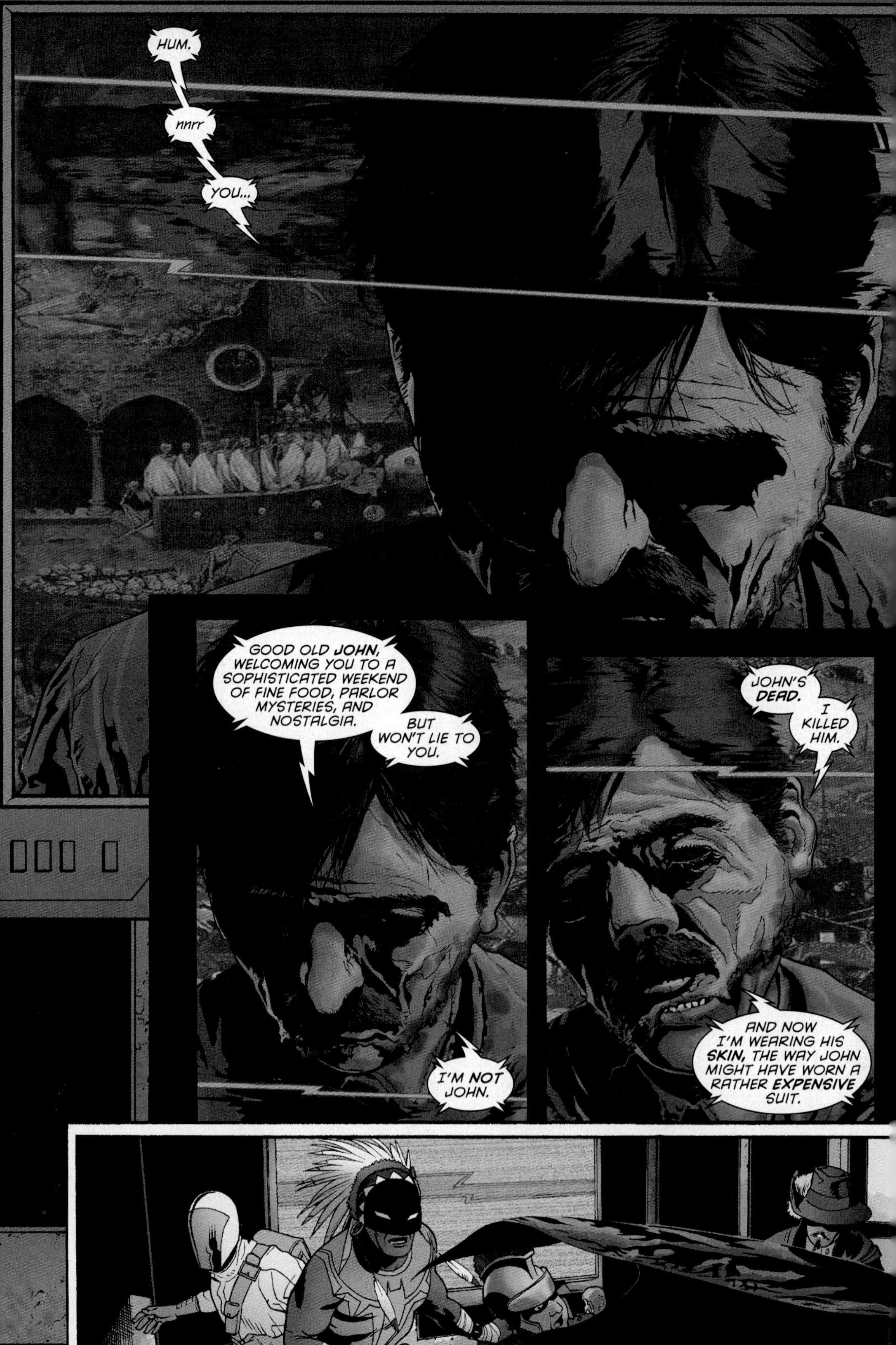
HUM.
nnrr
YOU...
GOOD OLD **JOHN**, WELCOMING YOU TO A SOPHISTICATED WEEKEND OF FINE FOOD, PARLOR MYSTERIES, AND NOSTALGIA.
BUT WON'T LIE TO YOU.
I'M **NOT** JOHN.
JOHN'S **DEAD.**
I KILLED HIM.
AND NOW I'M WEARING HIS **SKIN,** THE WAY JOHN MIGHT HAVE WORN A RATHER **EXPENSIVE** SUIT.

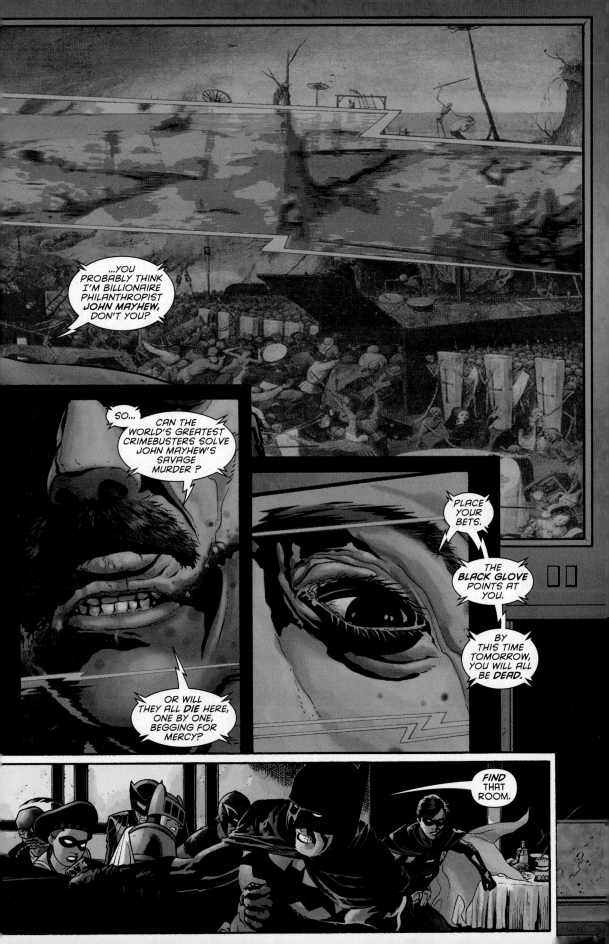

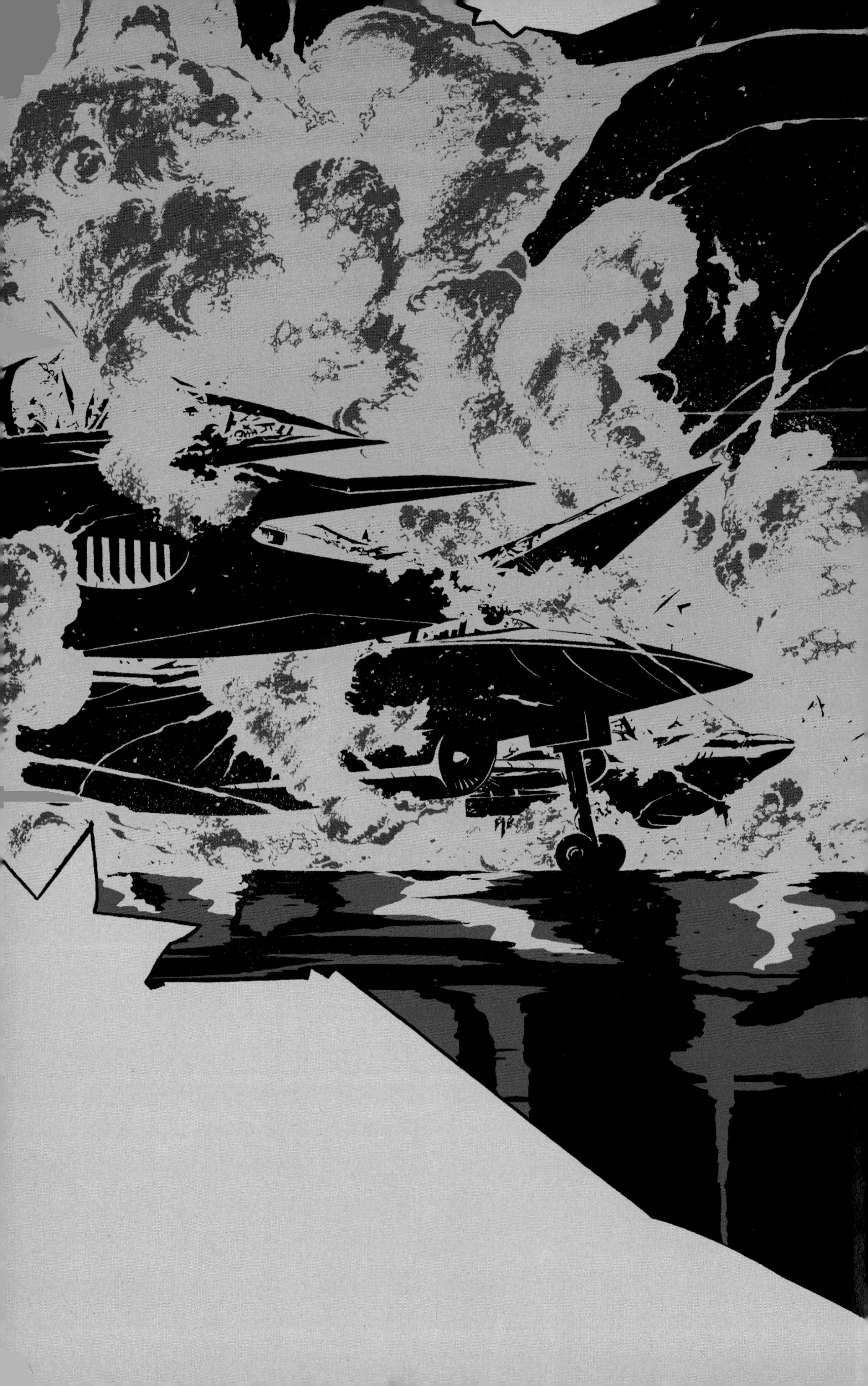

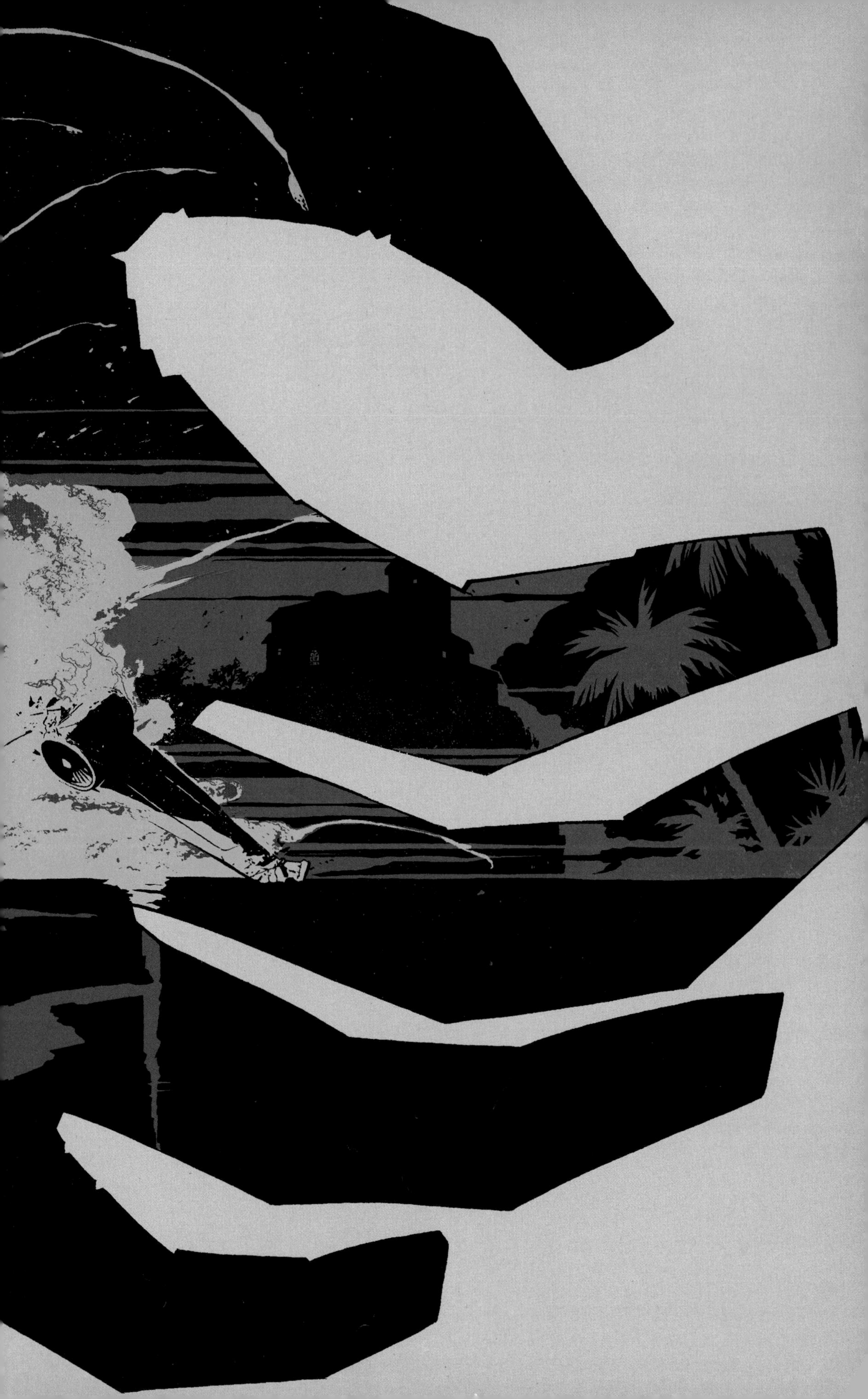

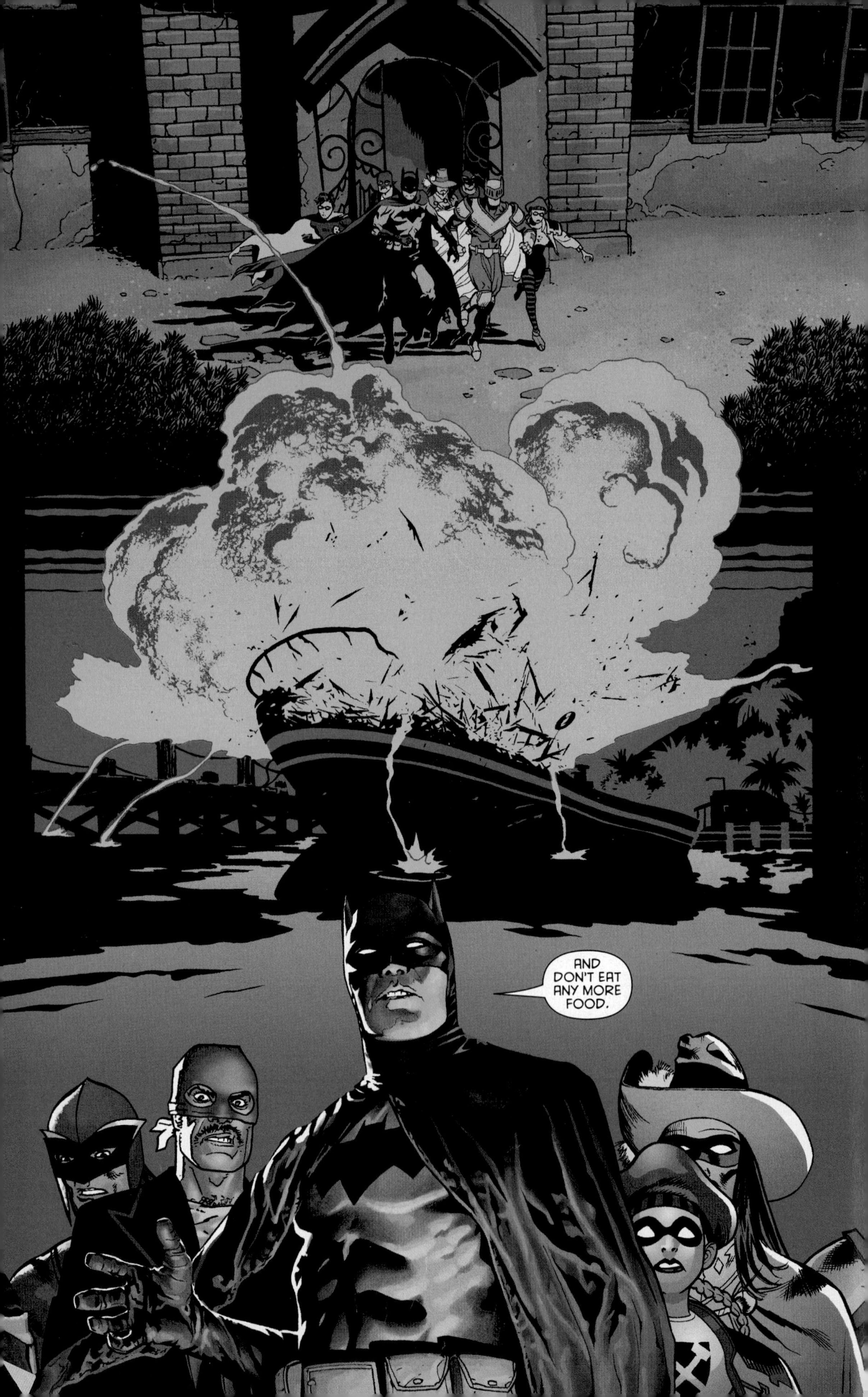
AND DON'T EAT ANY MORE FOOD.

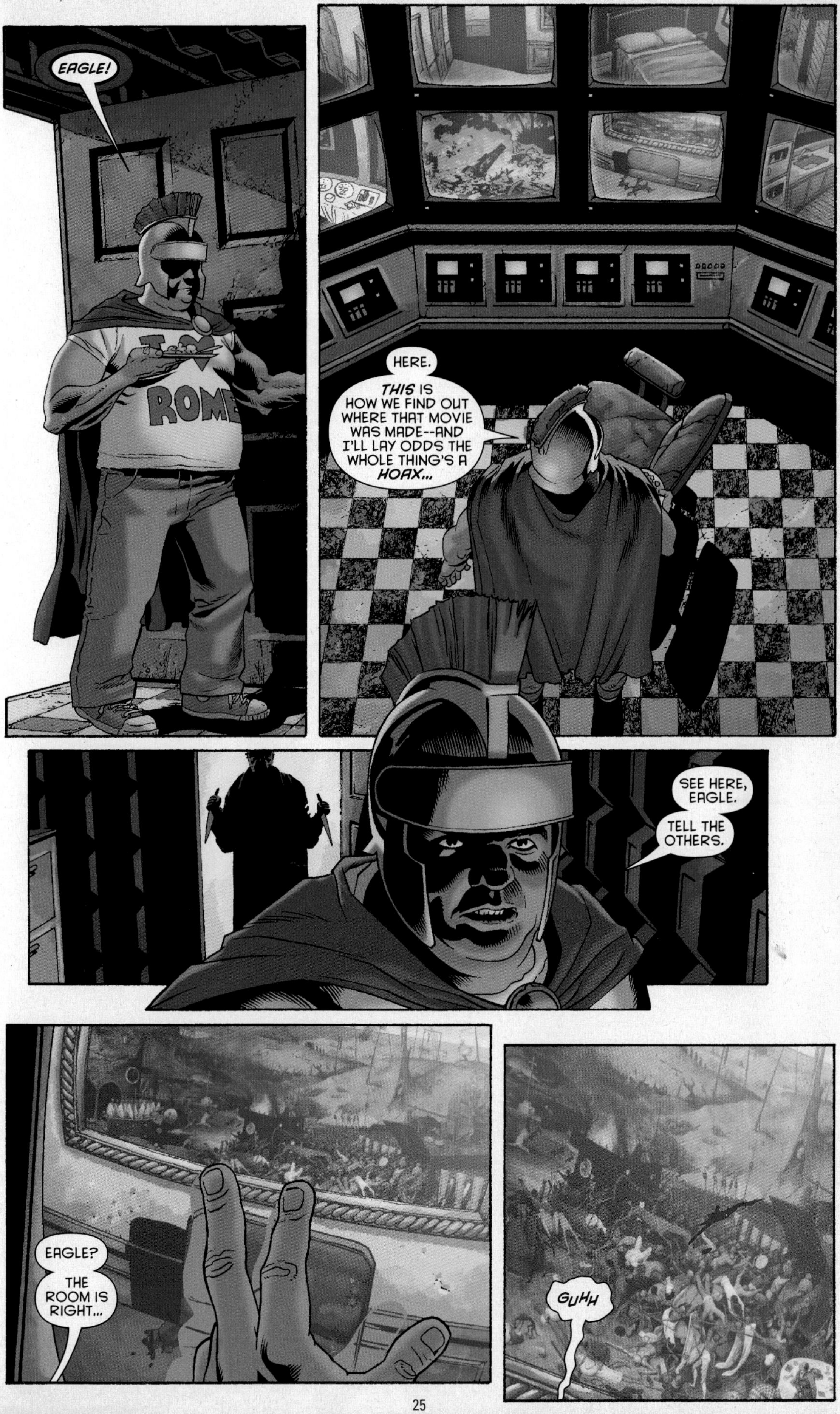
EAGLE!
HERE.
THIS IS HOW WE FIND OUT WHERE THAT MOVIE WAS MADE--AND I'LL LAY ODDS THE WHOLE THING'S A HOAX...
SEE HERE, EAGLE.
TELL THE OTHERS.
EAGLE?
THE ROOM IS RIGHT...
GUHH

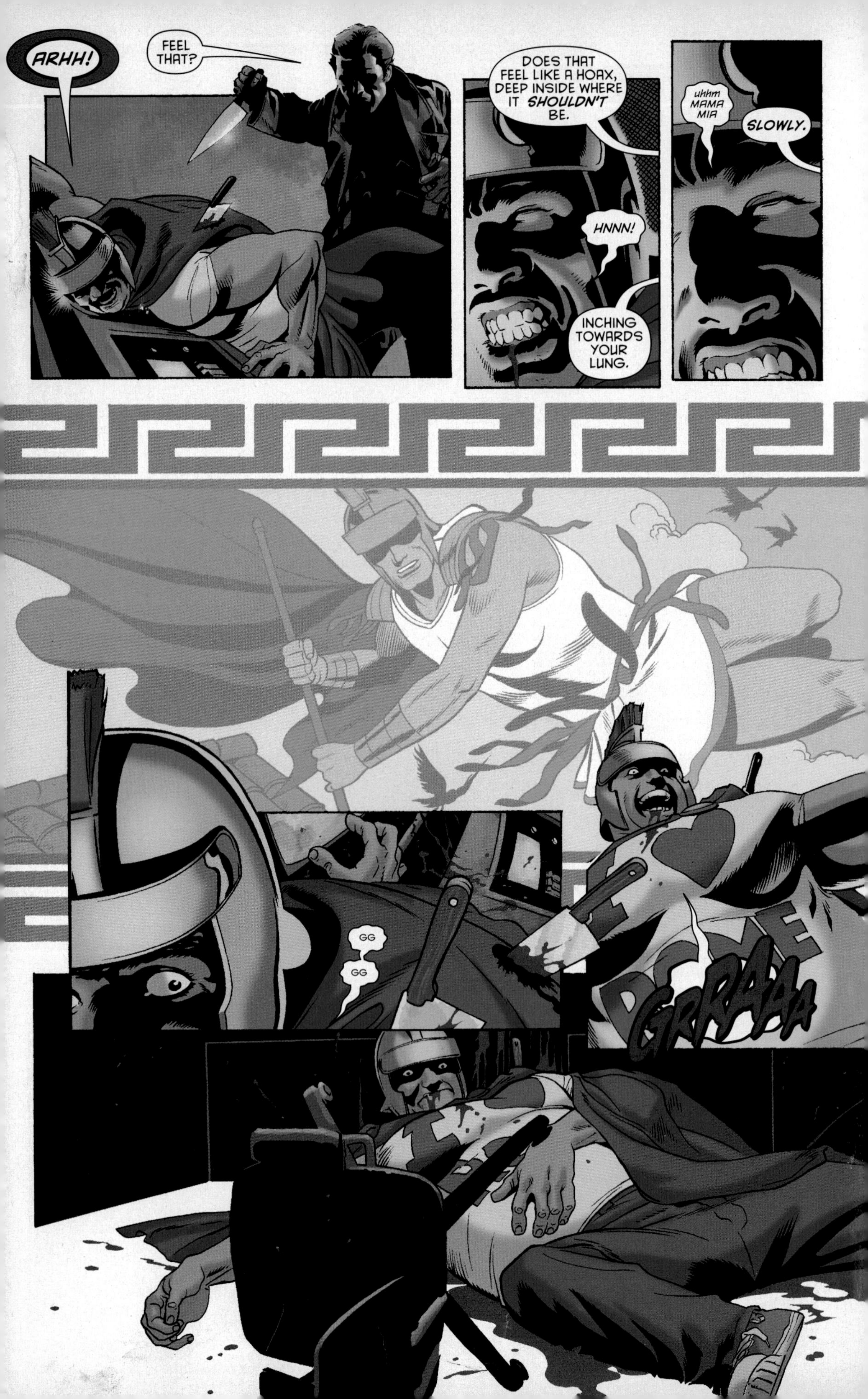
ARHH!
FEEL THAT?
DOES THAT FEEL LIKE A HOAX, DEEP INSIDE WHERE IT SHOULDN'T BE.
HNNN!
INCHING TOWARDS YOUR LUNG.
uhhm MAMA MIA
SLOWLY.
GG
GG
GRRAAA

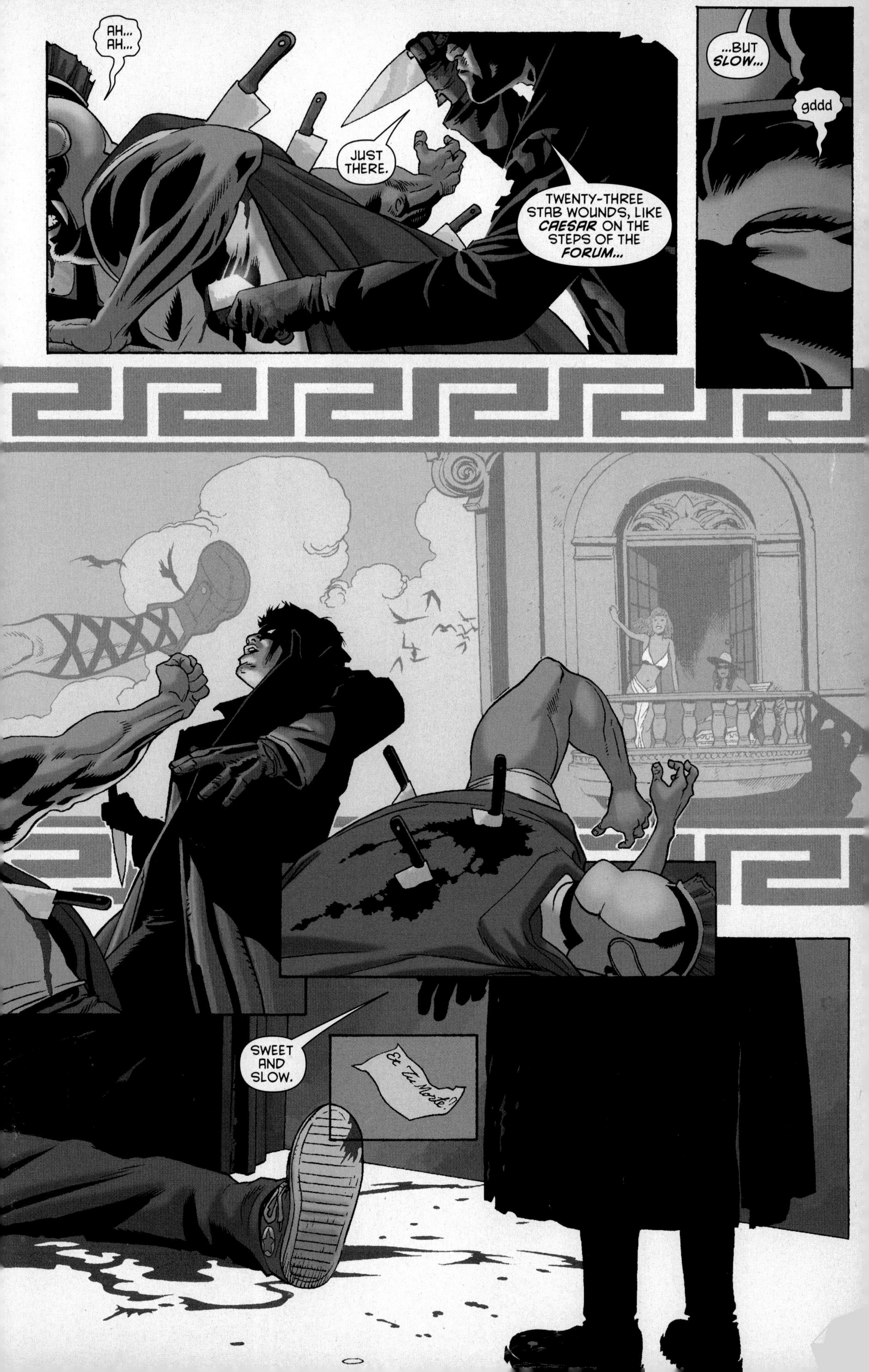
AH... AH...
JUST THERE.
TWENTY-THREE STAB WOUNDS, LIKE CAESAR ON THE STEPS OF THE FORUM...
...BUT SLOW...
gddd
SWEET AND SLOW.
Et Tu Morte?

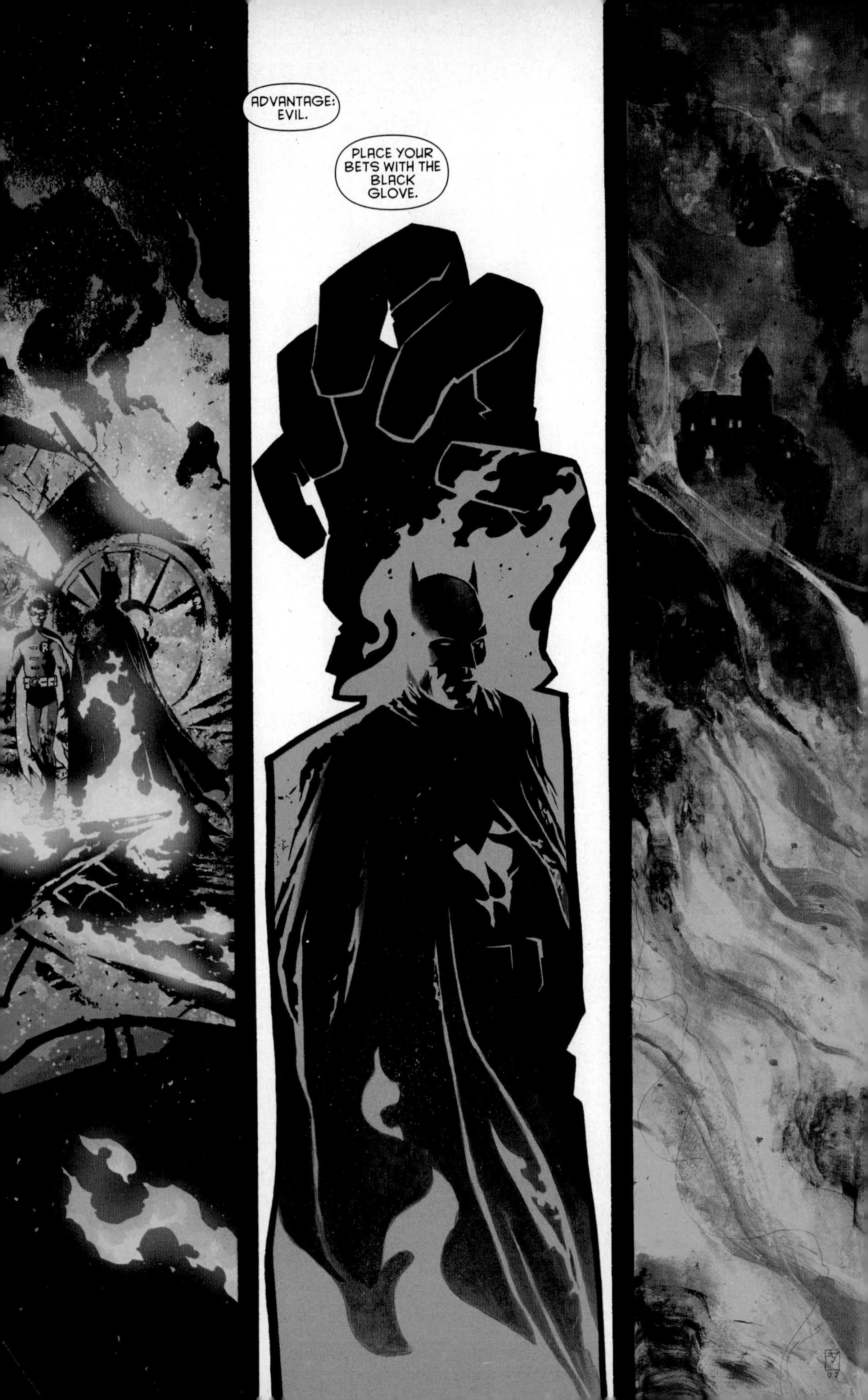
ADVANTAGE: EVIL.
PLACE YOUR BETS WITH THE BLACK GLOVE.

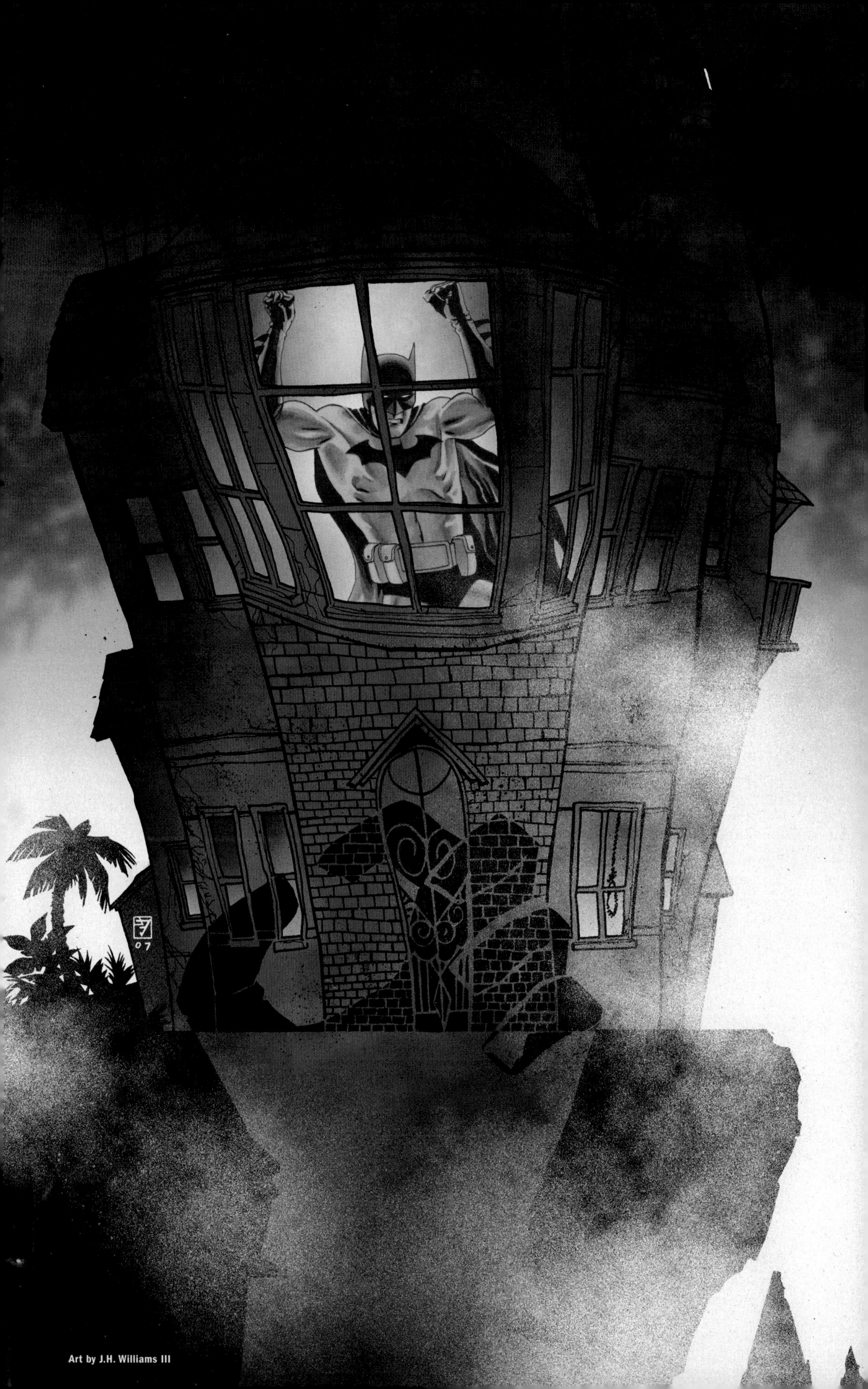

Art by J.H. Williams III

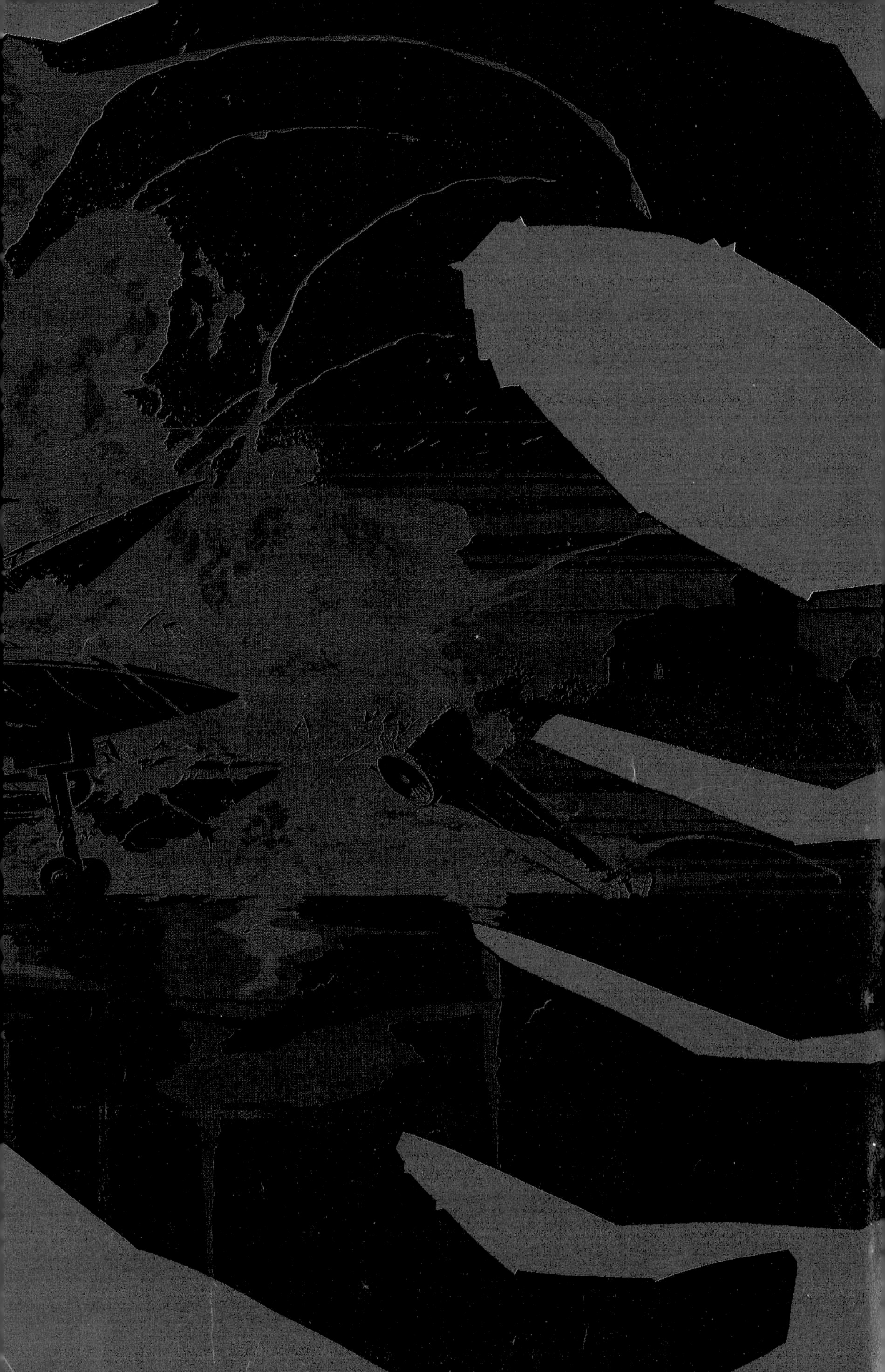

Chapter art by J.H. Williams III

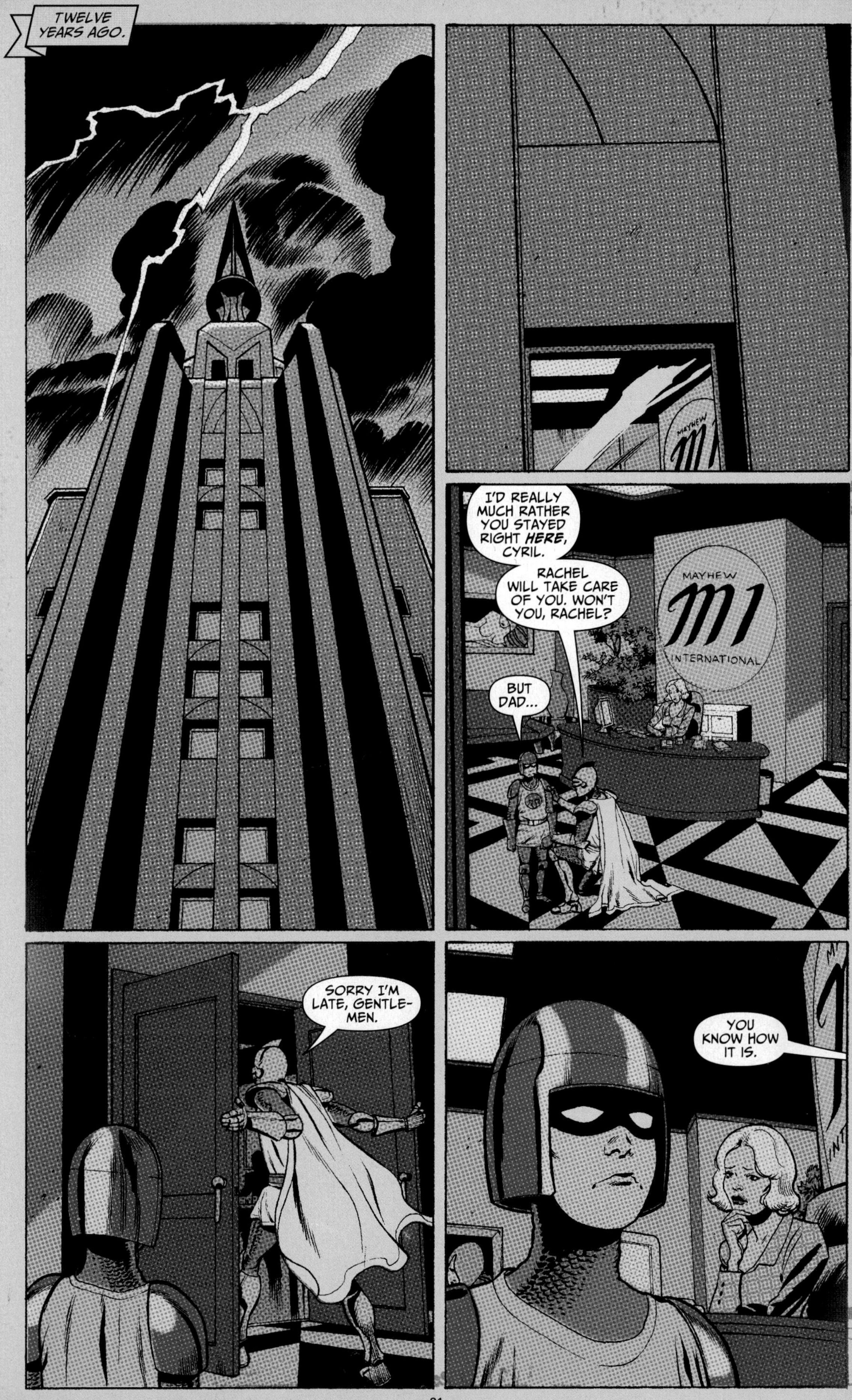
TWELVE YEARS AGO.
MAYHEW M1
I'D REALLY MUCH RATHER YOU STAYED RIGHT *HERE*, CYRIL.
RACHEL WILL TAKE CARE OF YOU. WON'T YOU, RACHEL?
MAYHEW M1 INTERNATIONAL
BUT DAD...
SORRY I'M LATE, GENTLE-MEN.
YOU KNOW HOW IT IS.

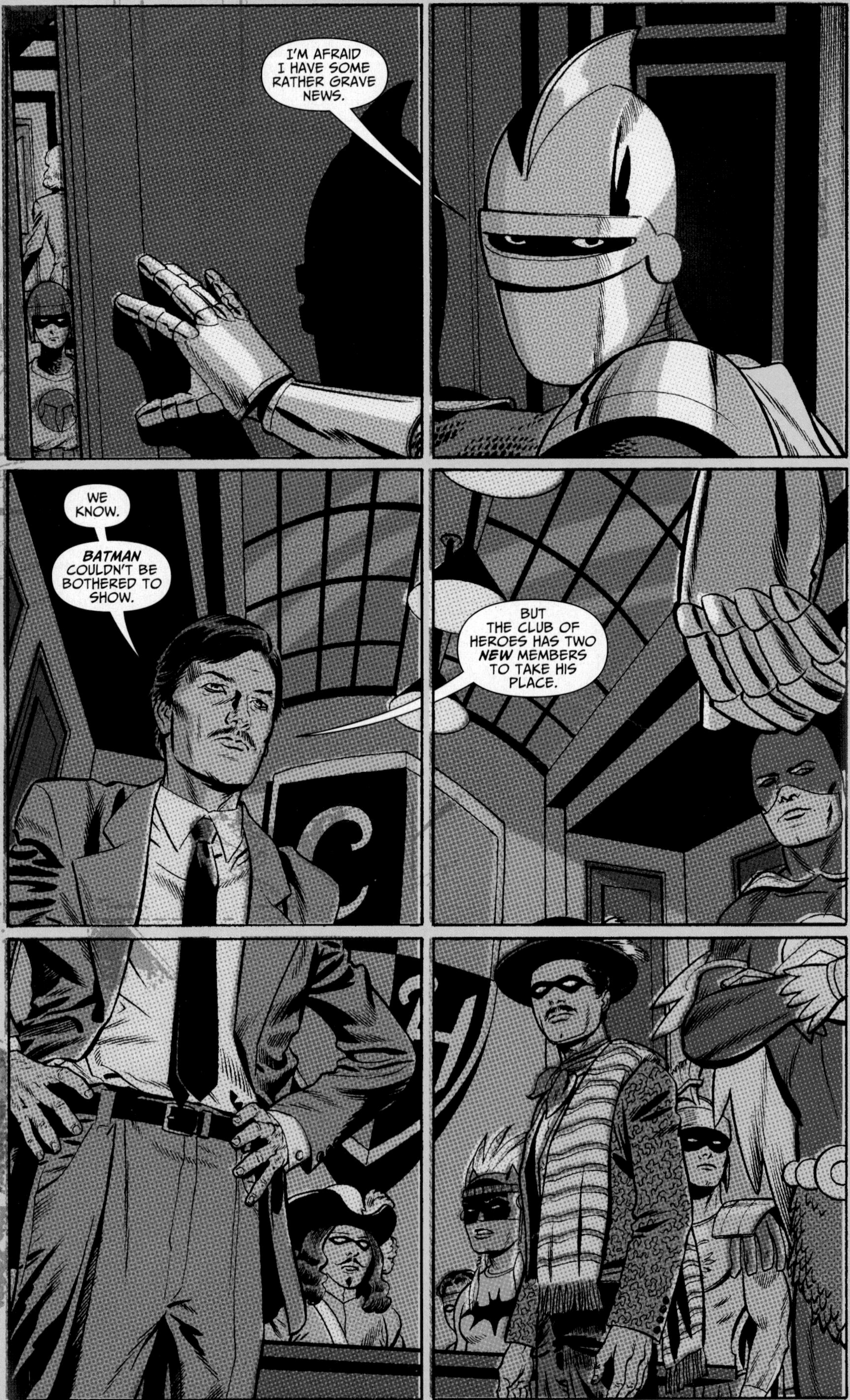
I'M AFRAID I HAVE SOME RATHER GRAVE NEWS.
WE KNOW.
BATMAN COULDN'T BE BOTHERED TO SHOW.
BUT THE CLUB OF HEROES HAS TWO NEW MEMBERS TO TAKE HIS PLACE.

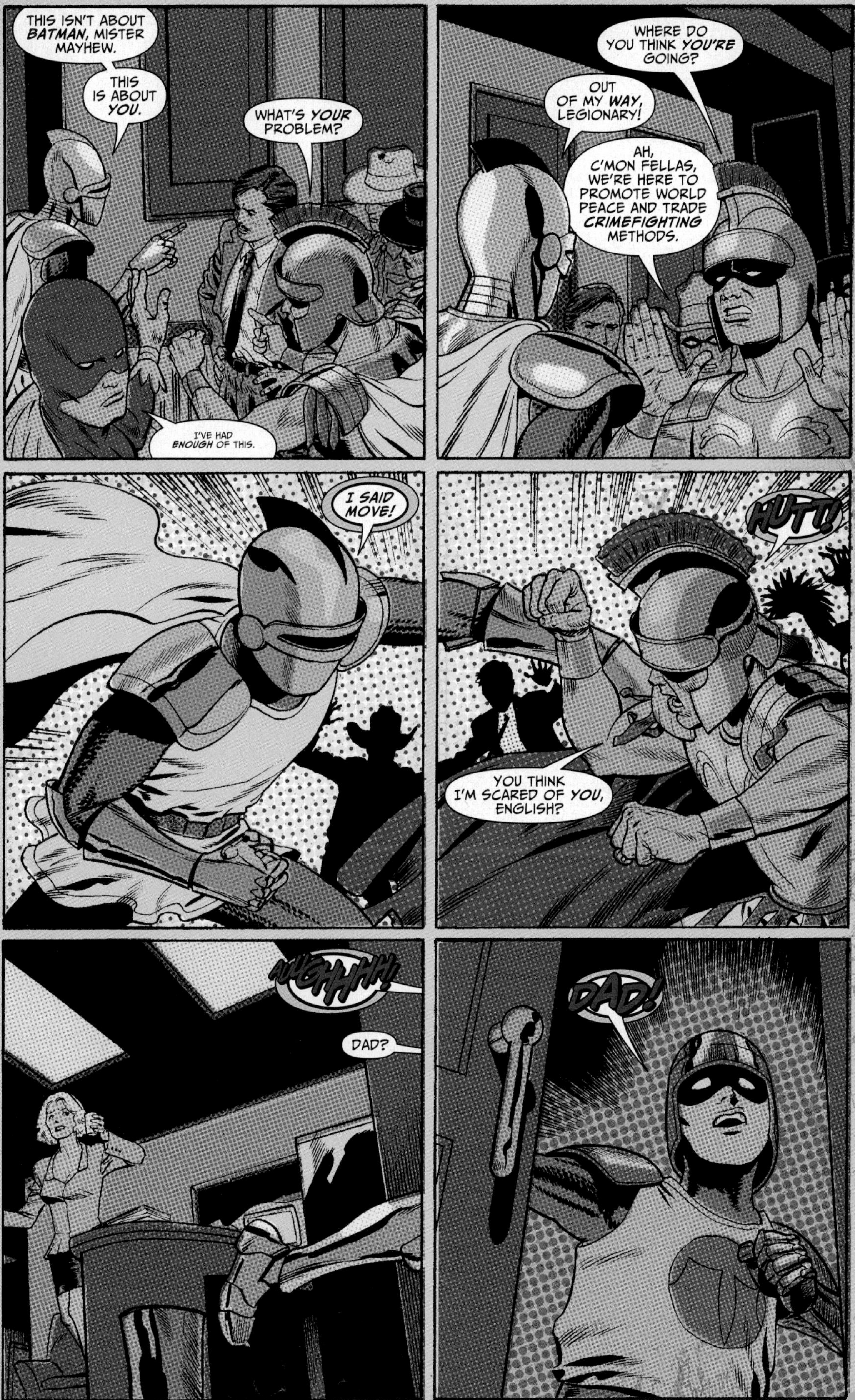

THIS ISN'T ABOUT BATMAN, MISTER MAYHEW.
THIS IS ABOUT YOU.
WHAT'S YOUR PROBLEM?
I'VE HAD ENOUGH OF THIS.
WHERE DO YOU THINK YOU'RE GOING?
OUT OF MY WAY, LEGIONARY!
AH, C'MON FELLAS, WE'RE HERE TO PROMOTE WORLD PEACE AND TRADE CRIMEFIGHTING METHODS.
I SAID MOVE!
HUTT!
YOU THINK I'M SCARED OF YOU, ENGLISH?
AUGHHHH!
DAD?
DAD!

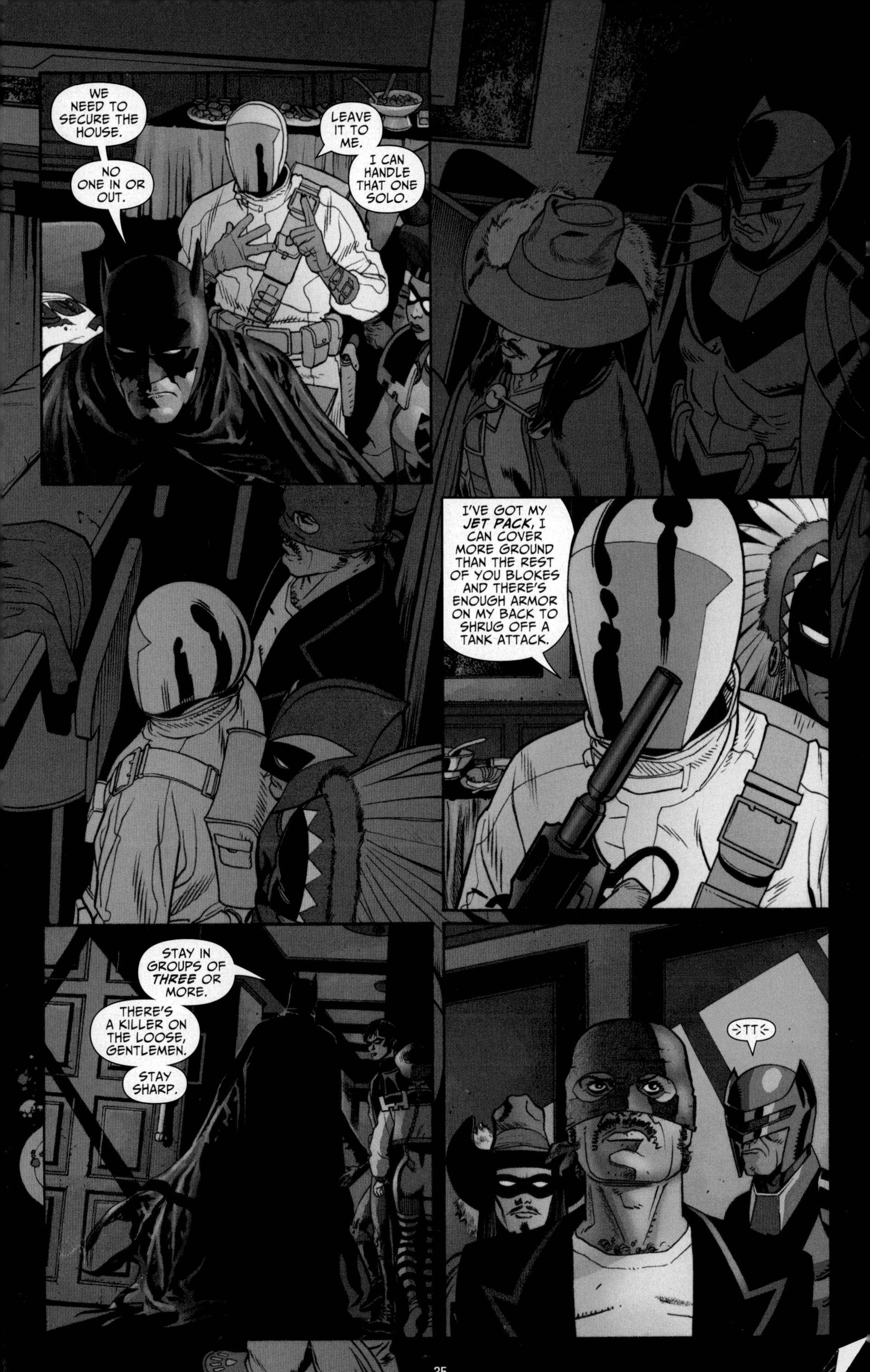
WE NEED TO SECURE THE HOUSE.
NO ONE IN OR OUT.
LEAVE IT TO ME.
I CAN HANDLE THAT ONE SOLO.
I'VE GOT MY JET PACK, I CAN COVER MORE GROUND THAN THE REST OF YOU BLOKES AND THERE'S ENOUGH ARMOR ON MY BACK TO SHRUG OFF A TANK ATTACK.
STAY IN GROUPS OF THREE OR MORE.
THERE'S A KILLER ON THE LOOSE, GENTLEMEN.
STAY SHARP.
TT

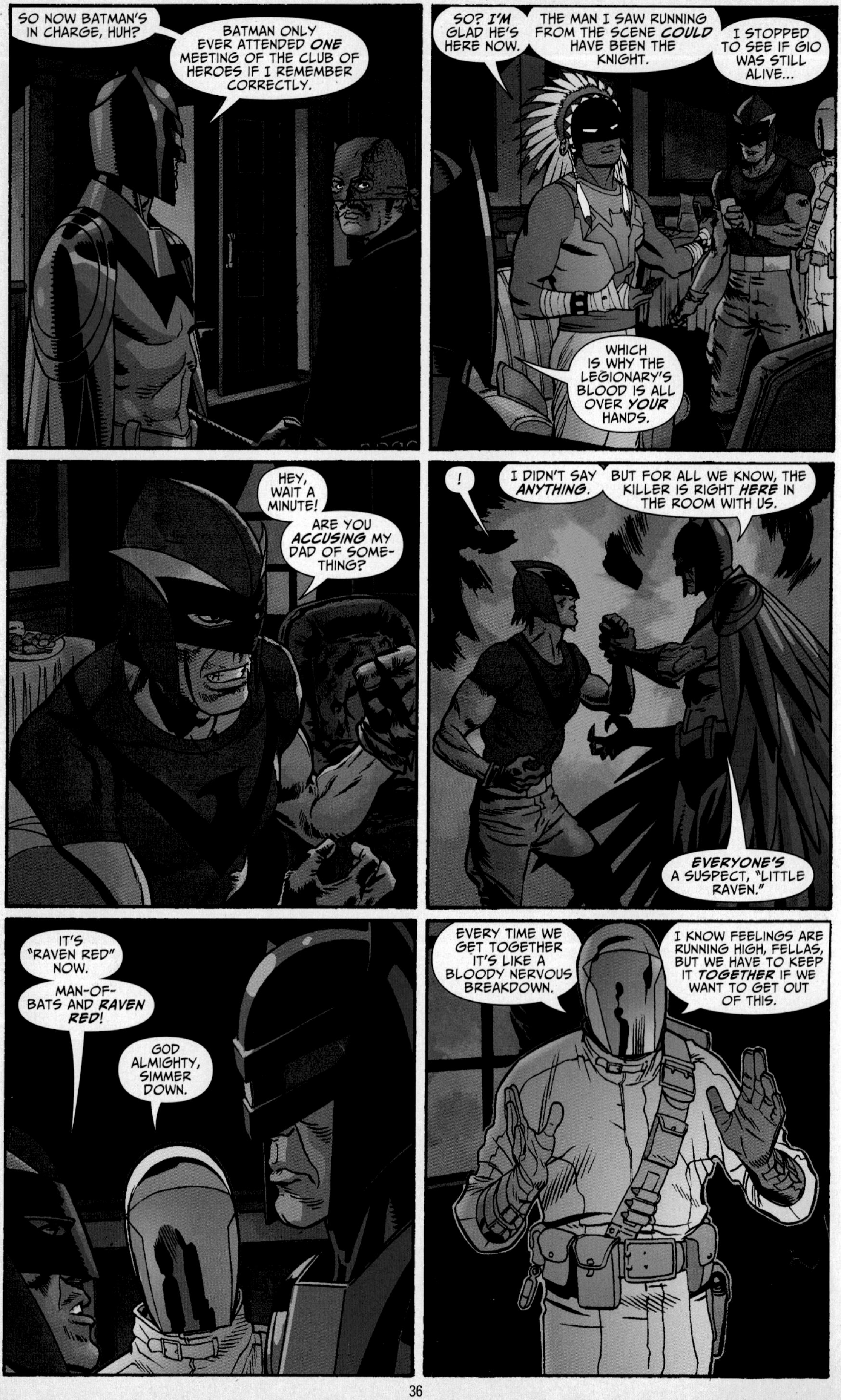
SO NOW BATMAN'S IN CHARGE, HUH?
BATMAN ONLY EVER ATTENDED ONE MEETING OF THE CLUB OF HEROES IF I REMEMBER CORRECTLY.
SO? I'M GLAD HE'S HERE NOW.
THE MAN I SAW RUNNING FROM THE SCENE COULD HAVE BEEN THE KNIGHT.
I STOPPED TO SEE IF GIO WAS STILL ALIVE...
WHICH IS WHY THE LEGIONARY'S BLOOD IS ALL OVER YOUR HANDS.
HEY, WAIT A MINUTE!
ARE YOU ACCUSING MY DAD OF SOME-THING?
!
I DIDN'T SAY ANYTHING.
BUT FOR ALL WE KNOW, THE KILLER IS RIGHT HERE IN THE ROOM WITH US.
EVERYONE'S A SUSPECT, "LITTLE RAVEN."
IT'S "RAVEN RED" NOW.
MAN-OF-BATS AND RAVEN RED!
GOD ALMIGHTY, SIMMER DOWN.
EVERY TIME WE GET TOGETHER IT'S LIKE A BLOODY NERVOUS BREAKDOWN.
I KNOW FEELINGS ARE RUNNING HIGH, FELLAS, BUT WE HAVE TO KEEP IT TOGETHER IF WE WANT TO GET OUT OF THIS.

NOM DE--!

I WAS STARTING TO *ENJOY* MY LIFE FOR THE FIRST TIME AFTER THOSE YEARS IN PRISON...

...NOW I'M TRAPPED ON AN *ISLAND* IN THE MIDDLE OF A TROPICAL STORM, BY A *MADMAN* WHO HAS KILLED AND *SKINNED* OUR HOST.

THE MADMAN COULD BE *ONE* OF US.

THEY SAY THE *KNIGHT'S* A RECOVERING DRUG ADDICT. I HEARD ON HIS LAST CASE HE WAS MIND-CONTROLLED BY A *GORILLA!*

CYRIL'S AWAYS BEEN A GOOD KID. YOU'D BETTER PRAY NOTHING'S HAPPENED TO HIM OR WE'RE DOWN ONE FIGHTER I WOULD RATHER HAVE AT MY SIDE.

ANYWAY, WHAT'S SO *FUNNY?*

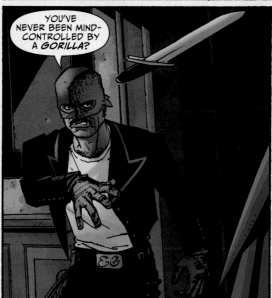

YOU'VE NEVER BEEN MIND-CONTROLLED BY A *GORILLA?*

THOK

NOT REALLY.

WE KNOW HE HAD THE *MOTIVE.*

YOU SAW IT.

WE *ALL* SAW WHAT HAPPENED THAT DAY.

THAK

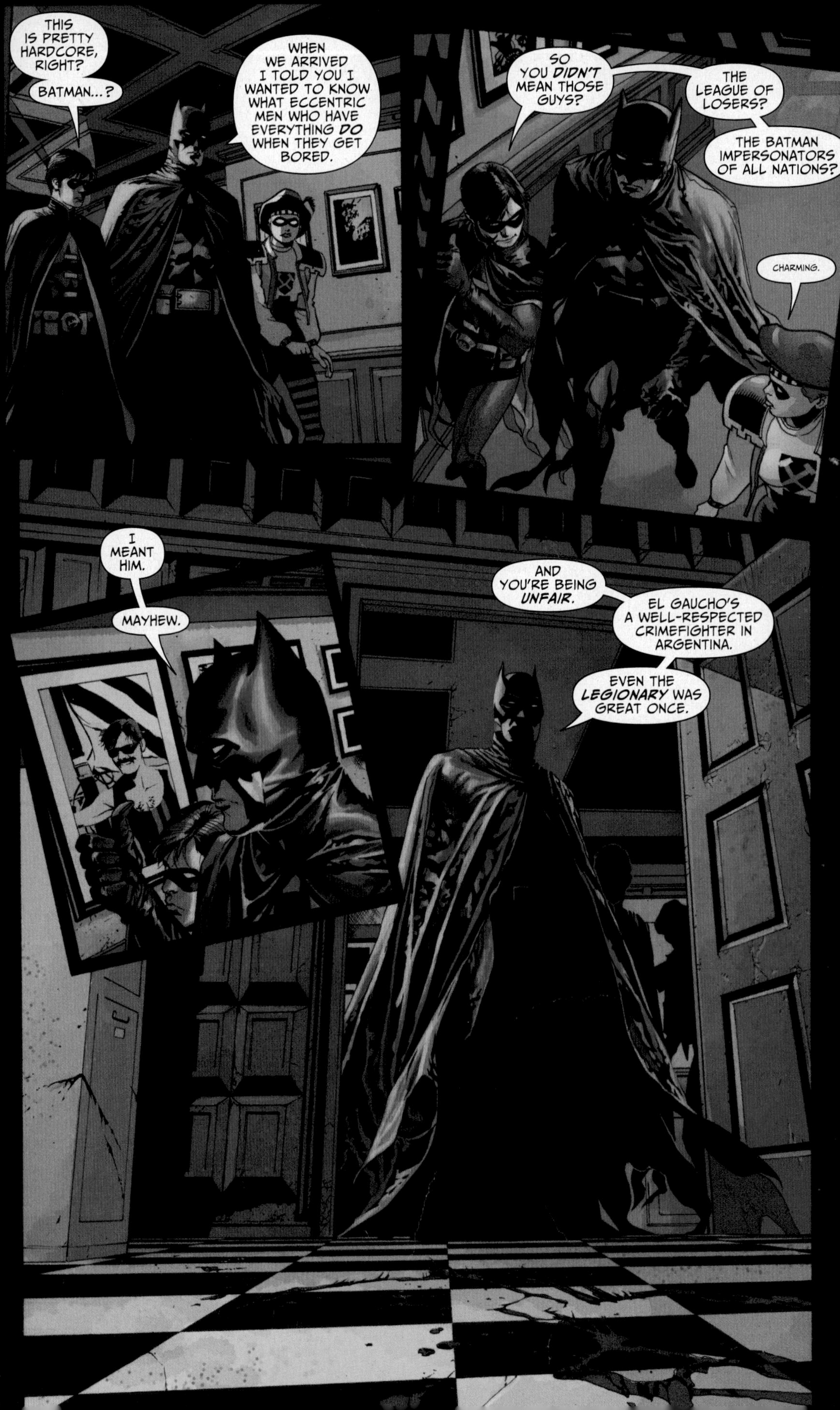
THIS IS PRETTY HARDCORE, RIGHT?
BATMAN...?
WHEN WE ARRIVED I TOLD YOU I WANTED TO KNOW WHAT ECCENTRIC MEN WHO HAVE EVERYTHING DO WHEN THEY GET BORED.
SO YOU DIDN'T MEAN THOSE GUYS?
THE LEAGUE OF LOSERS?
THE BATMAN IMPERSONATORS OF ALL NATIONS?
CHARMING.
I MEANT HIM.
MAYHEW.
AND YOU'RE BEING UNFAIR.
EL GAUCHO'S A WELL-RESPECTED CRIMEFIGHTER IN ARGENTINA.
EVEN THE LEGIONARY WAS GREAT ONCE.

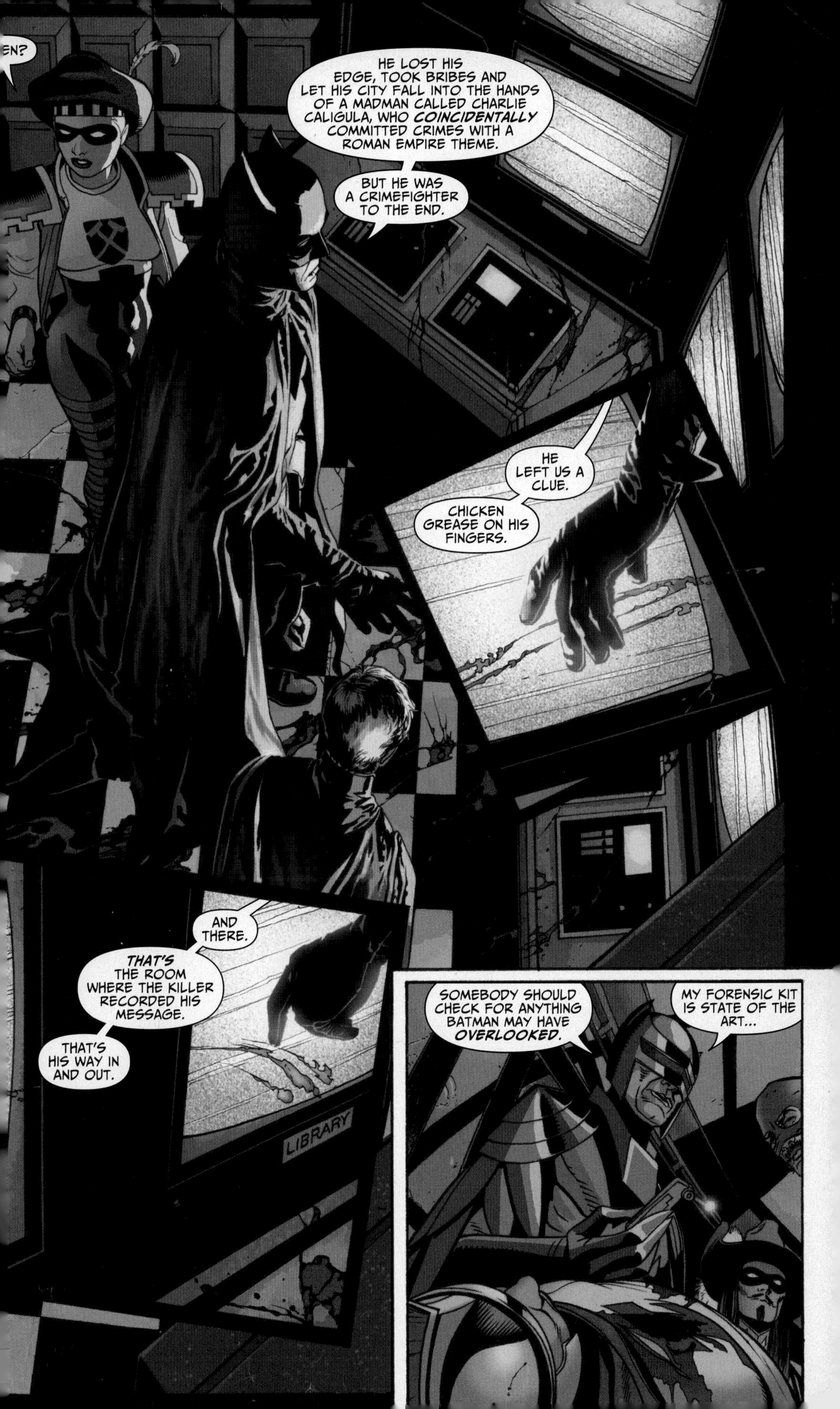

EN?
HE LOST HIS EDGE, TOOK BRIBES AND LET HIS CITY FALL INTO THE HANDS OF A MADMAN CALLED CHARLIE CALIGULA, WHO *COINCIDENTALLY* COMMITTED CRIMES WITH A ROMAN EMPIRE THEME.
BUT HE WAS A CRIMEFIGHTER TO THE END.
HE LEFT US A CLUE.
CHICKEN GREASE ON HIS FINGERS.
AND THERE.
THAT'S THE ROOM WHERE THE KILLER RECORDED HIS MESSAGE.
THAT'S HIS WAY IN AND OUT.
LIBRARY
SOMEBODY SHOULD CHECK FOR ANYTHING BATMAN MAY HAVE *OVERLOOKED*.
MY FORENSIC KIT IS STATE OF THE ART...

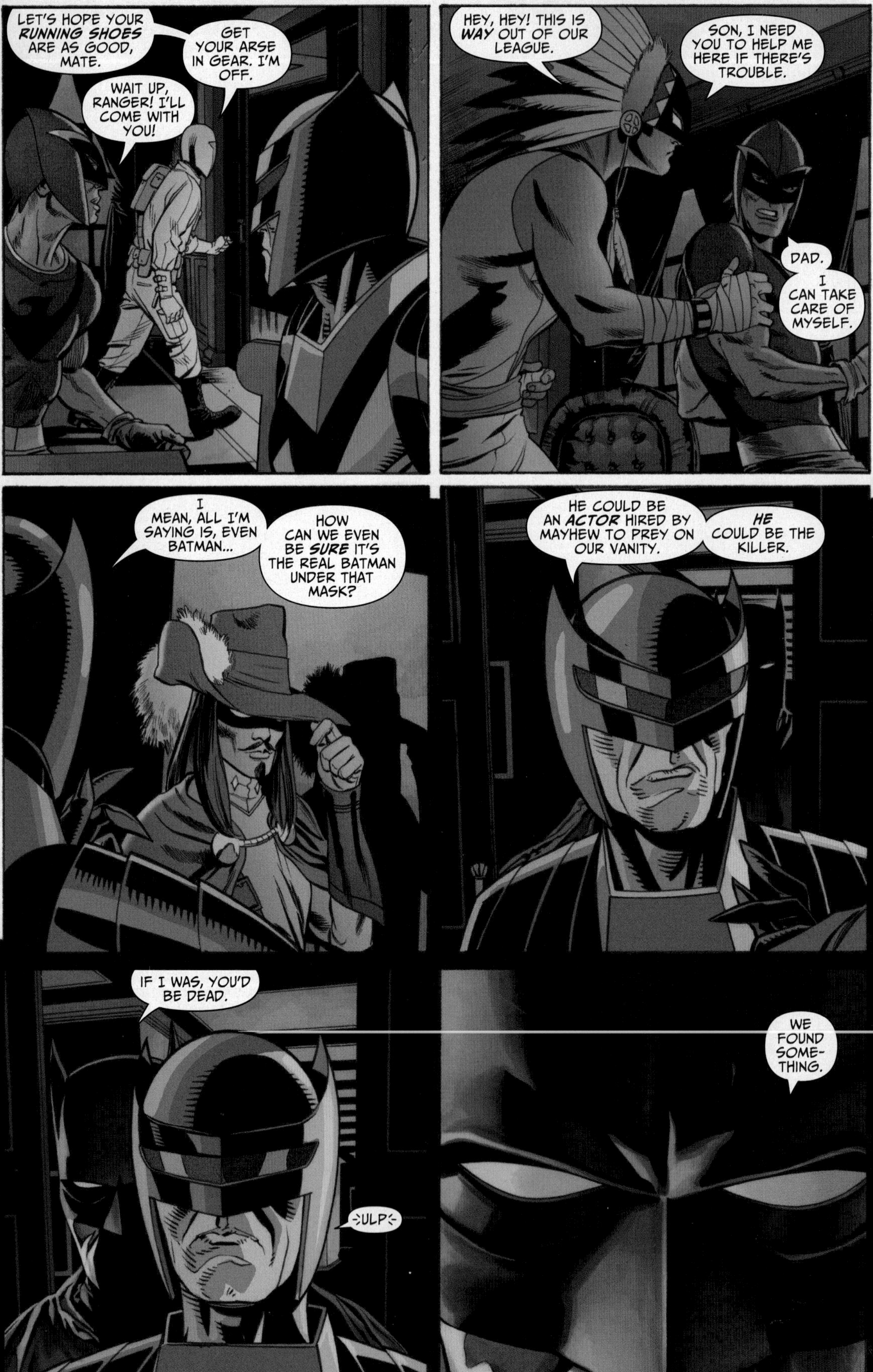
LET'S HOPE YOUR RUNNING SHOES ARE AS GOOD, MATE.
GET YOUR ARSE IN GEAR. I'M OFF.
WAIT UP, RANGER! I'LL COME WITH YOU!
HEY, HEY! THIS IS WAY OUT OF OUR LEAGUE.
SON, I NEED YOU TO HELP ME HERE IF THERE'S TROUBLE.
DAD.
I CAN TAKE CARE OF MYSELF.
I MEAN, ALL I'M SAYING IS, EVEN BATMAN...
HOW CAN WE EVEN BE SURE IT'S THE REAL BATMAN UNDER THAT MASK?
HE COULD BE AN ACTOR HIRED BY MAYHEW TO PREY ON OUR VANITY.
HE COULD BE THE KILLER.
IF I WAS, YOU'D BE DEAD.
ULP
WE FOUND SOME-THING.

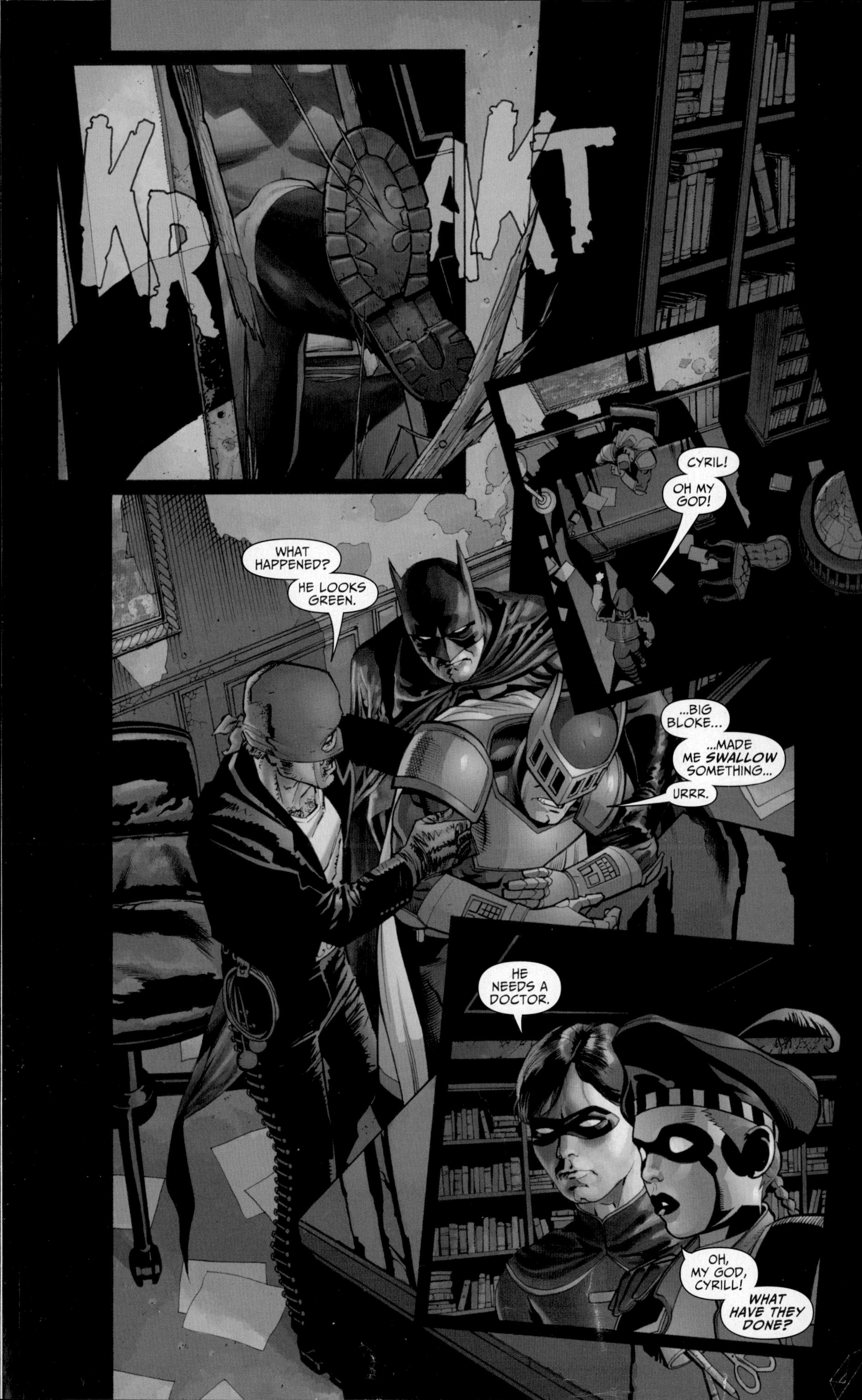
CYRIL!
OH MY GOD!
WHAT HAPPENED?
HE LOOKS GREEN.
...BIG BLOKE...
...MADE ME *SWALLOW* SOMETHING...
URRR.
HE NEEDS A DOCTOR.
OH, MY GOD, CYRILL!
WHAT HAVE THEY DONE?

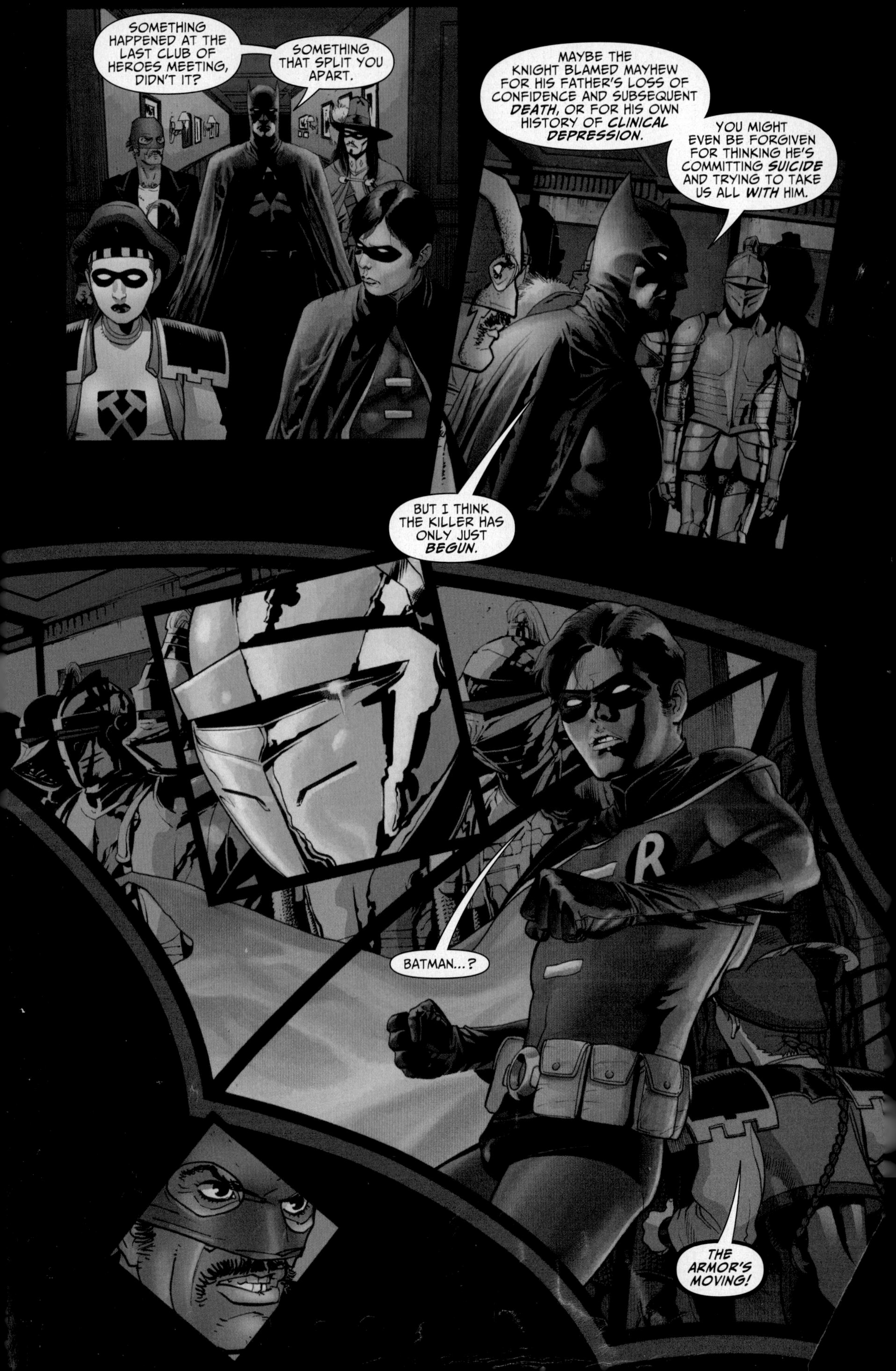
SOMETHING HAPPENED AT THE LAST CLUB OF HEROES MEETING, DIDN'T IT?
SOMETHING THAT SPLIT YOU APART.
MAYBE THE KNIGHT BLAMED MAYHEW FOR HIS FATHER'S LOSS OF CONFIDENCE AND SUBSEQUENT *DEATH*, OR FOR HIS OWN HISTORY OF *CLINICAL DEPRESSION*.
YOU MIGHT EVEN BE FORGIVEN FOR THINKING HE'S COMMITTING *SUICIDE* AND TRYING TO TAKE US ALL *WITH* HIM.
BUT I THINK THE KILLER HAS ONLY JUST *BEGUN*.
BATMAN...?
THE ARMOR'S MOVING!

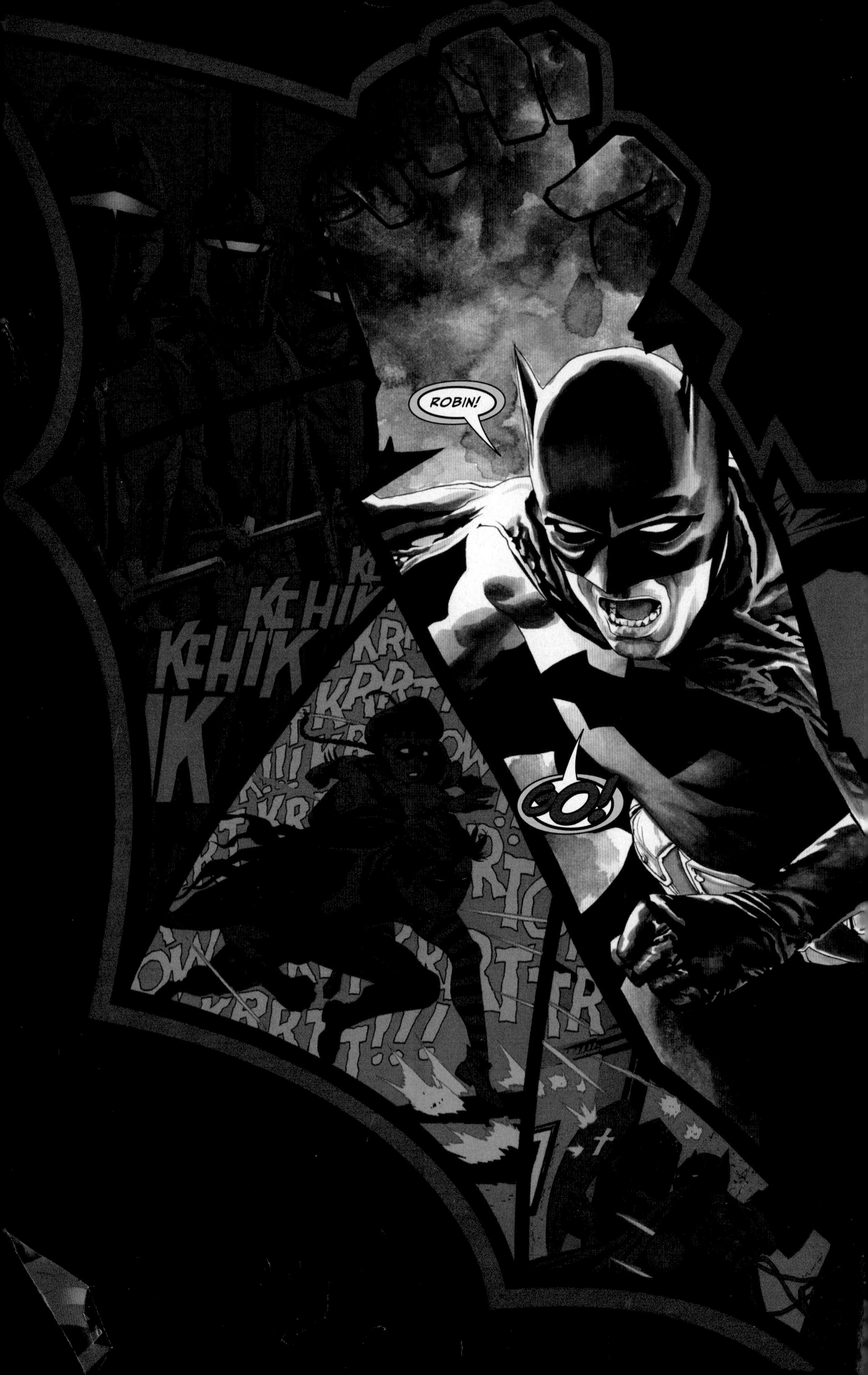
ROBIN!
KCHIK

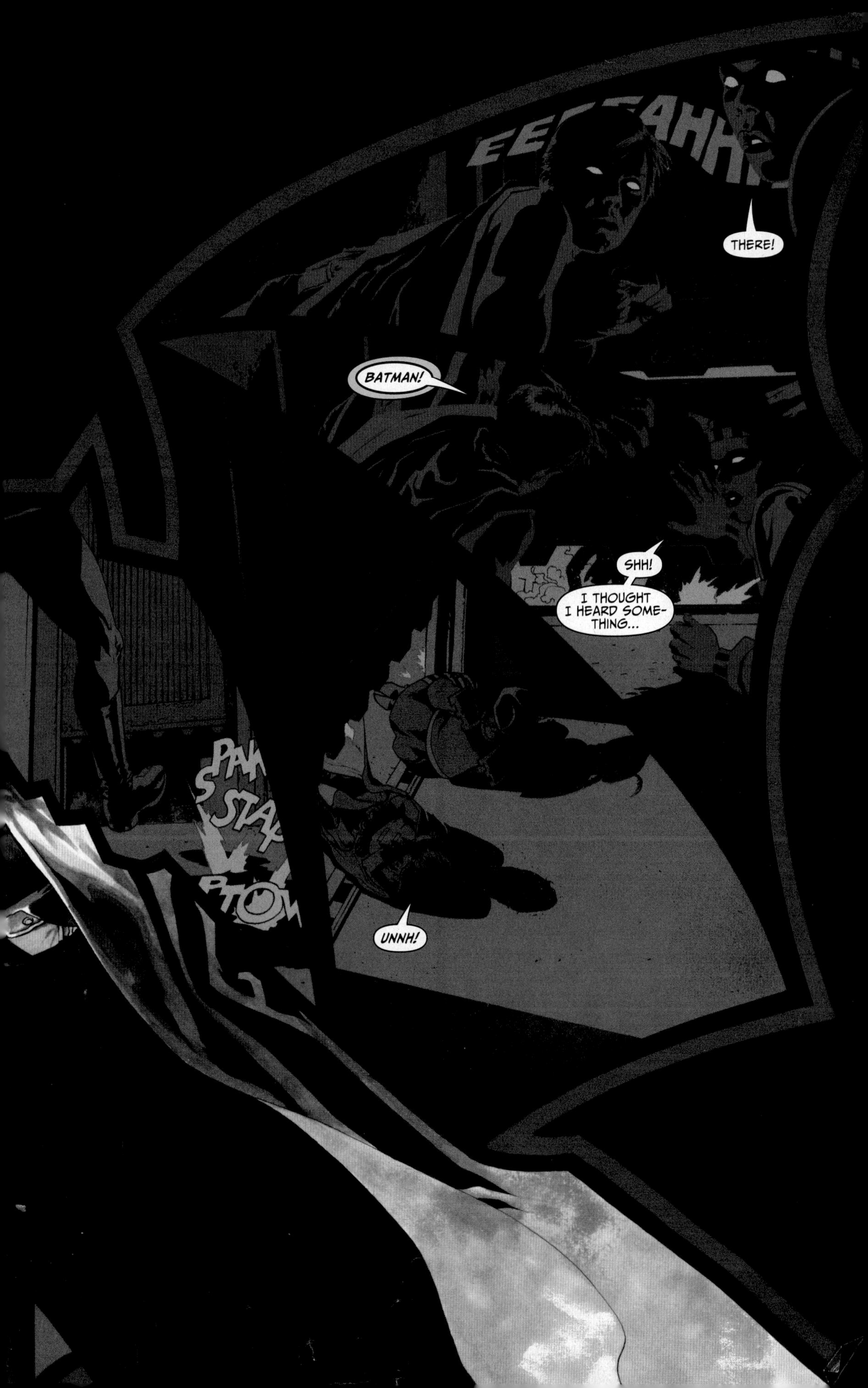
THERE!
BATMAN!
SHH!
I THOUGHT I HEARD SOME-THING...
UNNH!

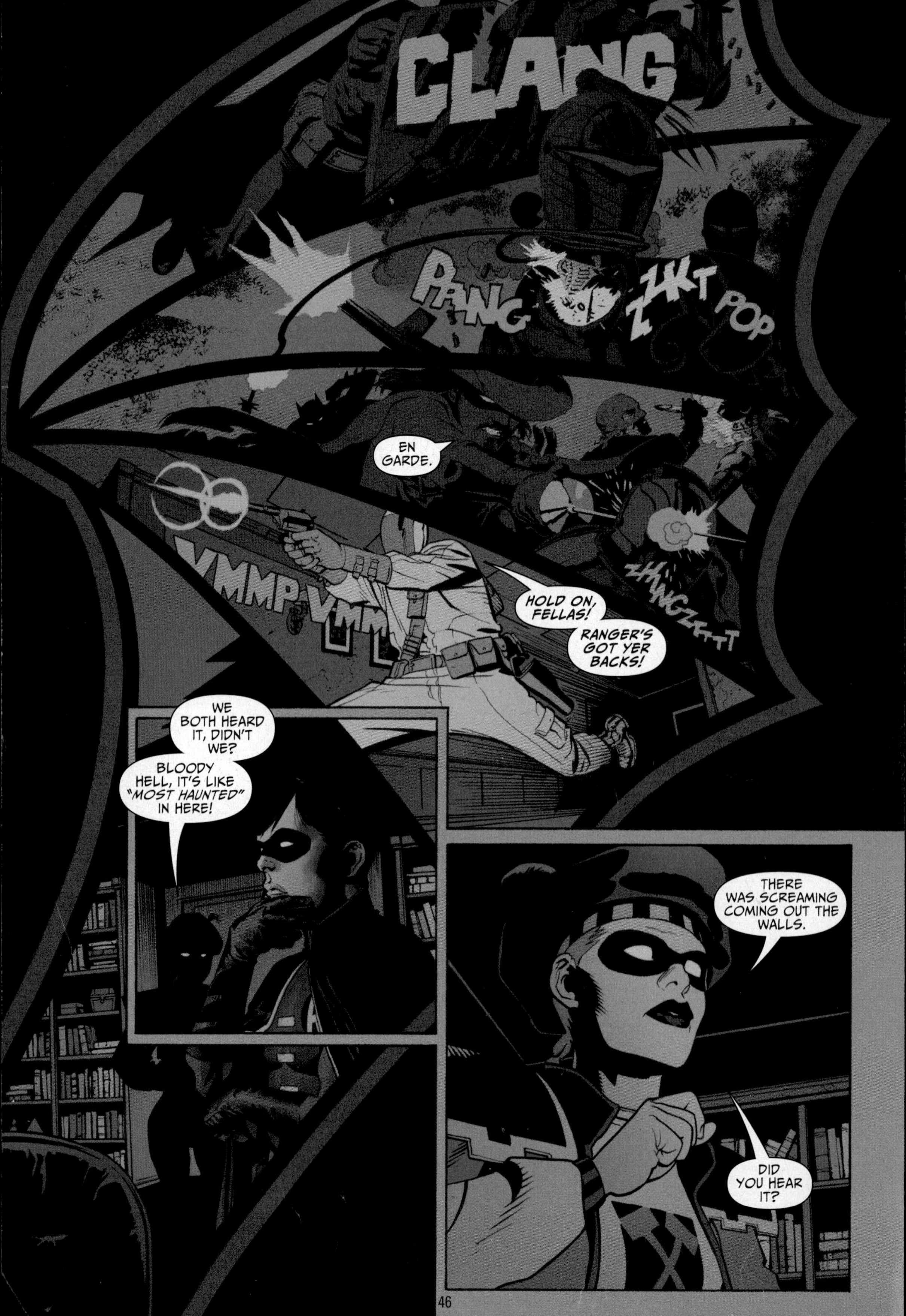

CLANG
PRANG
ZZKT
POP
EN GARDE.
VMMP VMM
ZHANGZKTTT
HOLD ON, FELLAS!
RANGER'S GOT YER BACKS!
WE BOTH HEARD IT, DIDN'T WE?
BLOODY HELL, IT'S LIKE *"MOST HAUNTED"* IN HERE!
THERE WAS SCREAMING COMING OUT THE WALLS.
DID YOU HEAR IT?

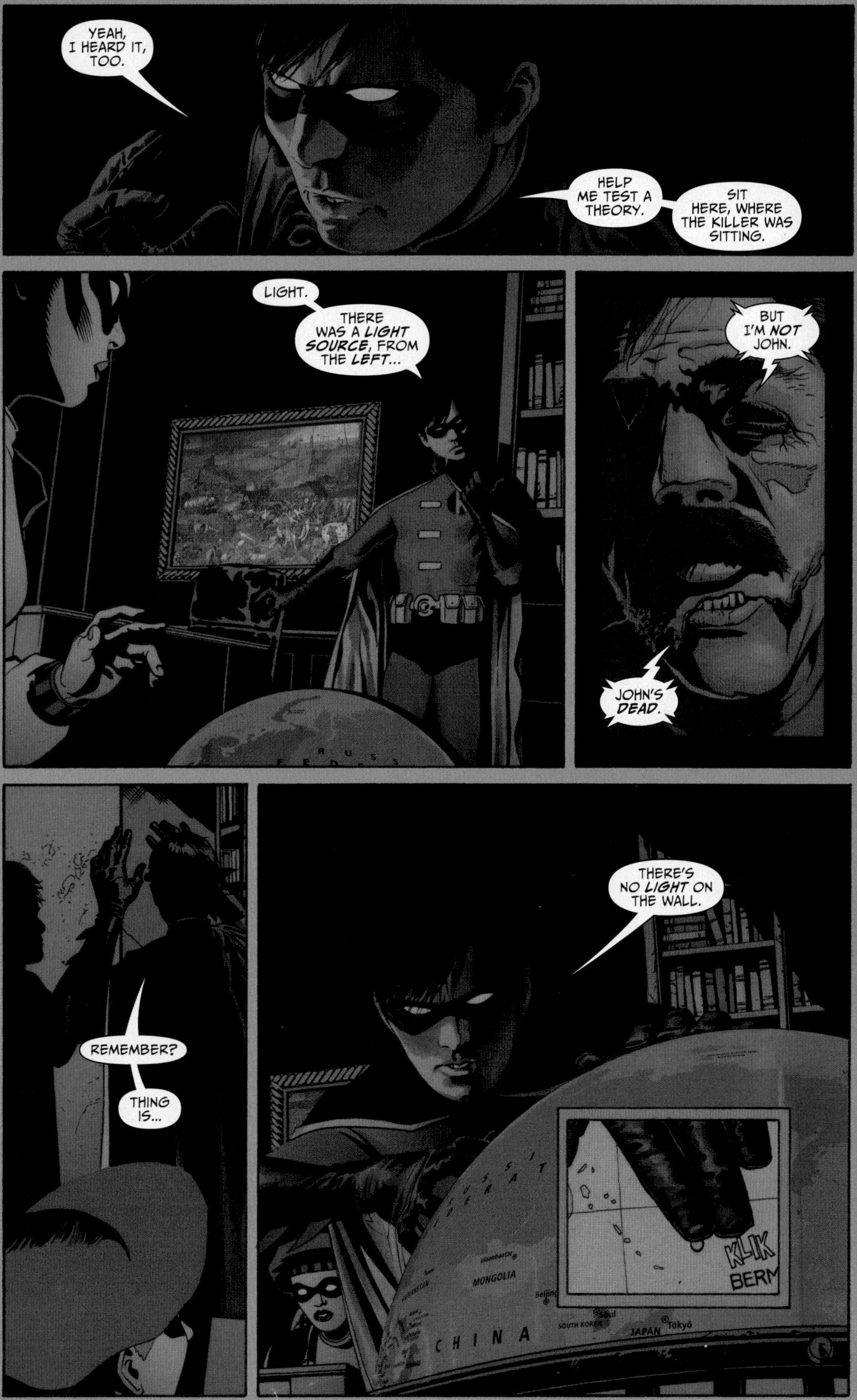
YEAH, I HEARD IT, TOO.
HELP ME TEST A THEORY.
SIT HERE, WHERE THE KILLER WAS SITTING.
LIGHT.
THERE WAS A LIGHT SOURCE, FROM THE LEFT...
BUT I'M NOT JOHN.
JOHN'S DEAD.
REMEMBER?
THING IS...
THERE'S NO LIGHT ON THE WALL.
KLIK
MONGOLIA
CHINA
SOUTH KOREA
JAPAN
Tōkyō
BERM

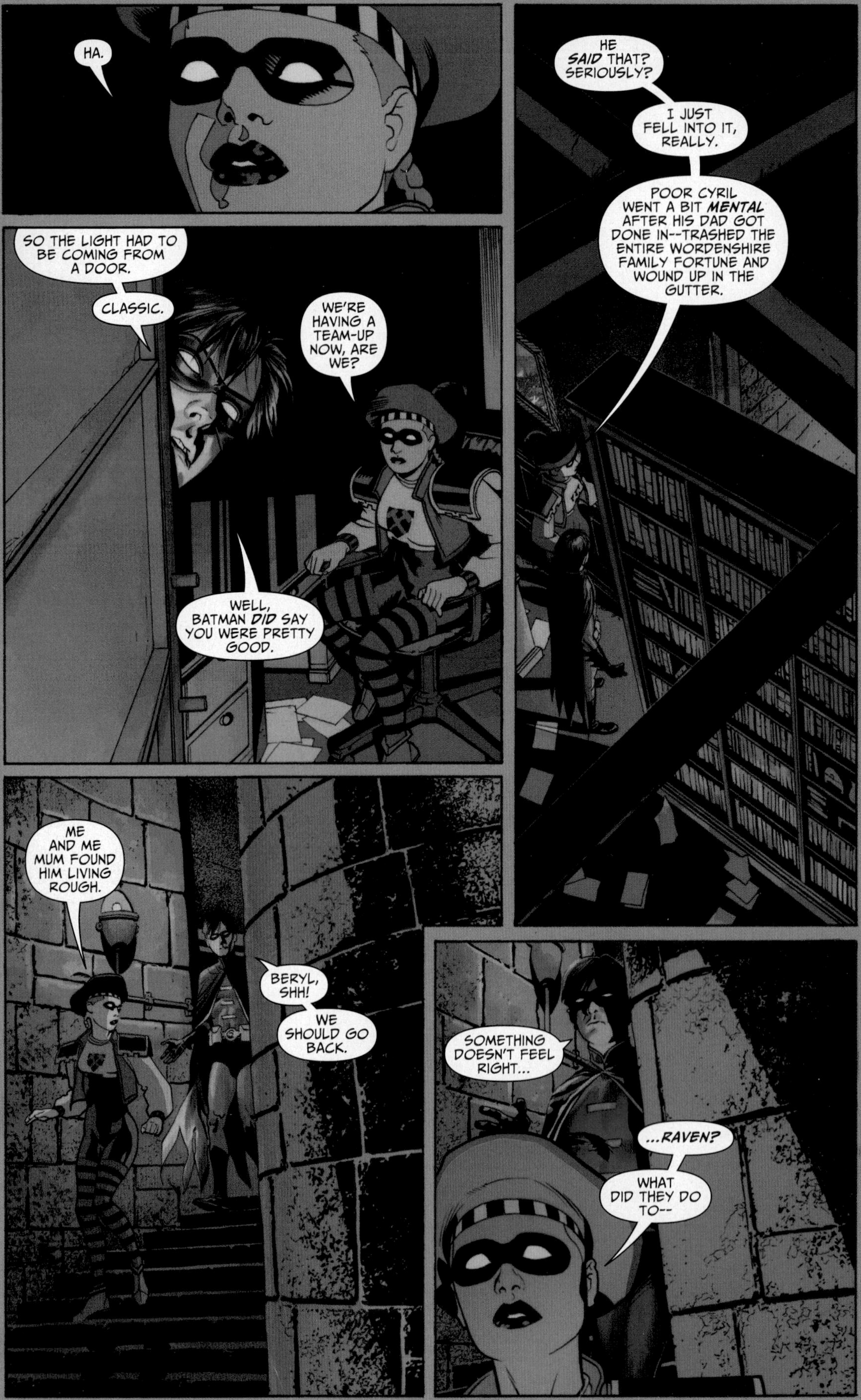
HA.
HE SAID THAT? SERIOUSLY?
I JUST FELL INTO IT, REALLY.
POOR CYRIL WENT A BIT MENTAL AFTER HIS DAD GOT DONE IN--TRASHED THE ENTIRE WORDENSHIRE FAMILY FORTUNE AND WOUND UP IN THE GUTTER.
SO THE LIGHT HAD TO BE COMING FROM A DOOR.
CLASSIC.
WE'RE HAVING A TEAM-UP NOW, ARE WE?
WELL, BATMAN DID SAY YOU WERE PRETTY GOOD.
ME AND ME MUM FOUND HIM LIVING ROUGH.
BERYL, SHH!
WE SHOULD GO BACK.
SOMETHING DOESN'T FEEL RIGHT...
...RAVEN?
WHAT DID THEY DO TO--

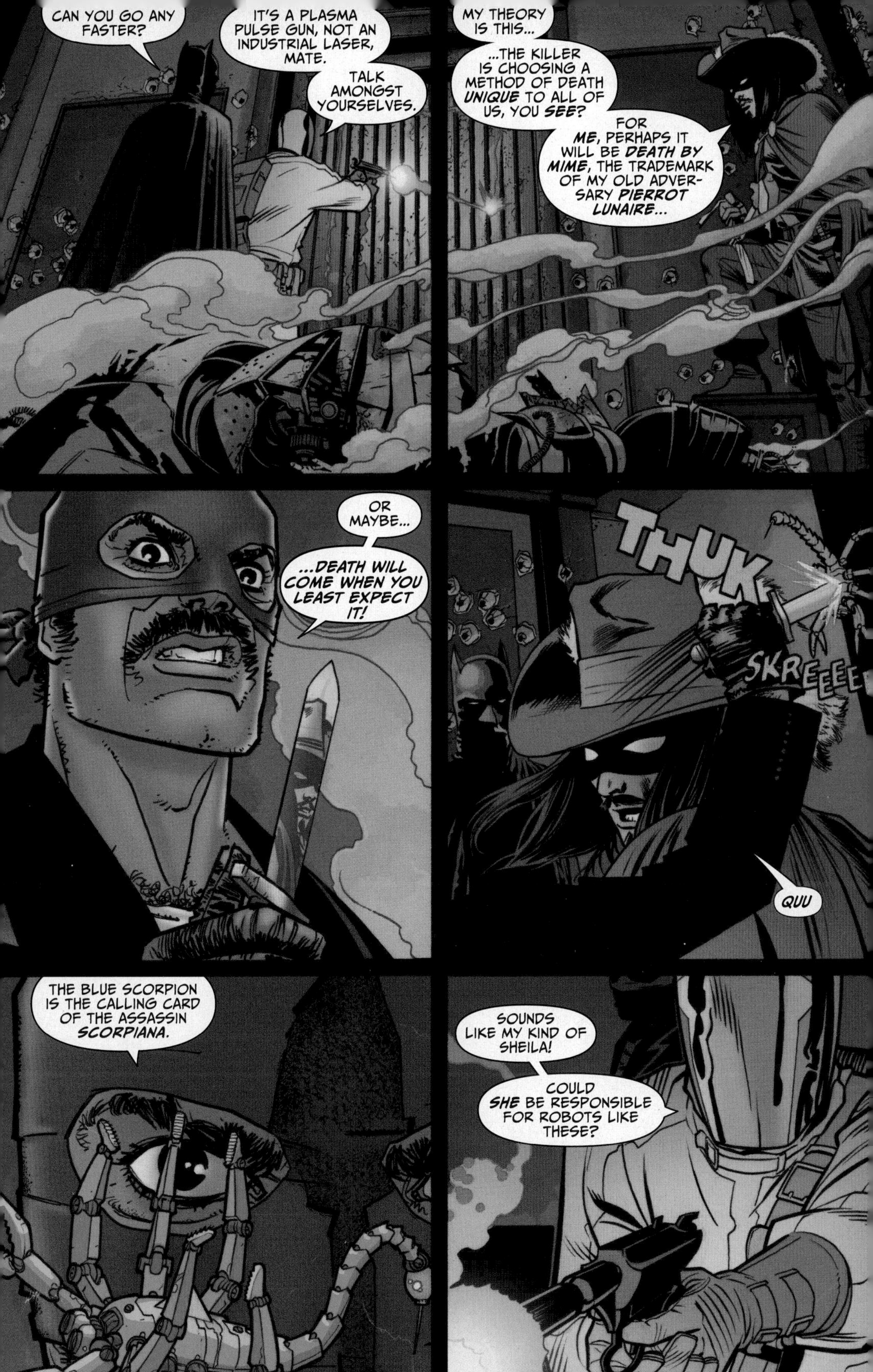
CAN YOU GO ANY FASTER?
IT'S A PLASMA PULSE GUN, NOT AN INDUSTRIAL LASER, MATE.
TALK AMONGST YOURSELVES.
MY THEORY IS THIS...
...THE KILLER IS CHOOSING A METHOD OF DEATH UNIQUE TO ALL OF US, YOU SEE?
FOR ME, PERHAPS IT WILL BE DEATH BY MIME, THE TRADEMARK OF MY OLD ADVERSARY PIERROT LUNAIRE...
OR MAYBE...
...DEATH WILL COME WHEN YOU LEAST EXPECT IT!
THUK
SKREEEEE
QUU
THE BLUE SCORPION IS THE CALLING CARD OF THE ASSASSIN SCORPIANA.
SOUNDS LIKE MY KIND OF SHEILA!
COULD SHE BE RESPONSIBLE FOR ROBOTS LIKE THESE?

NO...

...THAT WOULD BE THE SPECIALTY OF *EL SOMBRERO.*

SOMBRERO IS A *LUNATIC* WHO DESIGNS AND CREATES FANTASTIC, ARTISTIC *DEATH TRAPS.* FOR CROOKS WHO DON'T HAVE THE IMAGINATION TO MAKE THEIR *OWN.*

YOU THINK HE COULD BUILD A DEATH TRAP AS BIG AS THIS *HOUSE?*

ALL HE NEEDS IS MONEY AND TIME.

THIS WHOLE *ISLAND* COULD BE HIS WORK.

YOU KNOW WHAT HAPPENED THAT DAY, BATMAN?

SOME MEN WHO LIKED TO FIGHT HAD A *FIGHT.* PAHFF!

JOHN MAYHEW'S "CLUB OF HEROES" WAS EXPOSED AS A SHAM.

AND SOMETHING THAT MIGHT HAVE LED TO GLOBAL MEDIA *EXPOSURE,* MAYBE EVEN *JUSTICE LEAGUE* STATUS, LED NOWHERE.

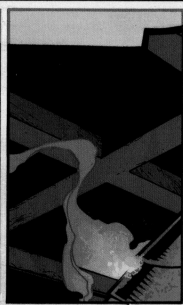

WE HAVE TO WONDER WHO HAD THE MOST TO LOSE WHEN THE CLUB OF HEROES WENT DOWN.

YOU STILL THINK *ONE MAN* IS DOING THIS?

MAYHEW *FAILED* WITH HIS CLUB OF *HEROES.* WHO CAN SAY...?

MAYBE HE THOUGHT HE COULD SUCCEED WITH A CLUB OF *VILLAINS?*

MOTHER OF GOD.

WINGMAN!

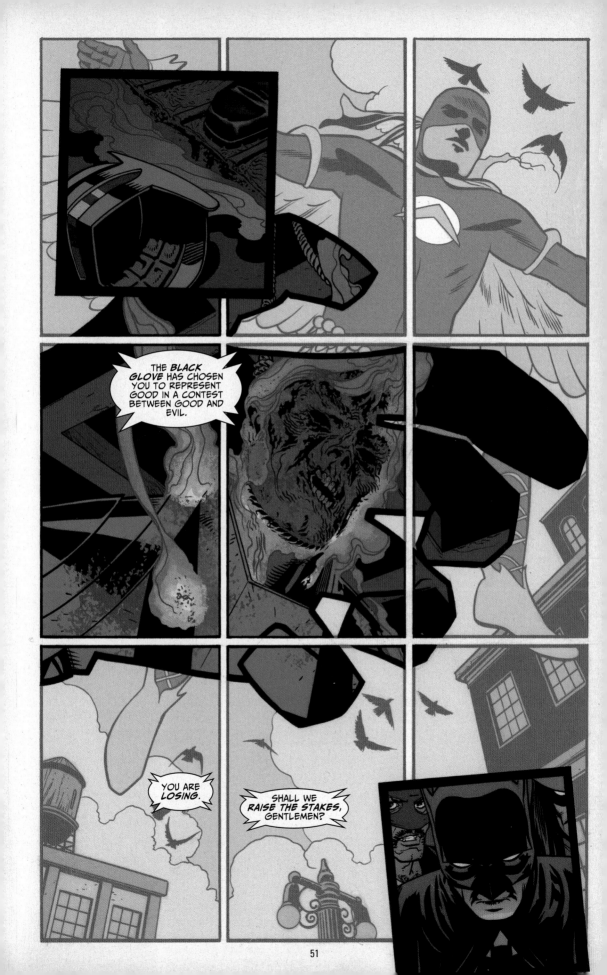

THE *BLACK GLOVE* HAS CHOSEN YOU TO REPRESENT GOOD IN A CONTEST BETWEEN GOOD AND EVIL.

YOU ARE *LOSING.*

SHALL WE *RAISE THE STAKES,* GENTLEMEN?

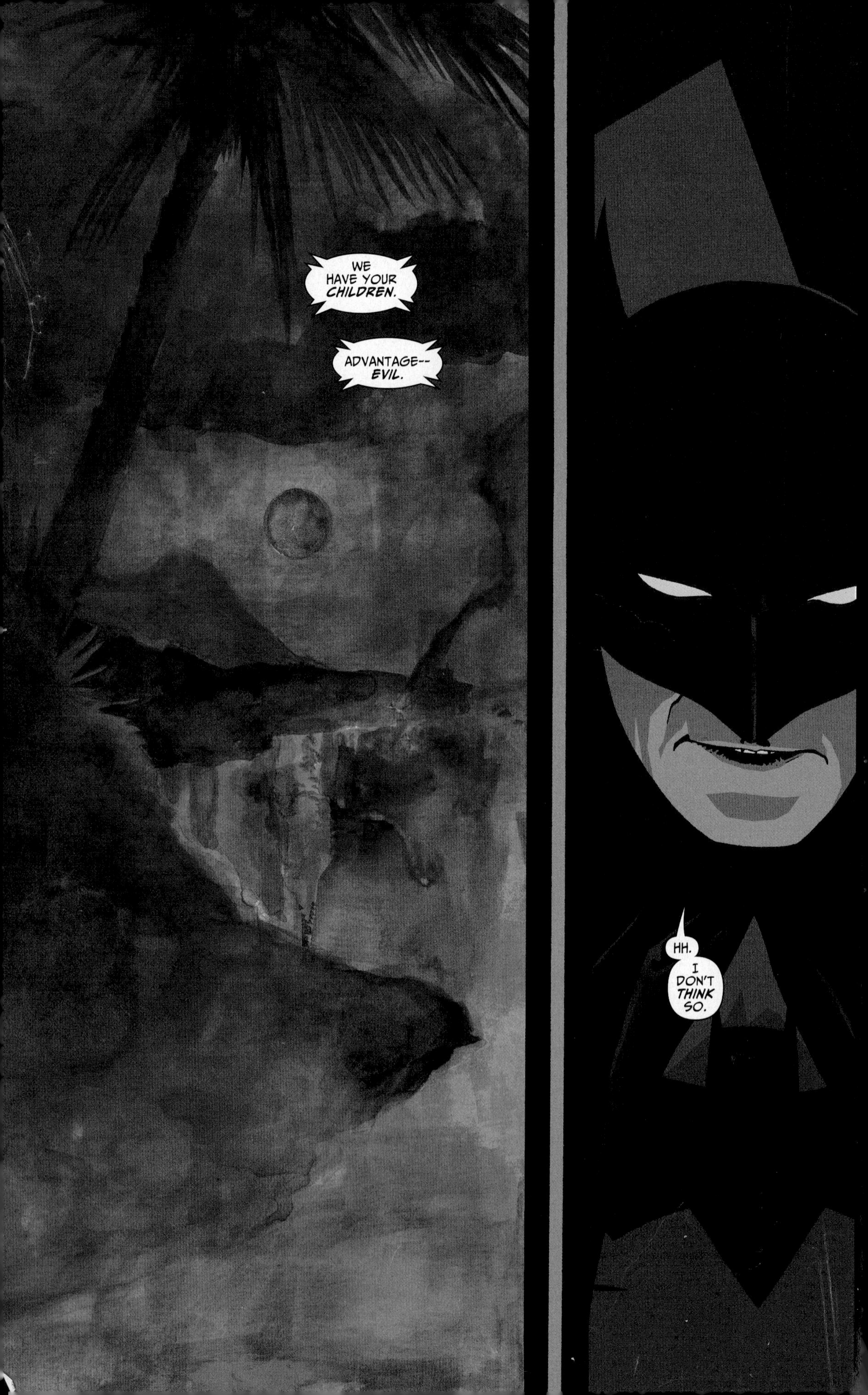
WE HAVE YOUR CHILDREN.
ADVANTAGE-- EVIL.
HH. I DON'T THINK SO.

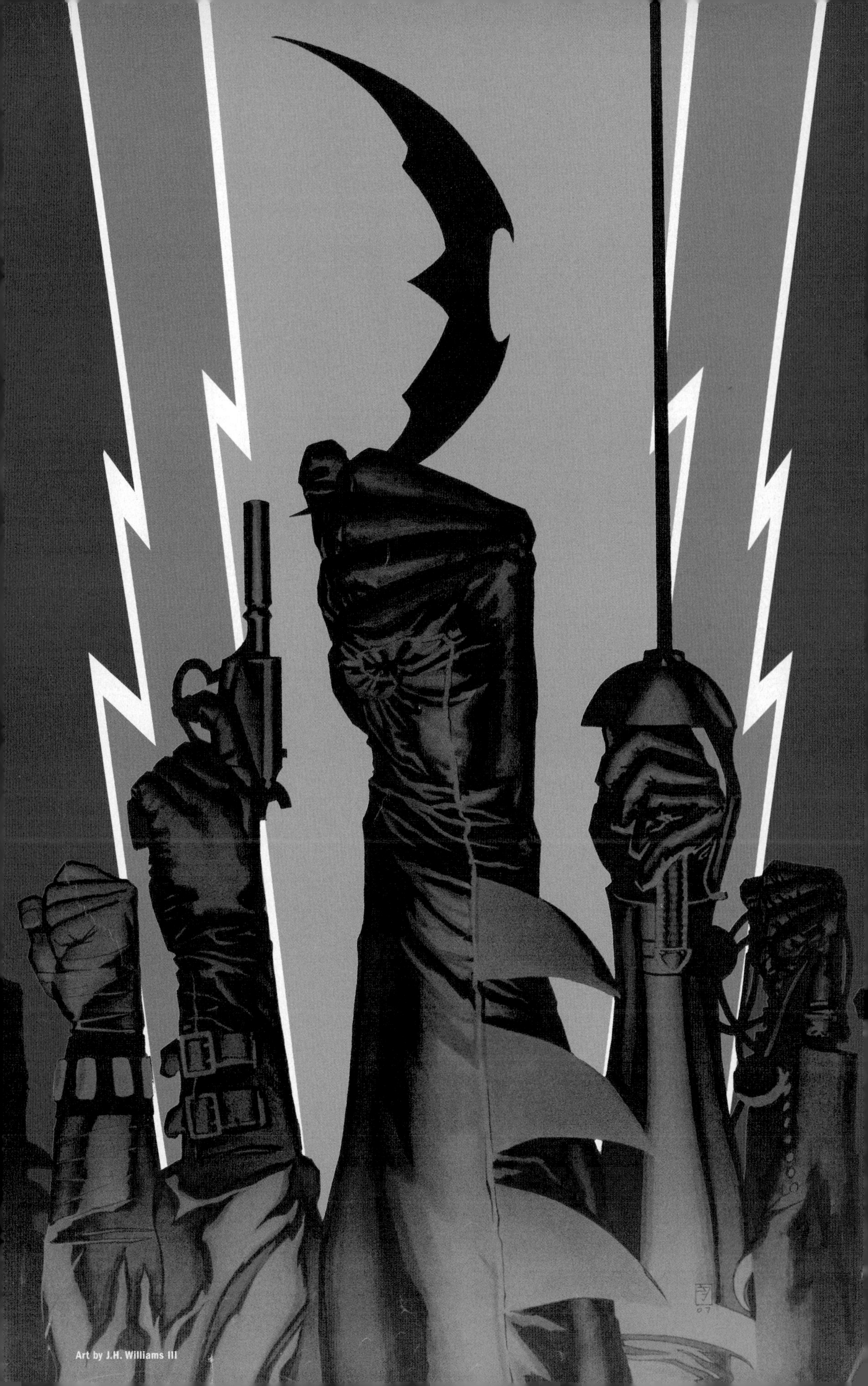

Art by J.H. Williams III

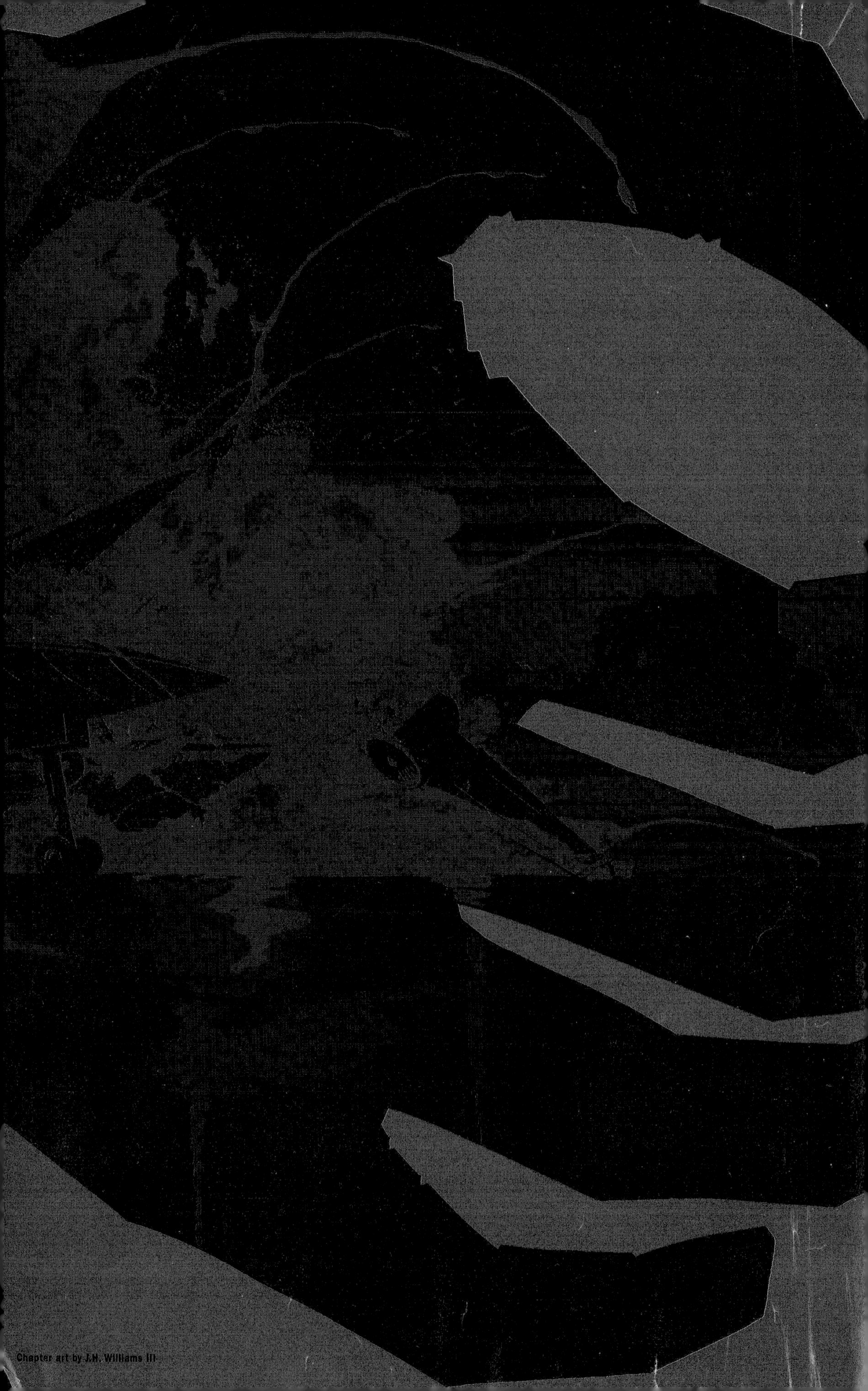

Chapter art by J.H. Williams III

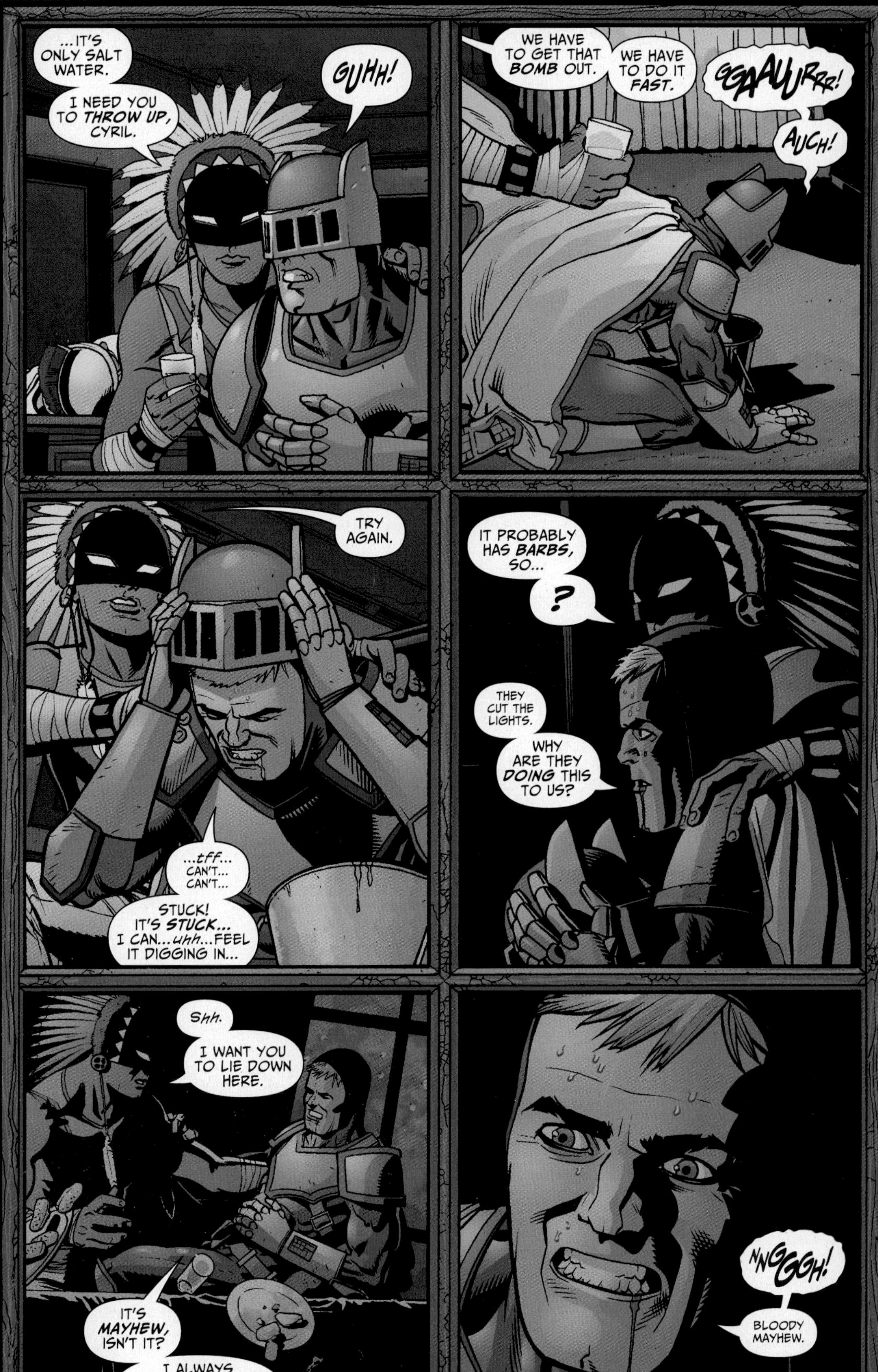

...IT'S ONLY SALT WATER.
I NEED YOU TO THROW UP, CYRIL.
GUHH!
WE HAVE TO GET THAT BOMB OUT.
WE HAVE TO DO IT FAST.
GGAAUURRR!
AUCH!
TRY AGAIN.
...tff... CAN'T... CAN'T...
STUCK! IT'S STUCK... I CAN...uhh...FEEL IT DIGGING IN...
IT PROBABLY HAS BARBS, SO...
?
THEY CUT THE LIGHTS.
WHY ARE THEY DOING THIS TO US?
Shh.
I WANT YOU TO LIE DOWN HERE.
IT'S MAYHEW, ISN'T IT?
I ALWAYS KNEW THERE WAS SOMETHING CREEPY ABOUT HIM.
NNGGGH!
BLOODY MAYHEW.

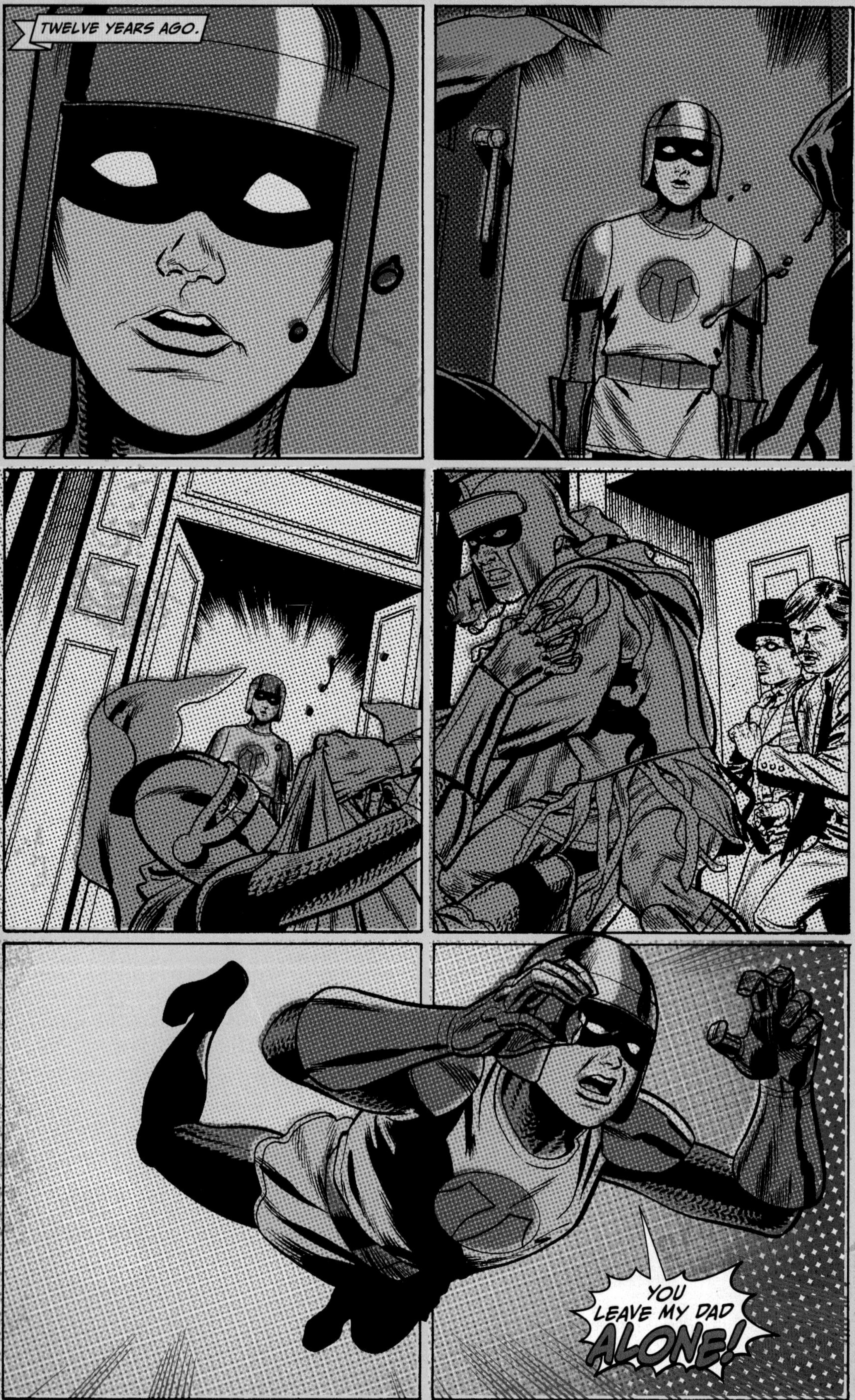
TWELVE YEARS AGO.
YOU LEAVE MY DAD ALONE!

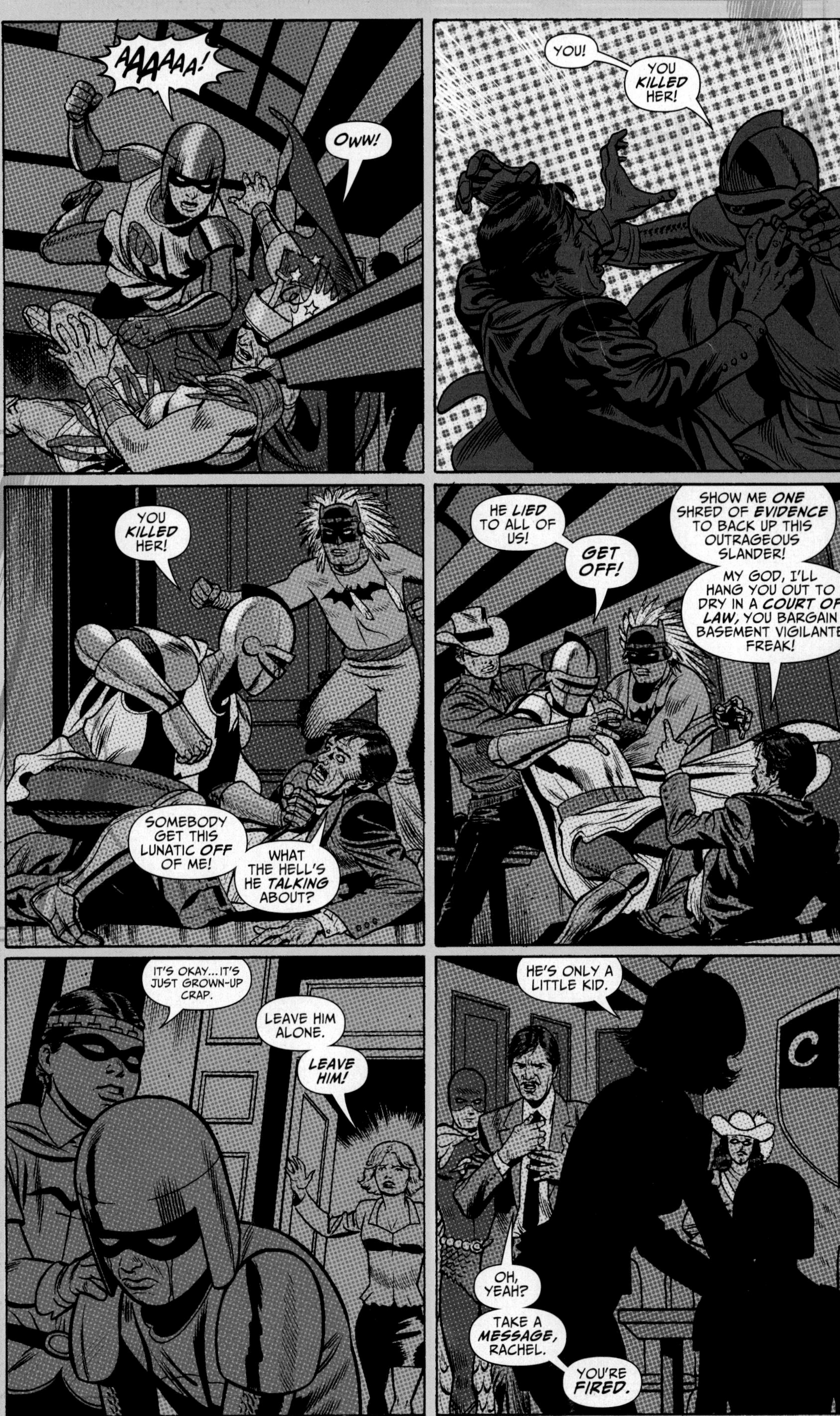
AAAAAA!
OWW!
YOU!
YOU KILLED HER!
YOU KILLED HER!
SOMEBODY GET THIS LUNATIC OFF OF ME!
WHAT THE HELL'S HE TALKING ABOUT?
HE LIED TO ALL OF US!
GET OFF!
SHOW ME ONE SHRED OF EVIDENCE TO BACK UP THIS OUTRAGEOUS SLANDER!
MY GOD, I'LL HANG YOU OUT TO DRY IN A COURT OF LAW, YOU BARGAIN BASEMENT VIGILANTE FREAK!
IT'S OKAY... IT'S JUST GROWN-UP CRAP.
LEAVE HIM ALONE.
LEAVE HIM!
HE'S ONLY A LITTLE KID.
OH, YEAH?
TAKE A MESSAGE, RACHEL.
YOU'RE FIRED.

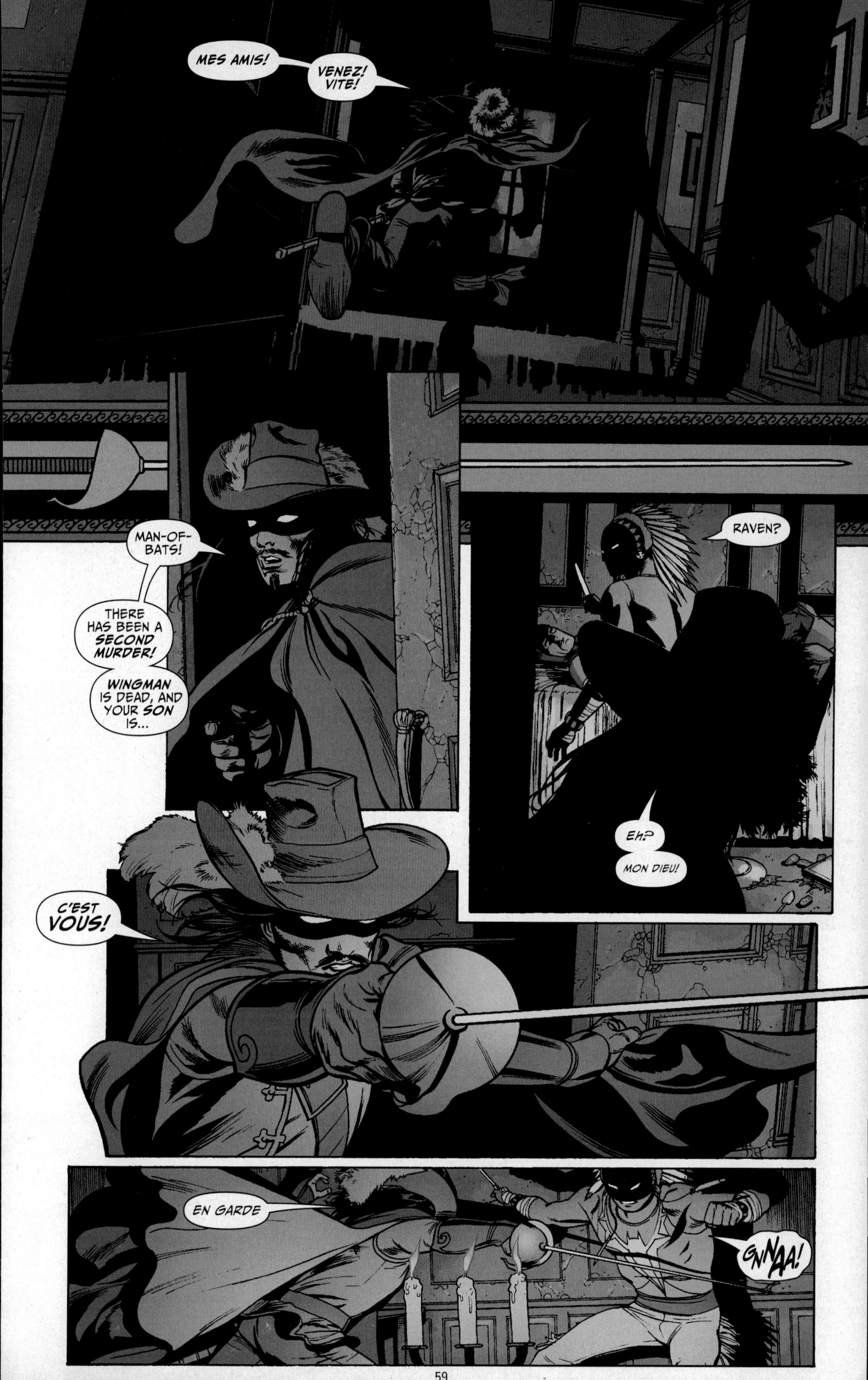
MES AMIS!
VENEZ! VITE!
MAN-OF-BATS!
THERE HAS BEEN A SECOND MURDER!
WINGMAN IS DEAD, AND YOUR SON IS...
RAVEN?
Eh?
MON DIEU!
C'EST VOUS!
EN GARDE
GNNAA!

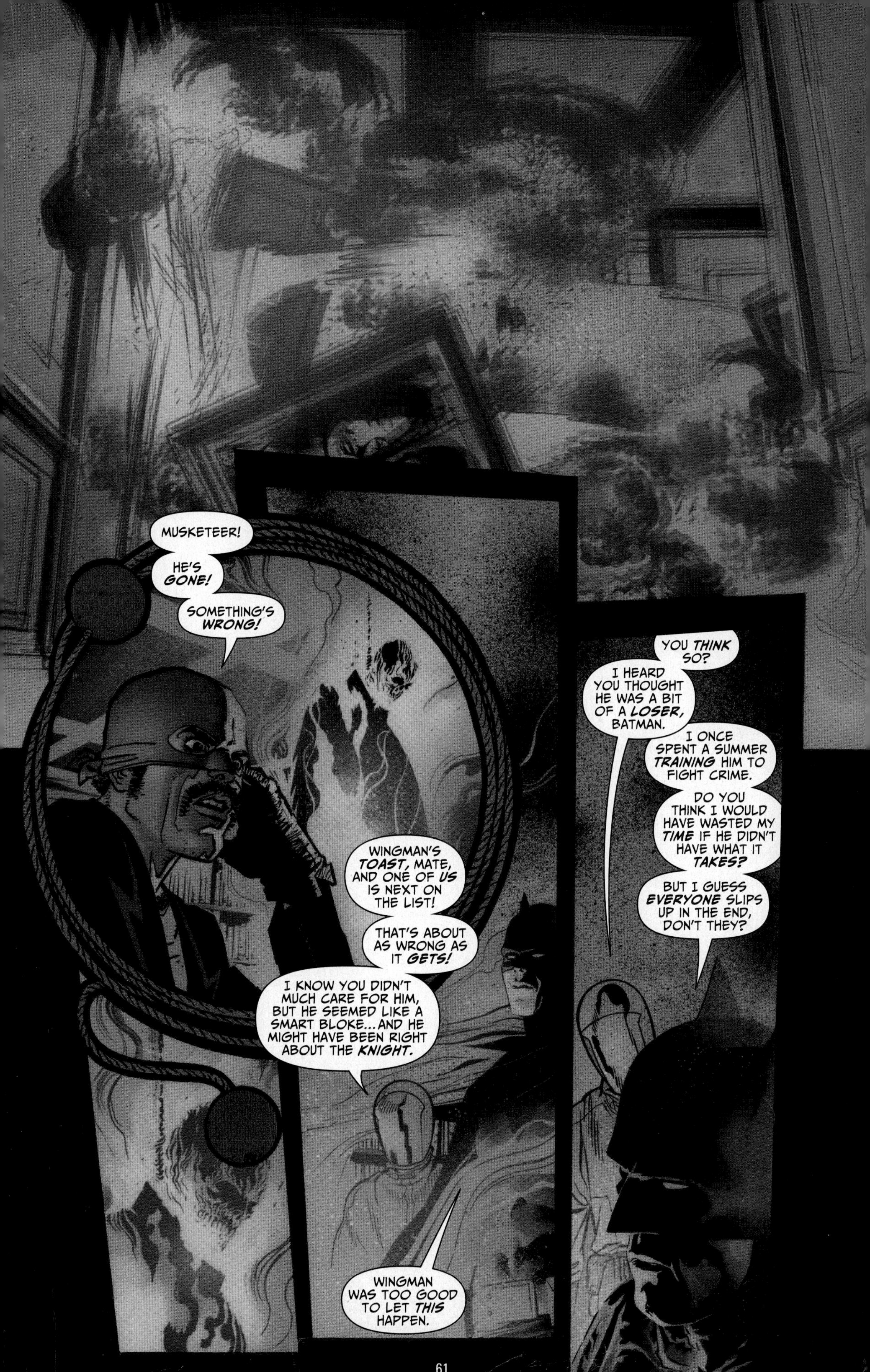
MUSKETEER!
HE'S GONE!
SOMETHING'S WRONG!
YOU THINK SO?
I HEARD YOU THOUGHT HE WAS A BIT OF A LOSER, BATMAN.
I ONCE SPENT A SUMMER TRAINING HIM TO FIGHT CRIME.
DO YOU THINK I WOULD HAVE WASTED MY TIME IF HE DIDN'T HAVE WHAT IT TAKES?
BUT I GUESS EVERYONE SLIPS UP IN THE END, DON'T THEY?
WINGMAN'S TOAST, MATE, AND ONE OF US IS NEXT ON THE LIST!
THAT'S ABOUT AS WRONG AS IT GETS!
I KNOW YOU DIDN'T MUCH CARE FOR HIM, BUT HE SEEMED LIKE A SMART BLOKE...AND HE MIGHT HAVE BEEN RIGHT ABOUT THE KNIGHT.
WINGMAN WAS TOO GOOD TO LET THIS HAPPEN.

WINGMAN HAD A FEW RUN-INS WITH A DISFIGURED DEEPSEA DIVER TURNED *PIRATE*.
THEY CALLED HIM ***KING KRAKEN.***
KRAKEN'S WEAPON OF CHOICE WAS A HIGH VOLTAGE ***ELECTRICAL RIFLE*** WHICH COULD EASILY CREATE THE KIND OF TRAUMA WE SEE HERE.
MORE EVIDENCE FOR THE *CLUB OF VILLAINS* THEORY?
OR ANOTHER RED HERRING?
GAUCHO?
THE DARK KNIGHT MUST DIE!

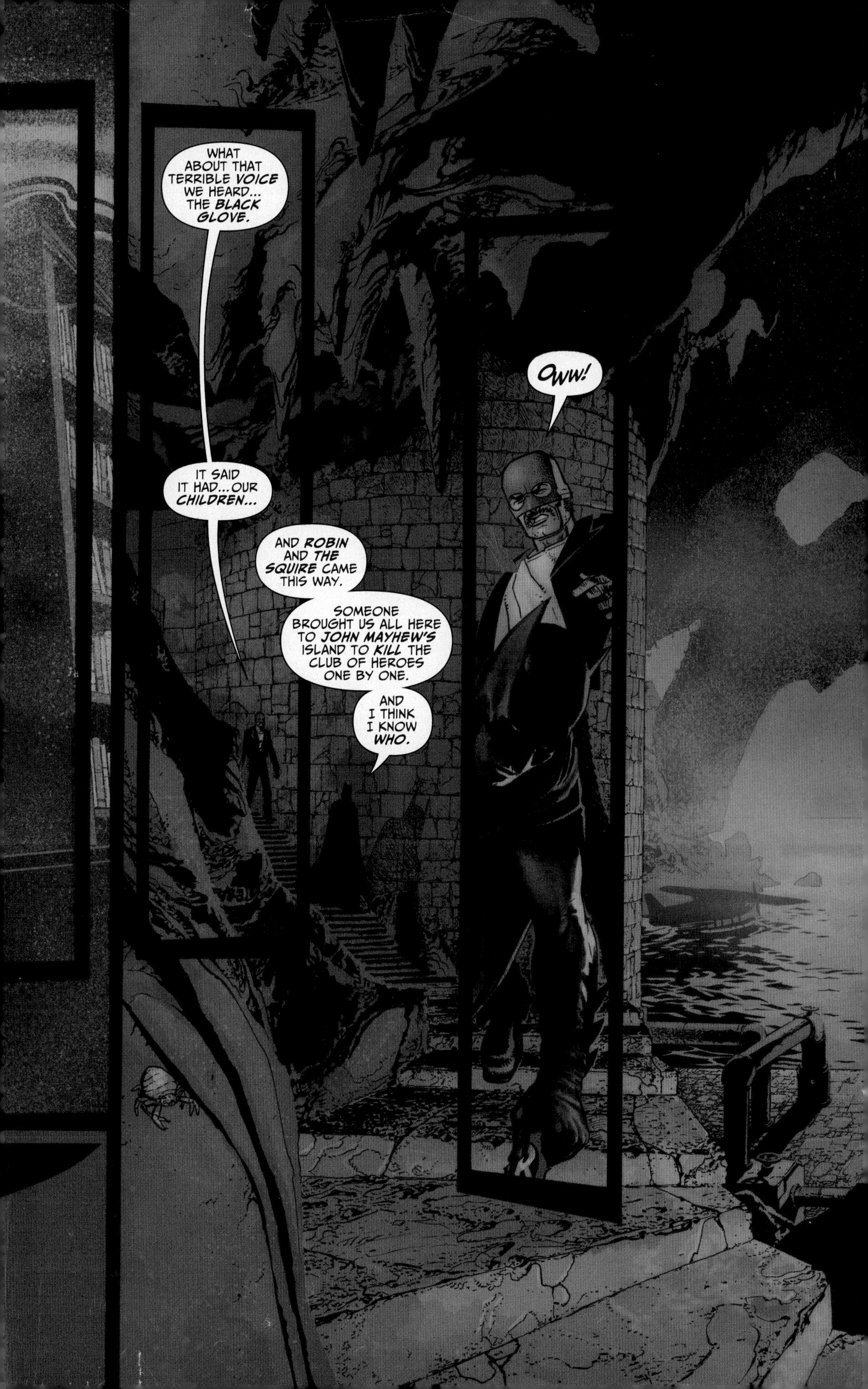
WHAT ABOUT THAT TERRIBLE VOICE WE HEARD... THE BLACK GLOVE.
IT SAID IT HAD...OUR CHILDREN...
AND ROBIN AND THE SQUIRE CAME THIS WAY.
SOMEONE BROUGHT US ALL HERE TO JOHN MAYHEW'S ISLAND TO KILL THE CLUB OF HEROES ONE BY ONE.
AND I THINK I KNOW WHO.
OWW!

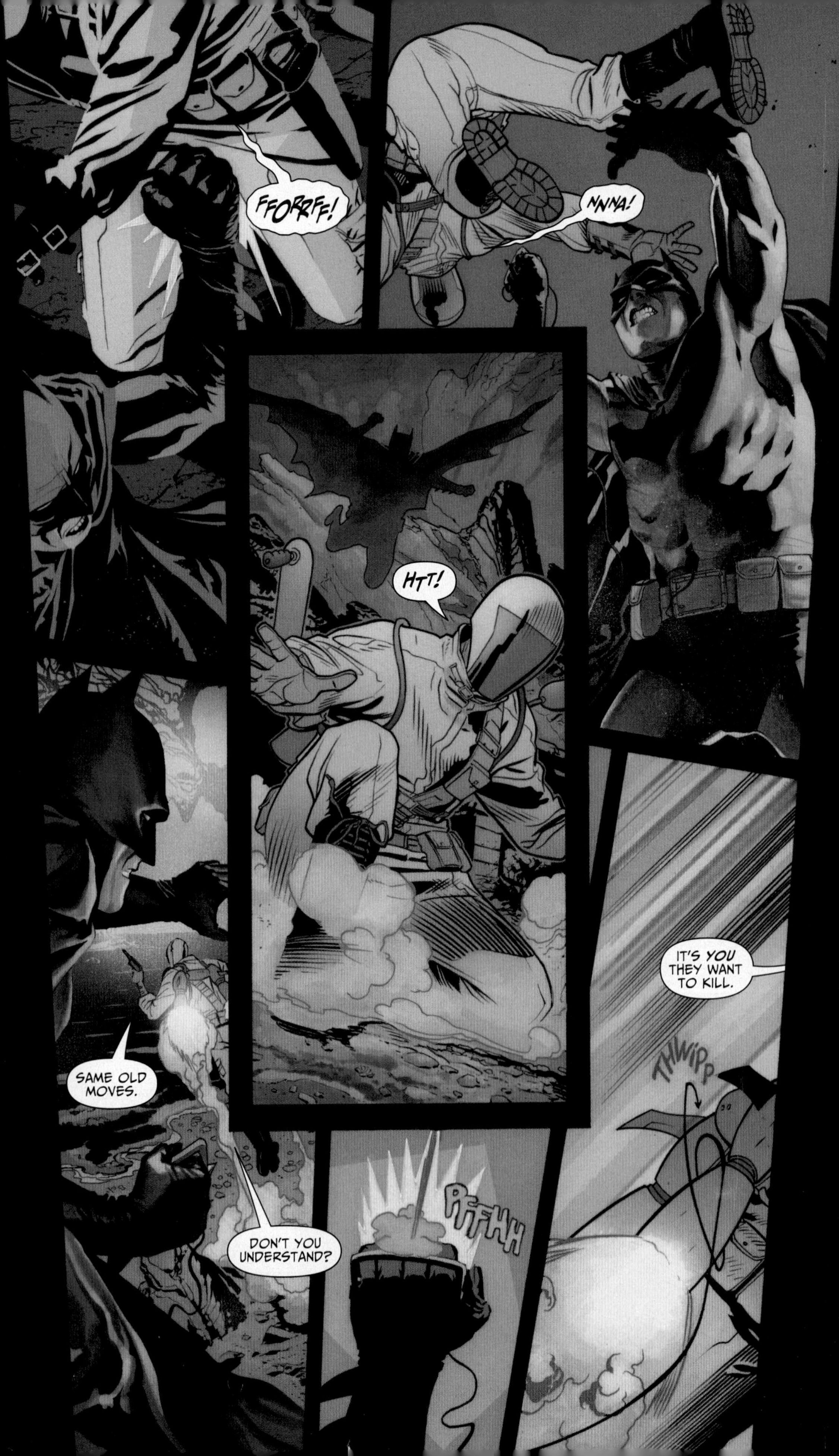
FFORRFF!
NNNA!
HTT!
SAME OLD MOVES.
DON'T YOU UNDERSTAND?
PFFHH
IT'S YOU THEY WANT TO KILL.
THWIPP

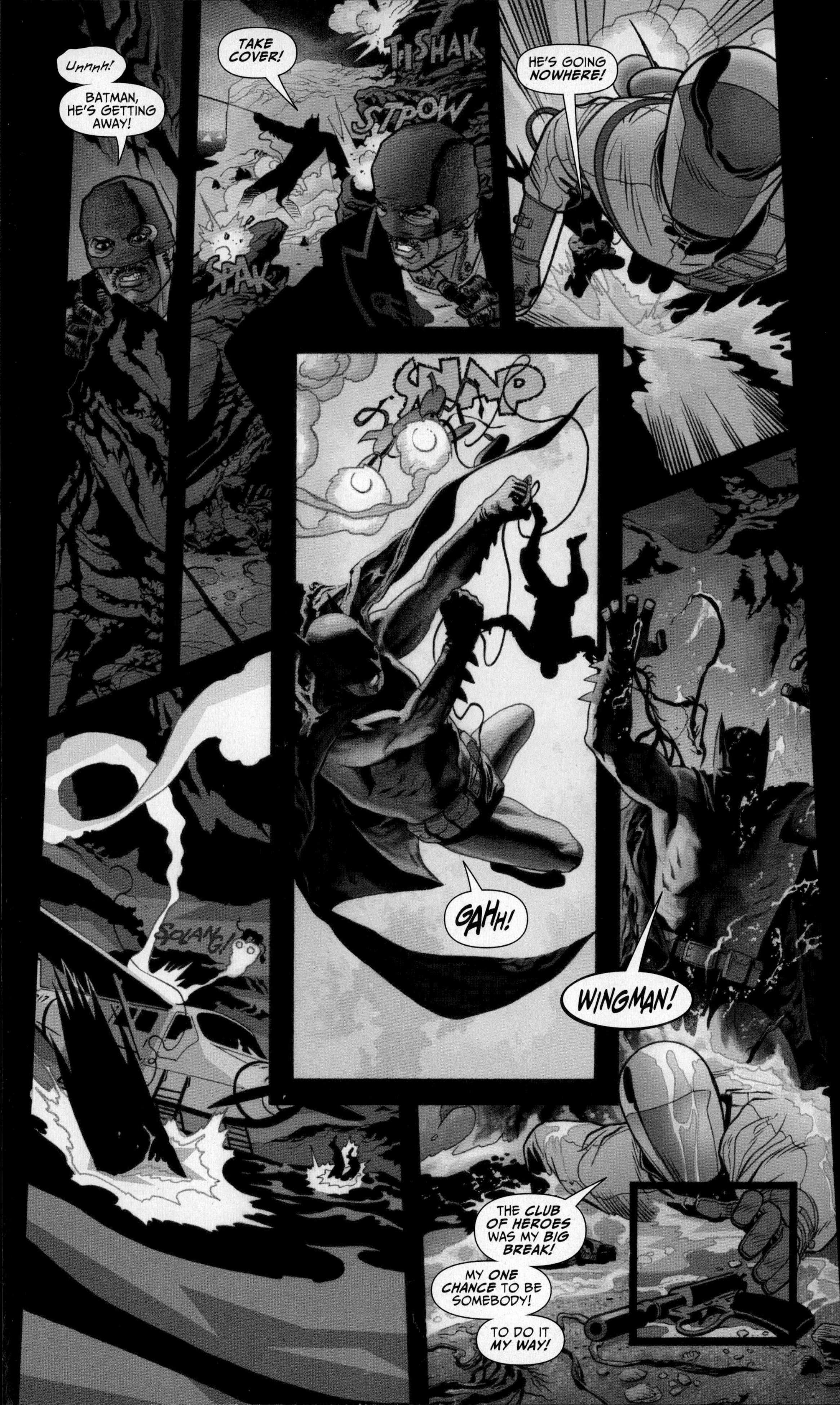
Unnnh!
BATMAN, HE'S GETTING AWAY!
TAKE COVER!
TI SHAK
SPAK
SITPOW
HE'S GOING NOWHERE!
SNAP
SPLANG!
GAHH!
WINGMAN!
THE CLUB OF HEROES WAS MY BIG BREAK!
MY ONE CHANCE TO BE SOMEBODY!
TO DO IT MY WAY!

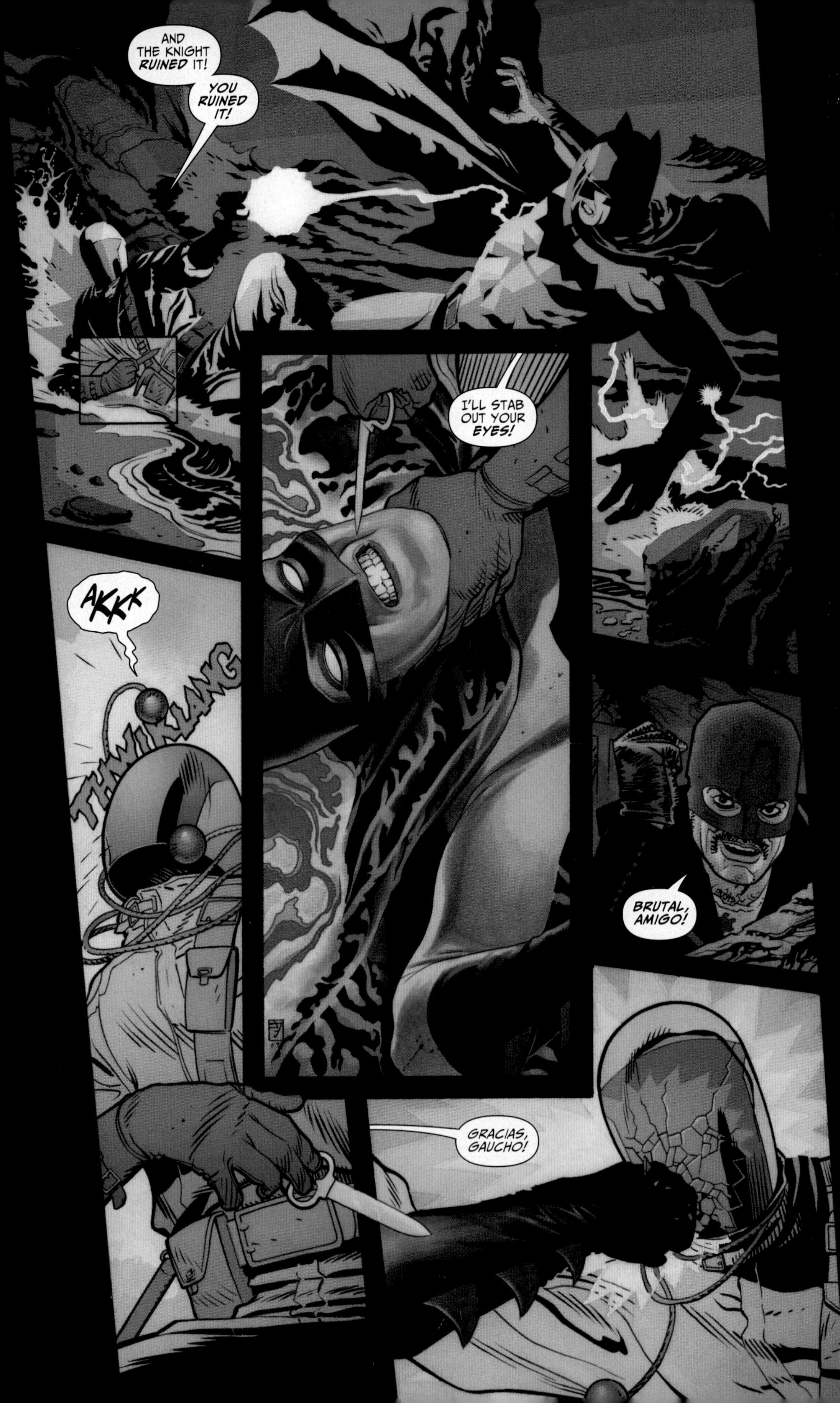
AND THE KNIGHT *RUINED* IT!
YOU RUINED IT!
I'LL STAB OUT YOUR *EYES!*
AKKK
THWIKLANG
BRUTAL, AMIGO!
GRACIAS, GAUCHO!

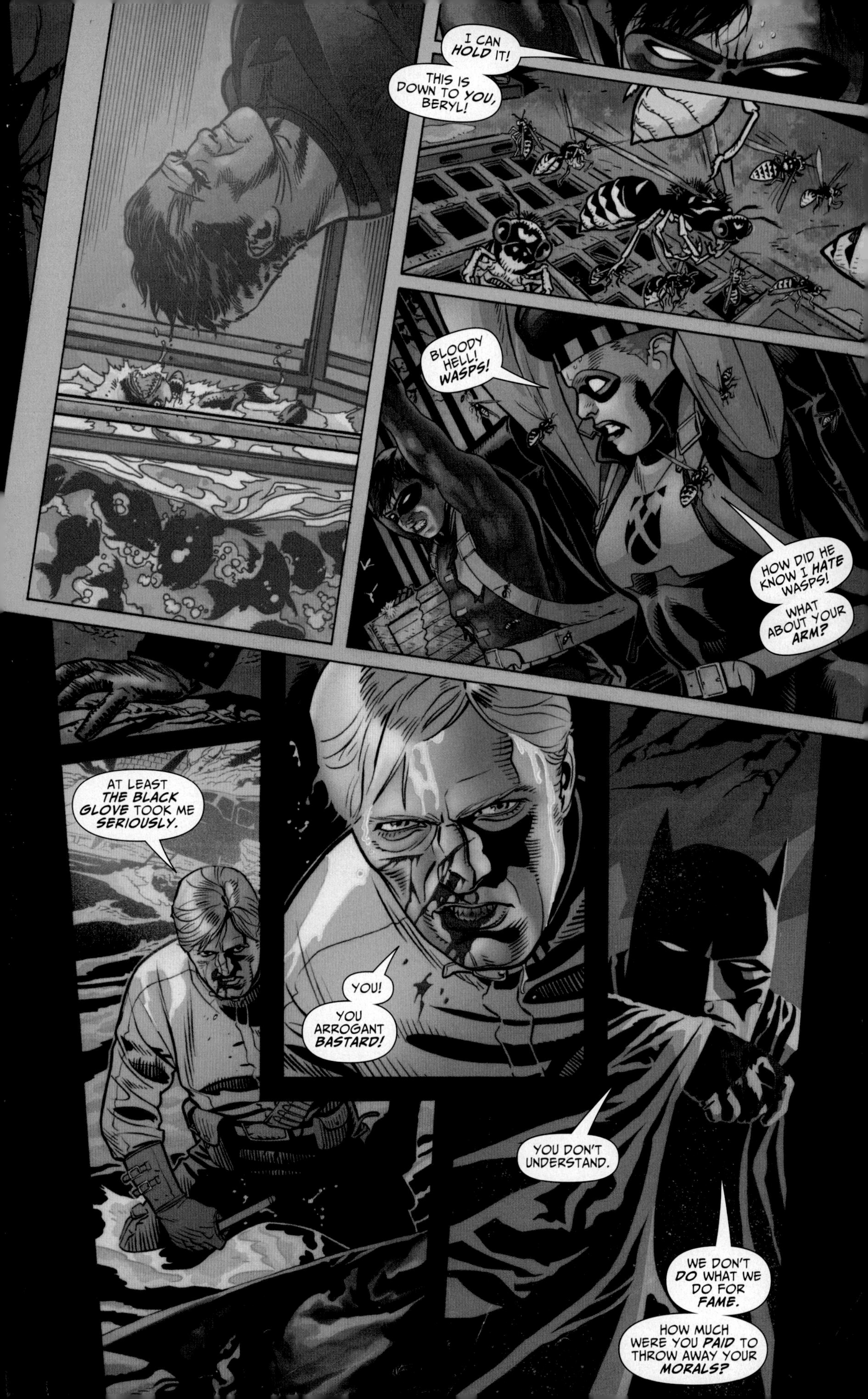
I CAN HOLD IT!
THIS IS DOWN TO YOU, BERYL!
BLOODY HELL! WASPS!
HOW DID HE KNOW I HATE WASPS!
WHAT ABOUT YOUR ARM?
AT LEAST THE BLACK GLOVE TOOK ME SERIOUSLY.
YOU!
YOU ARROGANT BASTARD!
YOU DON'T UNDERSTAND.
WE DON'T DO WHAT WE DO FOR FAME.
HOW MUCH WERE YOU PAID TO THROW AWAY YOUR MORALS?

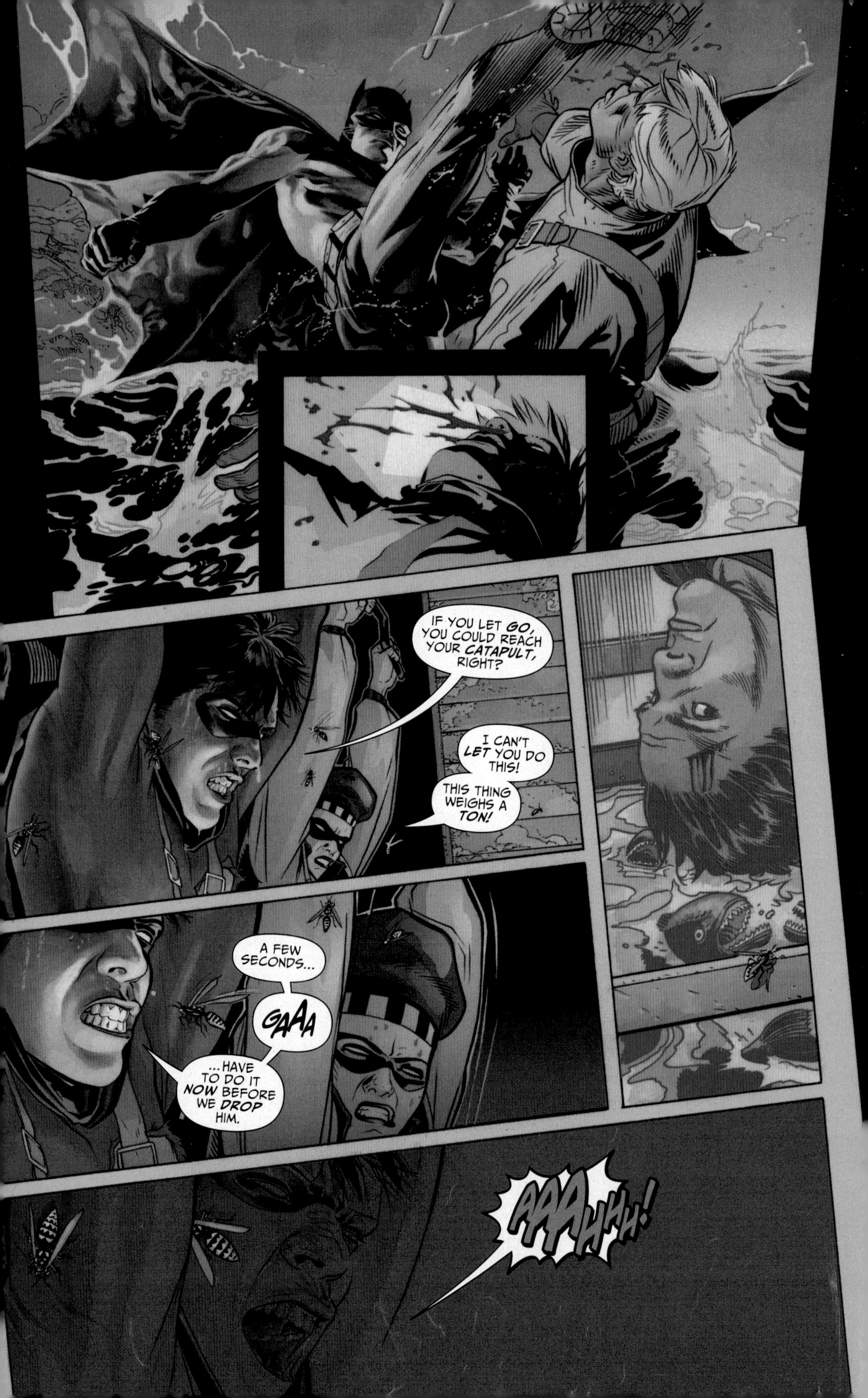
IF YOU LET GO, YOU COULD REACH YOUR CATAPULT, RIGHT?
I CAN'T LET YOU DO THIS!
THIS THING WEIGHS A TON!
A FEW SECONDS...
GAAA
...HAVE TO DO IT NOW BEFORE WE DROP HIM.
AAAUHHH!

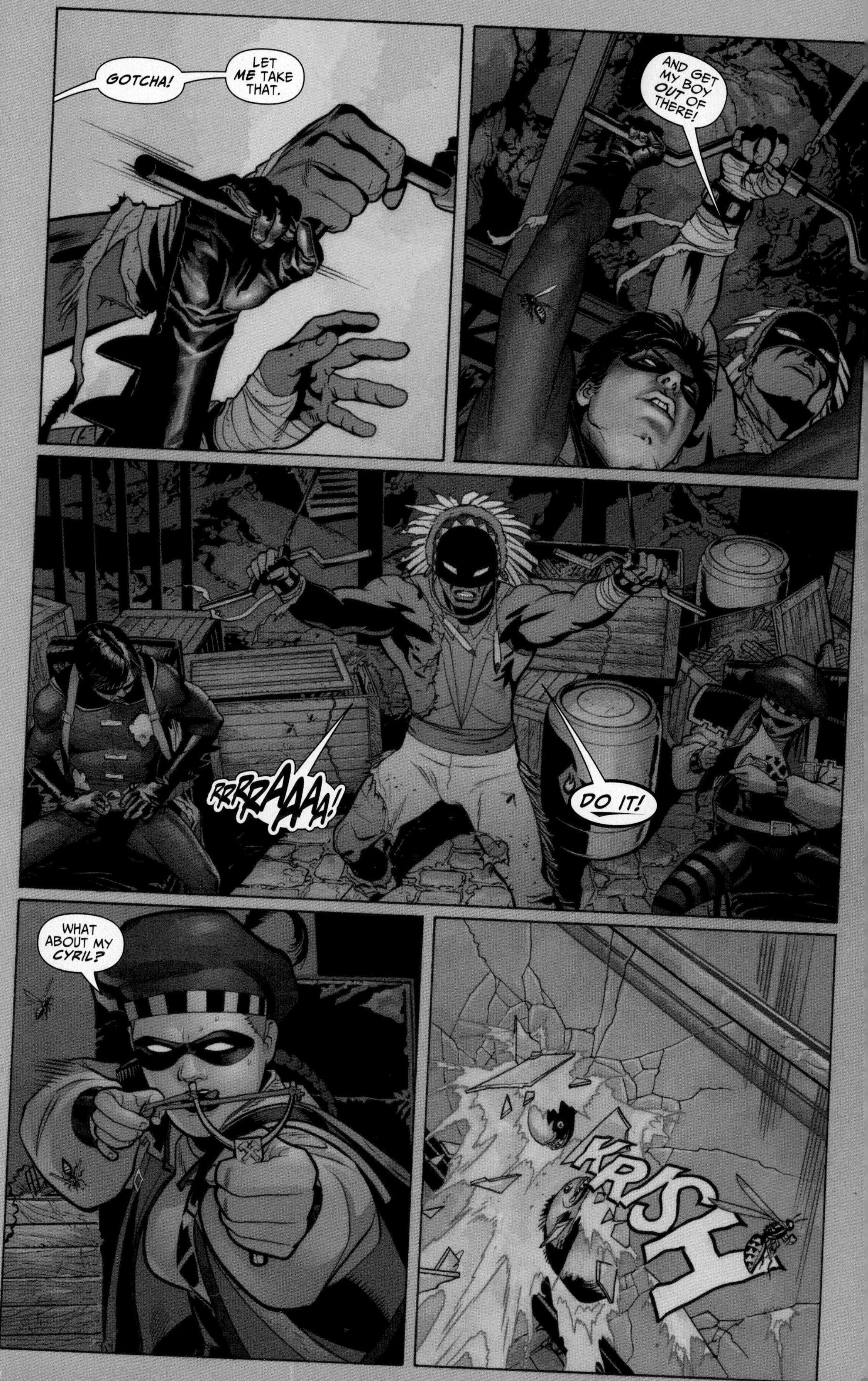
GOTCHA!
LET ME TAKE THAT.
AND GET MY BOY OUT OF THERE!
RRRRAAAAA!
DO IT!
WHAT ABOUT MY CYRIL?
KRISH

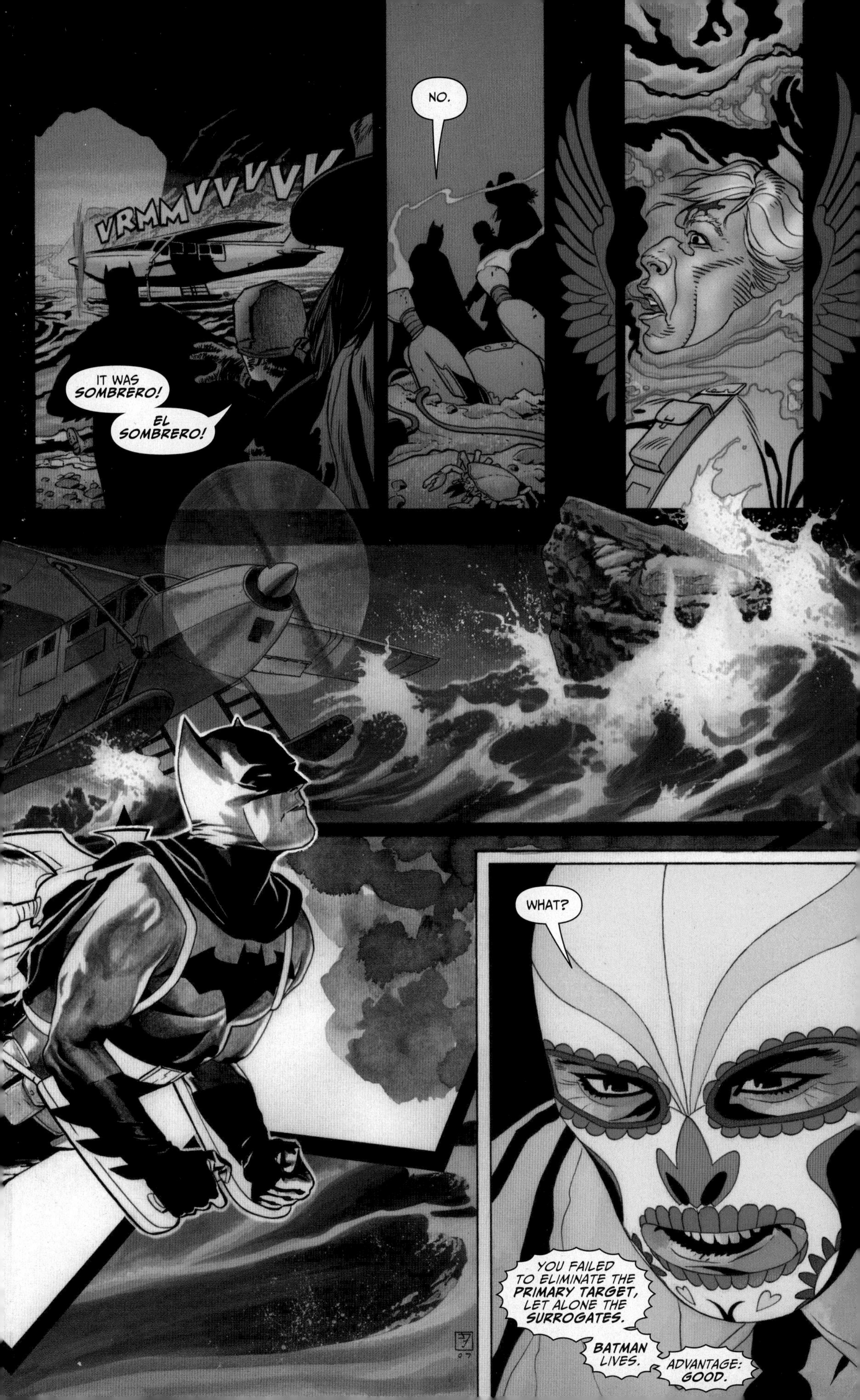
VRMMVVVVVV
IT WAS SOMBRERO!
EL SOMBRERO!
NO.
WHAT?
YOU FAILED TO ELIMINATE THE PRIMARY TARGET, LET ALONE THE SURROGATES.
BATMAN LIVES.
ADVANTAGE: GOOD.

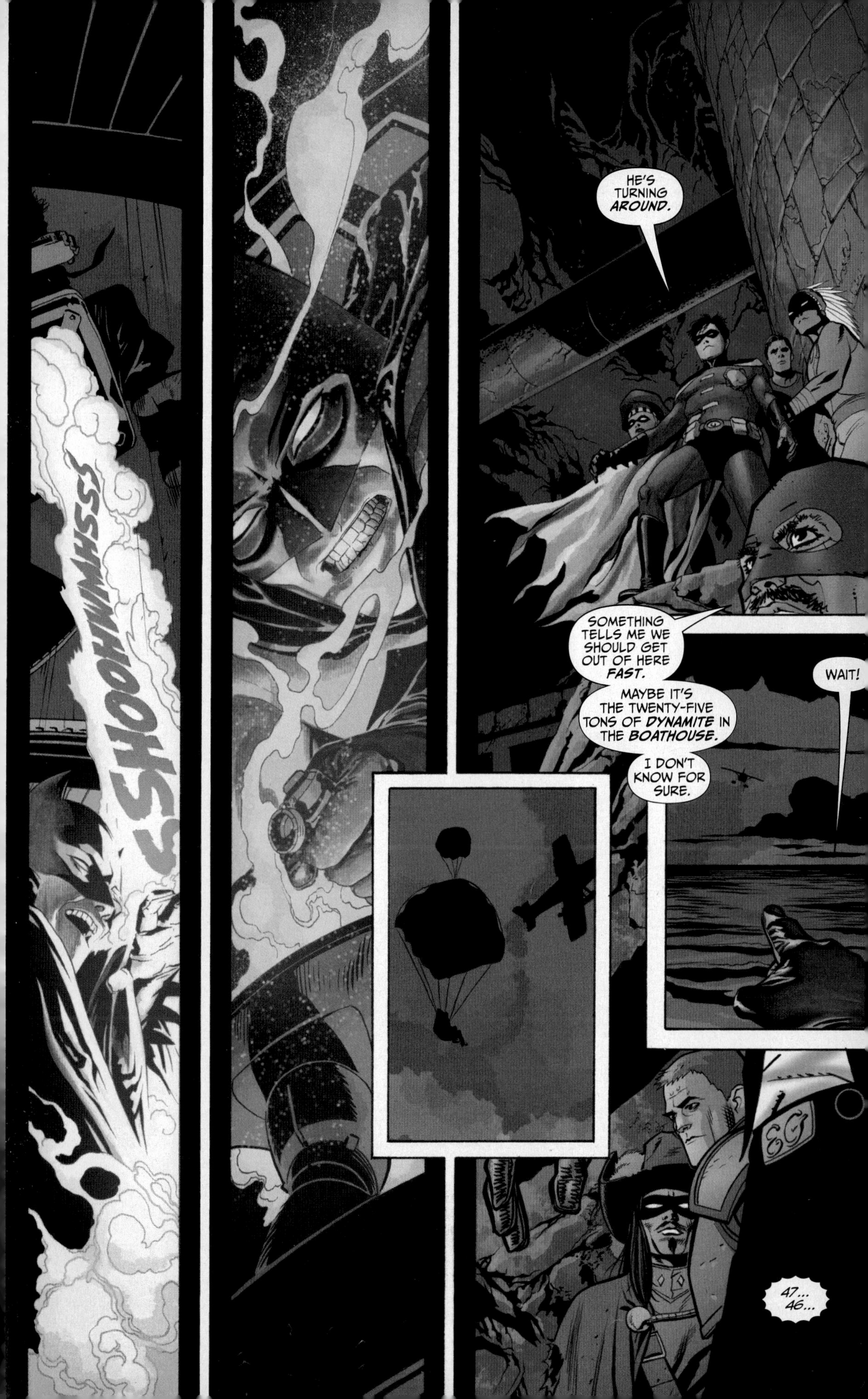
SHOOHWWHHSSSS
HE'S TURNING AROUND.
SOMETHING TELLS ME WE SHOULD GET OUT OF HERE FAST.
MAYBE IT'S THE TWENTY-FIVE TONS OF DYNAMITE IN THE BOATHOUSE.
I DON'T KNOW FOR SURE.
WAIT!
47... 46...

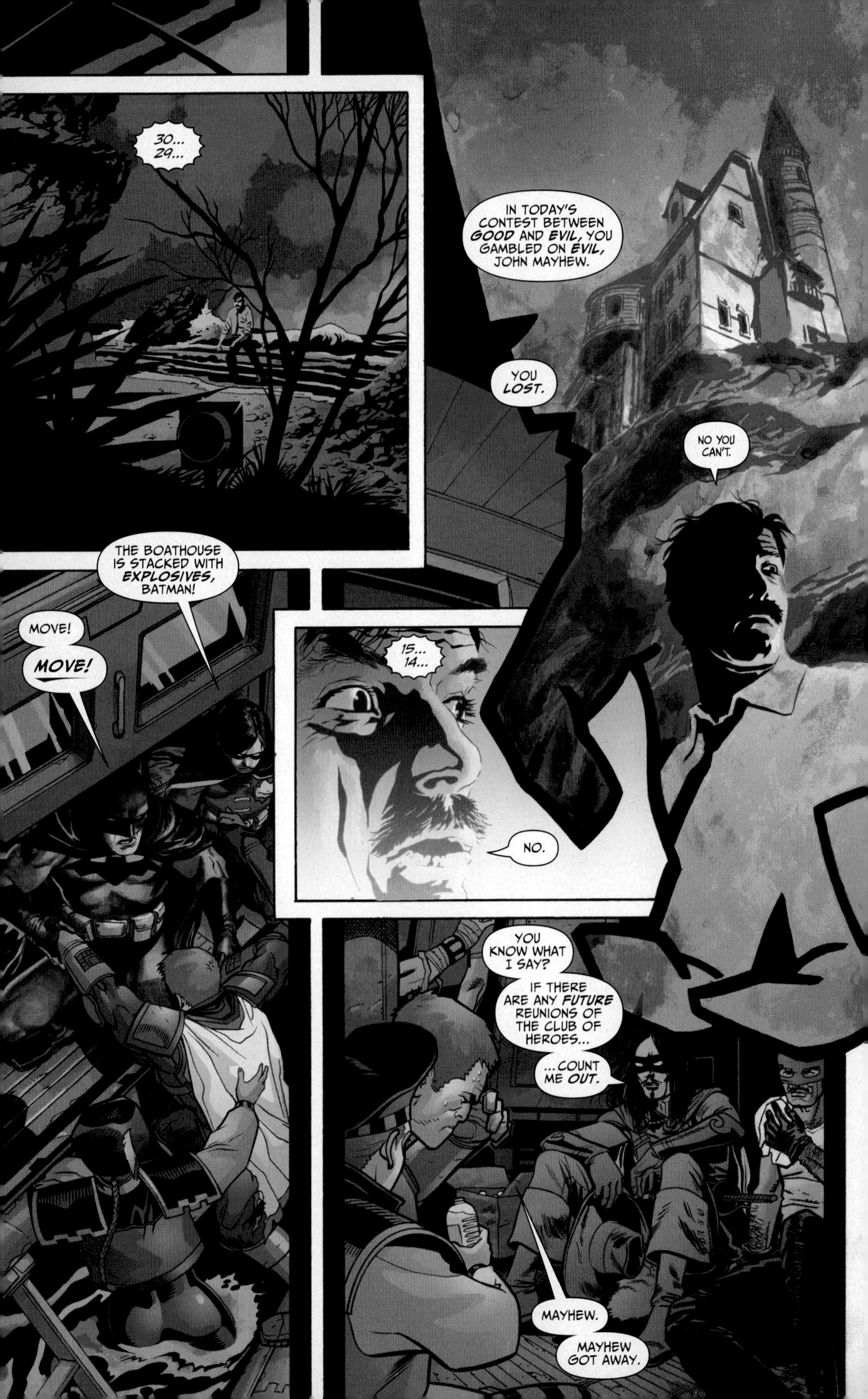
30...
29...
IN TODAY'S CONTEST BETWEEN GOOD AND EVIL, YOU GAMBLED ON EVIL, JOHN MAYHEW.
YOU LOST.
NO YOU CAN'T.
THE BOATHOUSE IS STACKED WITH EXPLOSIVES, BATMAN!
MOVE!
MOVE!
15...
14...
NO.
YOU KNOW WHAT I SAY?
IF THERE ARE ANY FUTURE REUNIONS OF THE CLUB OF HEROES...
...COUNT ME OUT.
MAYHEW.
MAYHEW GOT AWAY.

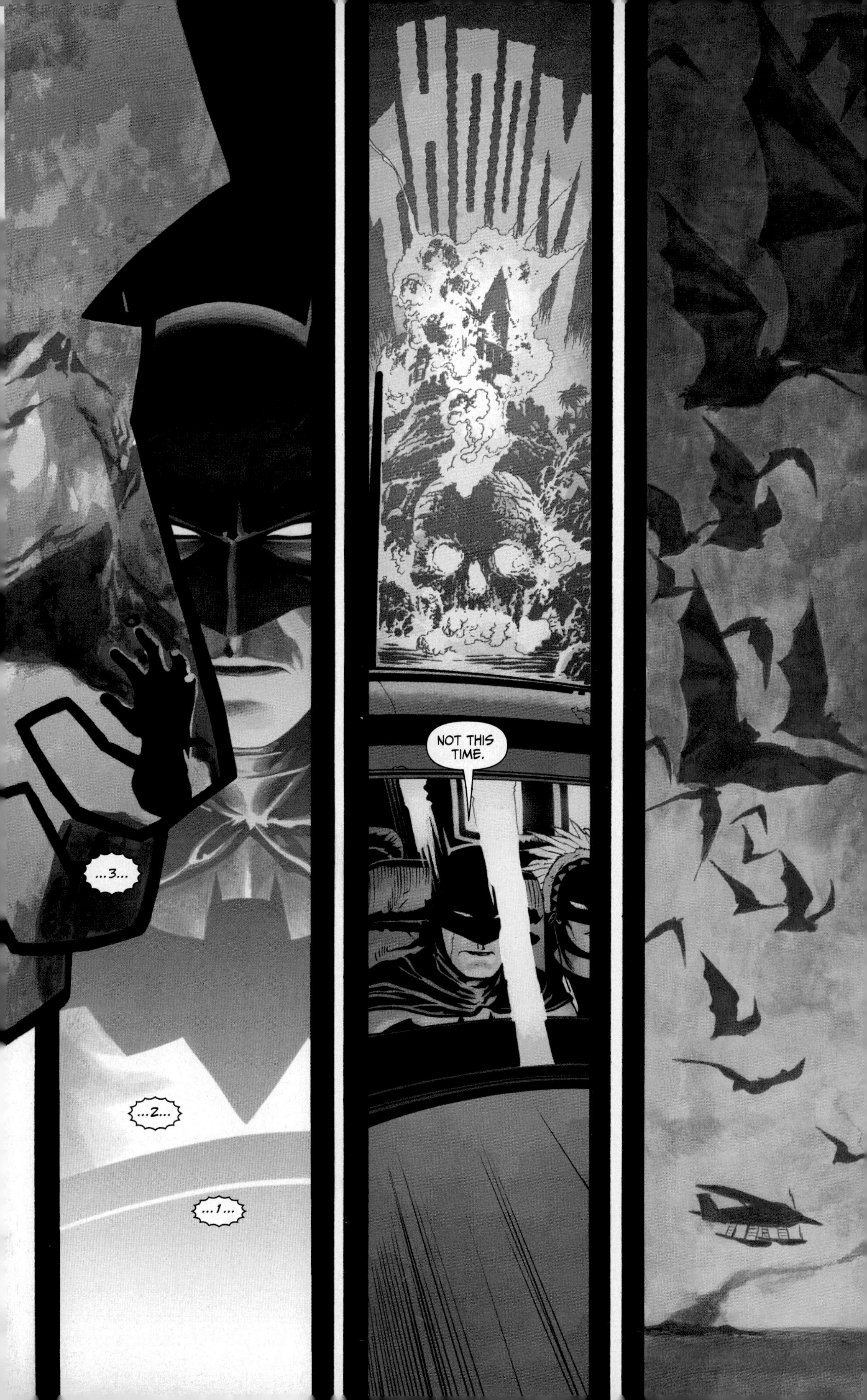
...3...
...2...
...1...
THOOM
NOT THIS TIME.

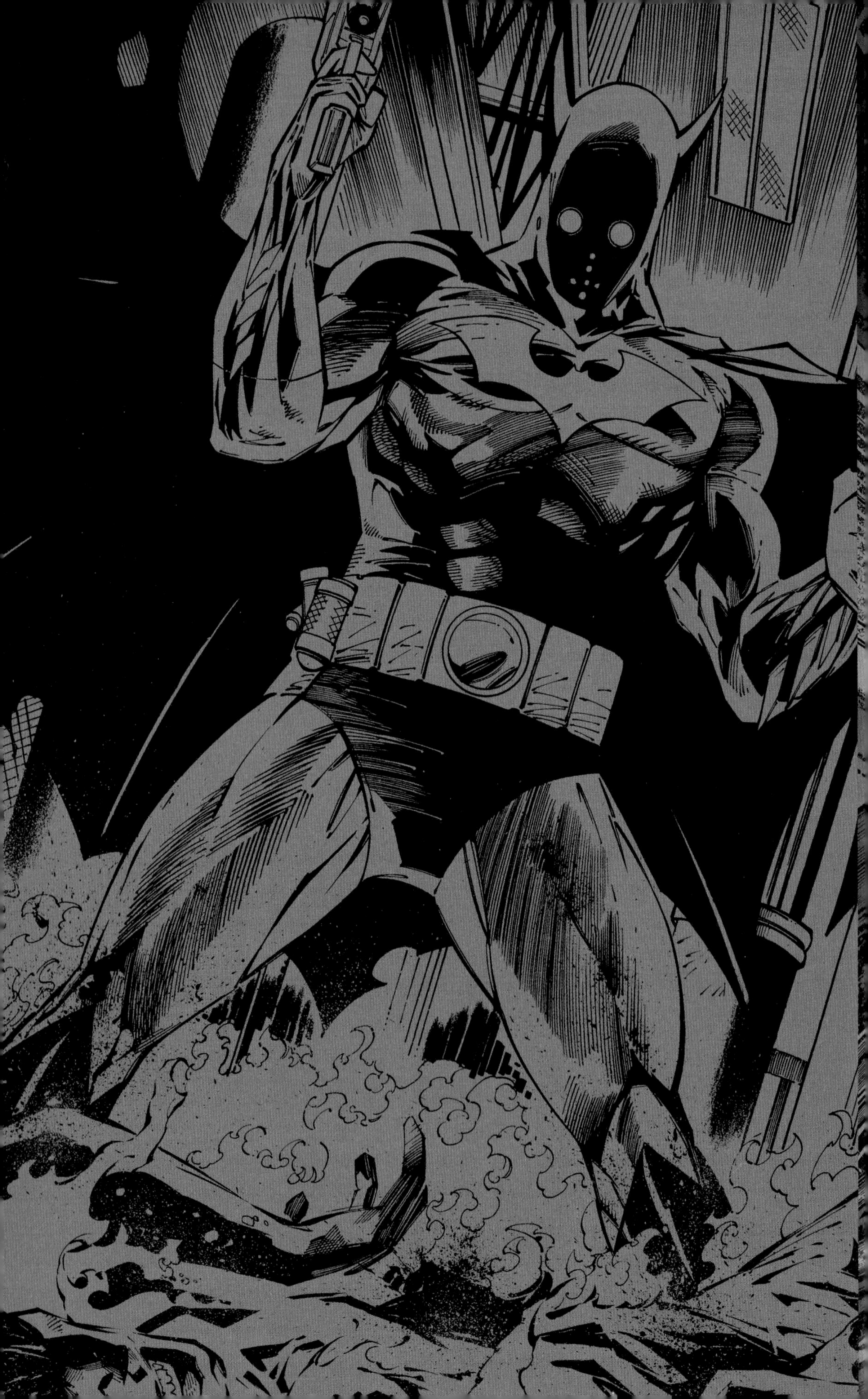

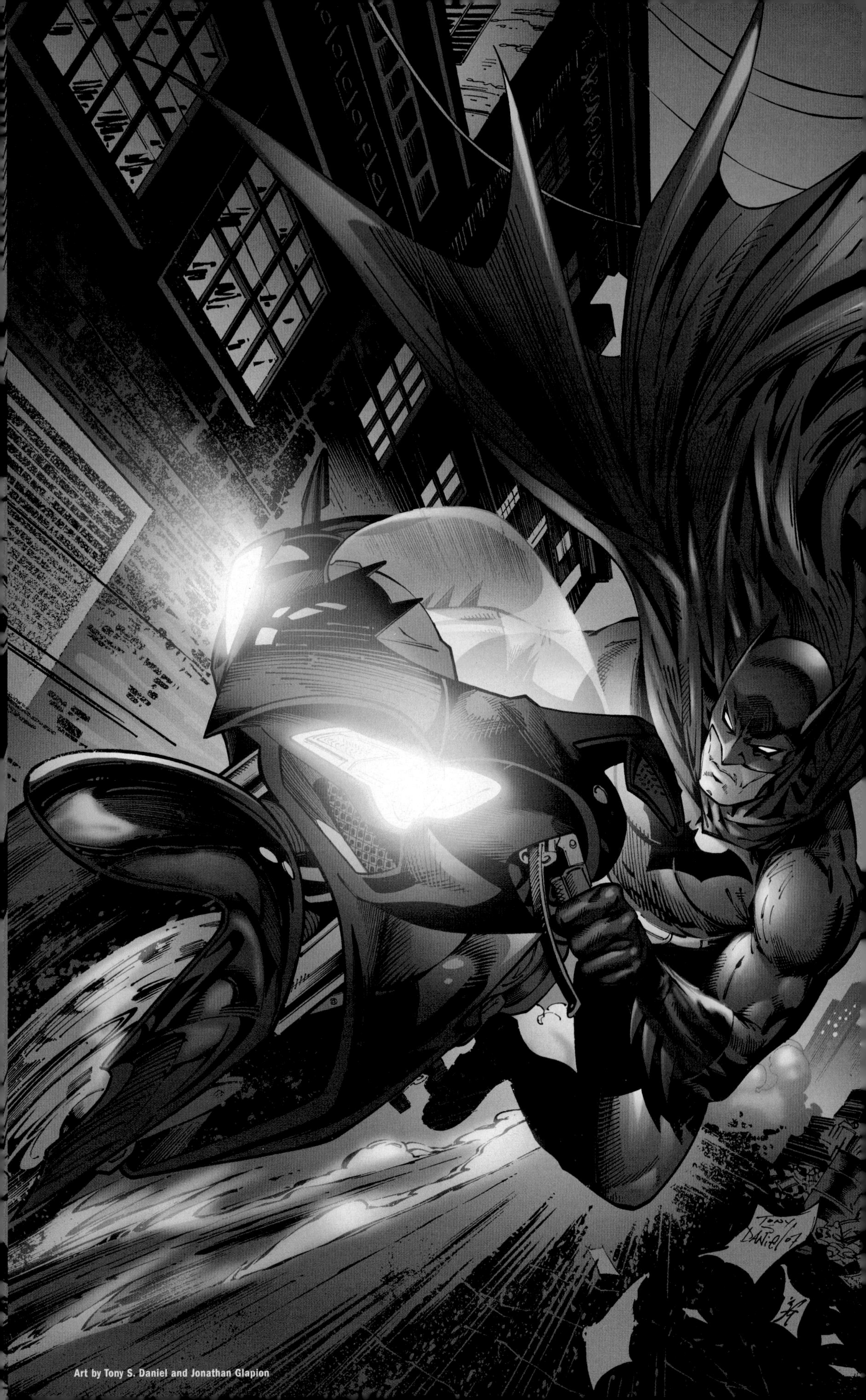

Art by Tony S. Daniel and Jonathan Glapion

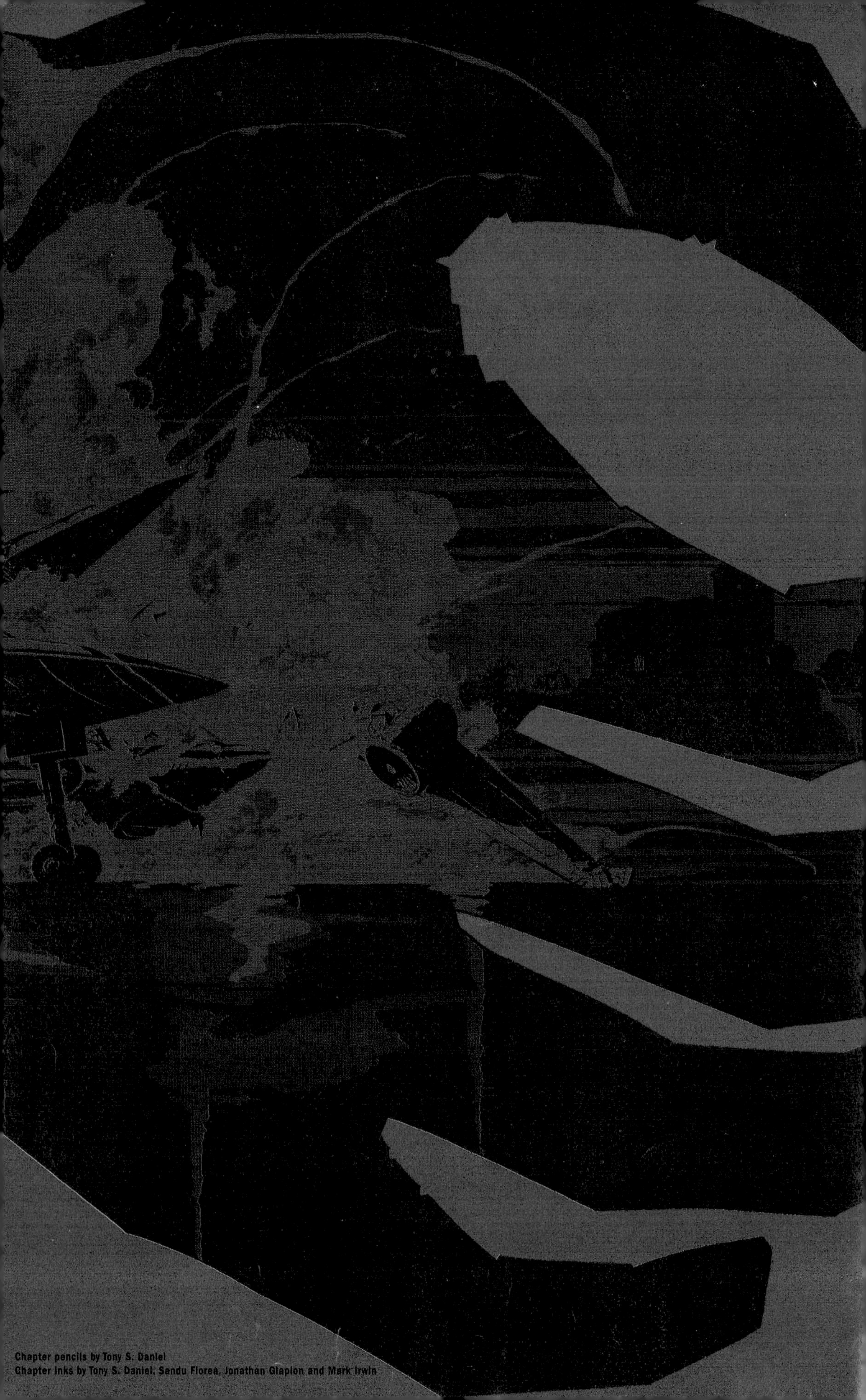

Chapter pencils by Tony S. Daniel
Chapter inks by Tony S. Daniel, Sandu Florea, Jonathan Glapion and Mark Irwin

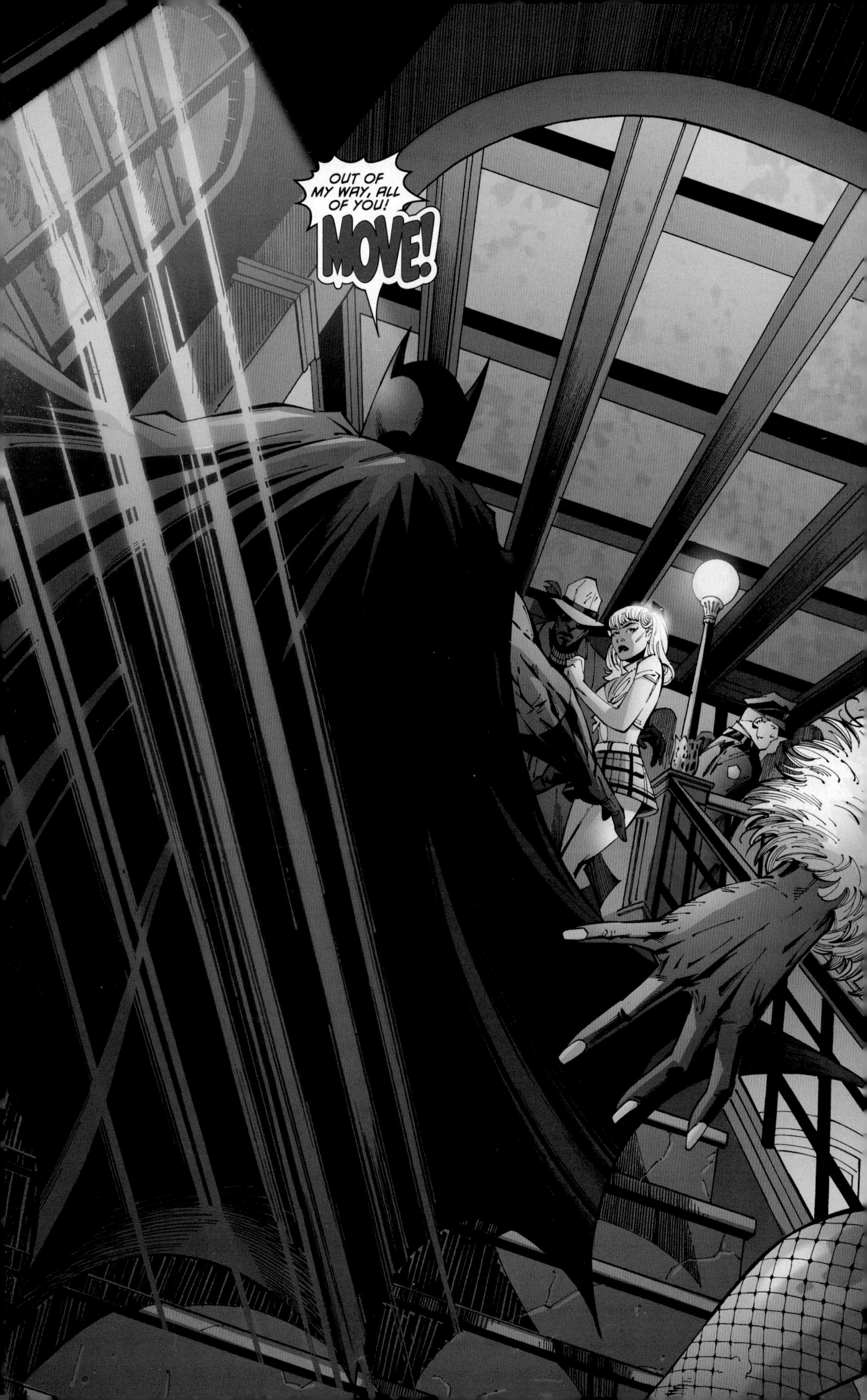
OUT OF MY WAY, ALL OF YOU!
MOVE!

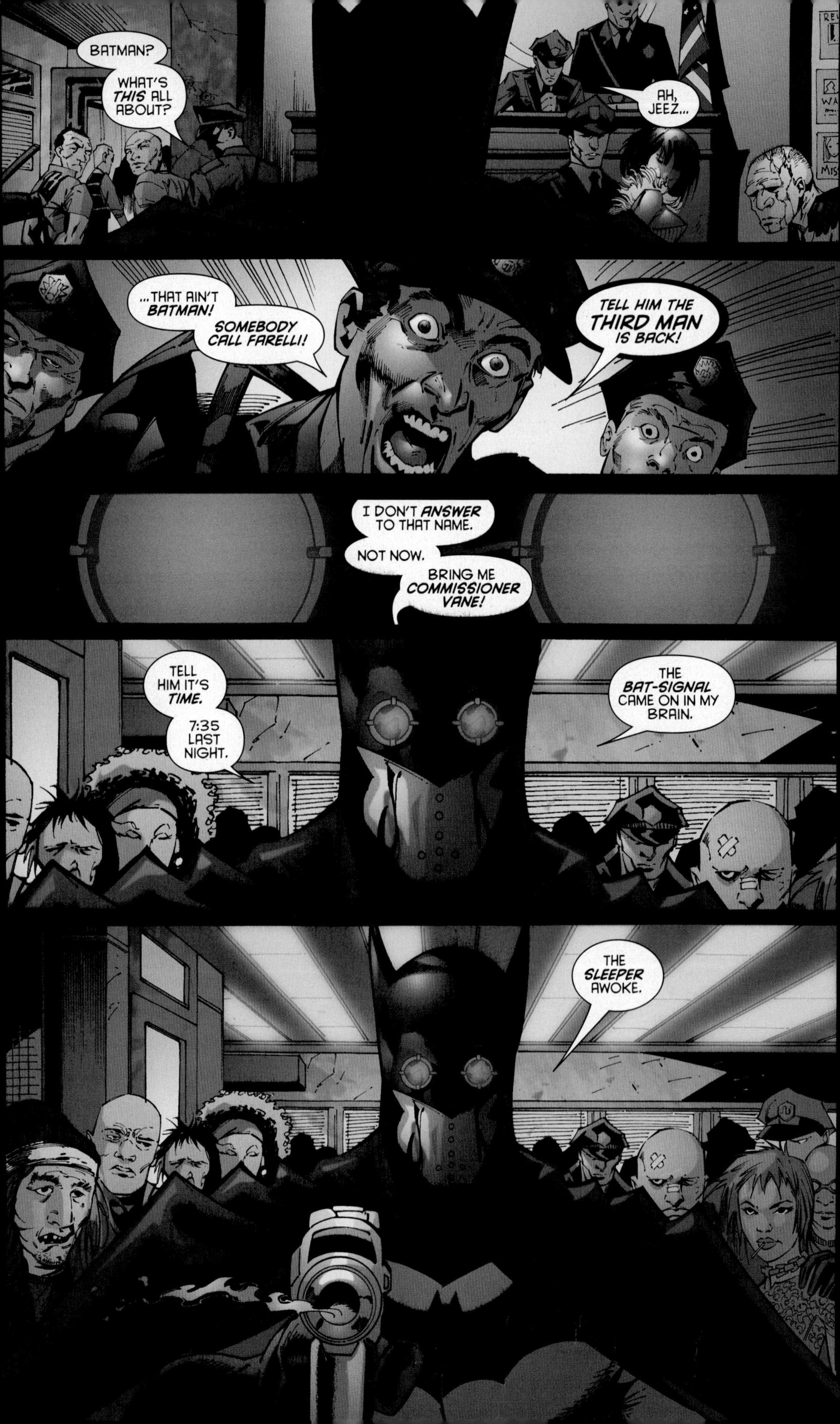
BATMAN?
WHAT'S THIS ALL ABOUT?
AH, JEEZ...
...THAT AIN'T BATMAN! SOMEBODY CALL FARELLI!
TELL HIM THE THIRD MAN IS BACK!
I DON'T ANSWER TO THAT NAME.
NOT NOW.
BRING ME COMMISSIONER VANE!
TELL HIM IT'S TIME.
7:35 LAST NIGHT.
THE BAT-SIGNAL CAME ON IN MY BRAIN.
THE SLEEPER AWOKE.

I WALKED ALL THE WAY FROM *HELL.*
WITH A *SECRET* TO TELL.
ABOUT *BATMAN* AND ME.
space medicine

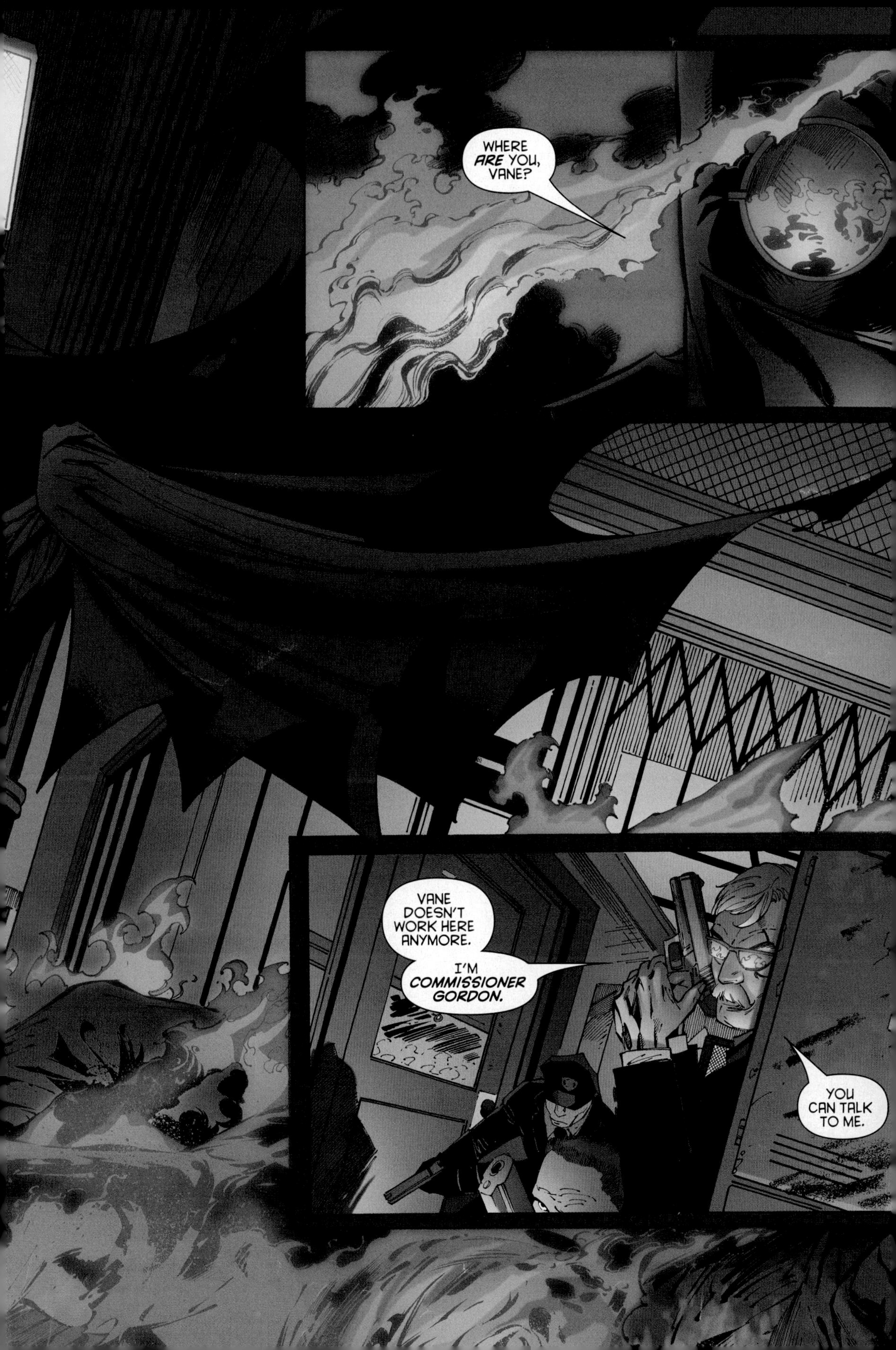
WHERE ARE YOU, VANE?
VANE DOESN'T WORK HERE ANYMORE.
I'M COMMISSIONER GORDON.
YOU CAN TALK TO ME.

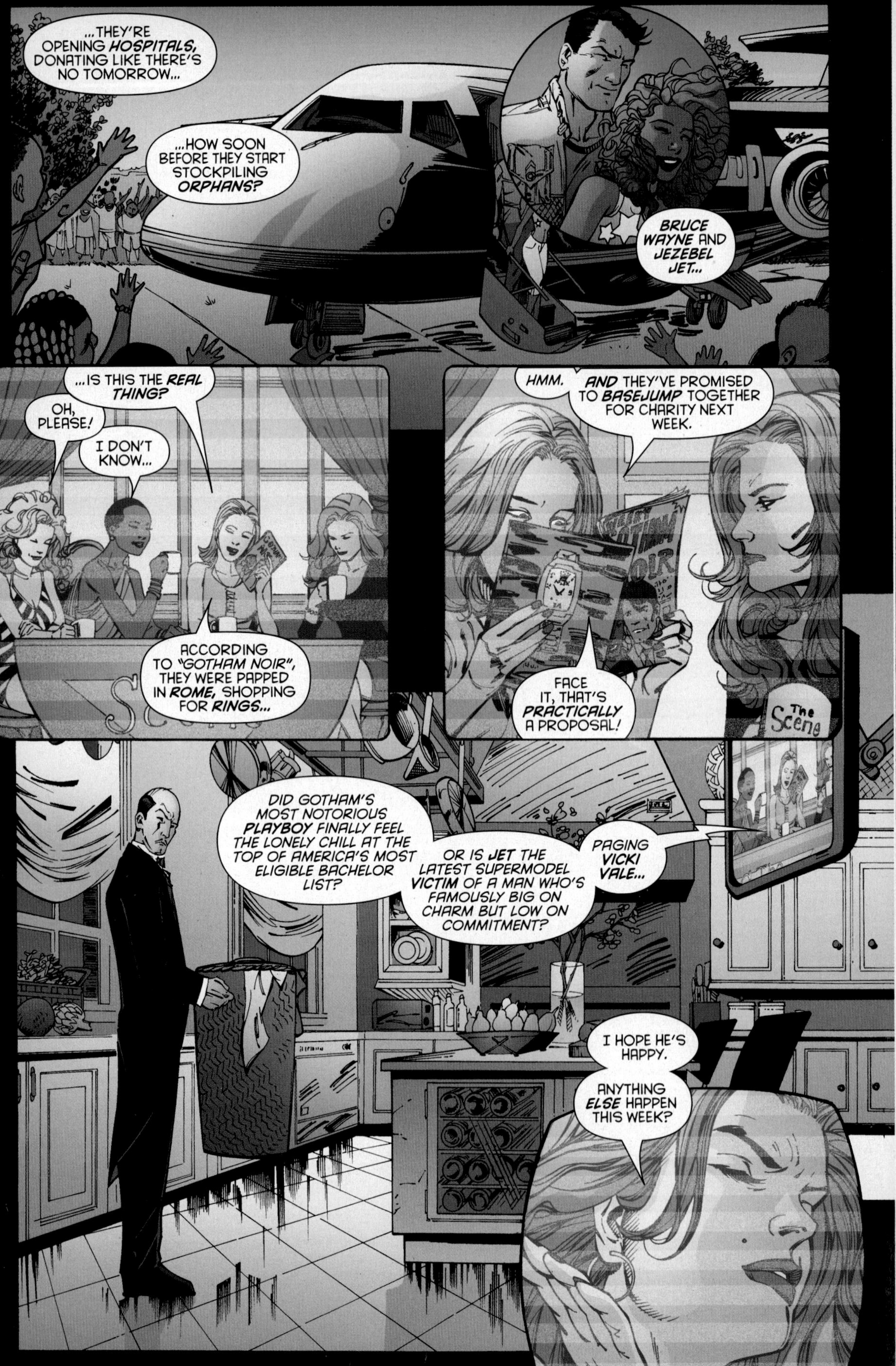
...THEY'RE OPENING HOSPITALS, DONATING LIKE THERE'S NO TOMORROW...
...HOW SOON BEFORE THEY START STOCKPILING ORPHANS?
BRUCE WAYNE AND JEZEBEL JET...
...IS THIS THE REAL THING?
OH, PLEASE!
I DON'T KNOW...
ACCORDING TO "GOTHAM NOIR", THEY WERE PAPPED IN ROME, SHOPPING FOR RINGS...
HMM.
AND THEY'VE PROMISED TO BASEJUMP TOGETHER FOR CHARITY NEXT WEEK.
FACE IT, THAT'S PRACTICALLY A PROPOSAL!
The Scene
DID GOTHAM'S MOST NOTORIOUS PLAYBOY FINALLY FEEL THE LONELY CHILL AT THE TOP OF AMERICA'S MOST ELIGIBLE BACHELOR LIST?
OR IS JET THE LATEST SUPERMODEL VICTIM OF A MAN WHO'S FAMOUSLY BIG ON CHARM BUT LOW ON COMMITMENT?
PAGING VICKI VALE...
I HOPE HE'S HAPPY.
ANYTHING ELSE HAPPEN THIS WEEK?

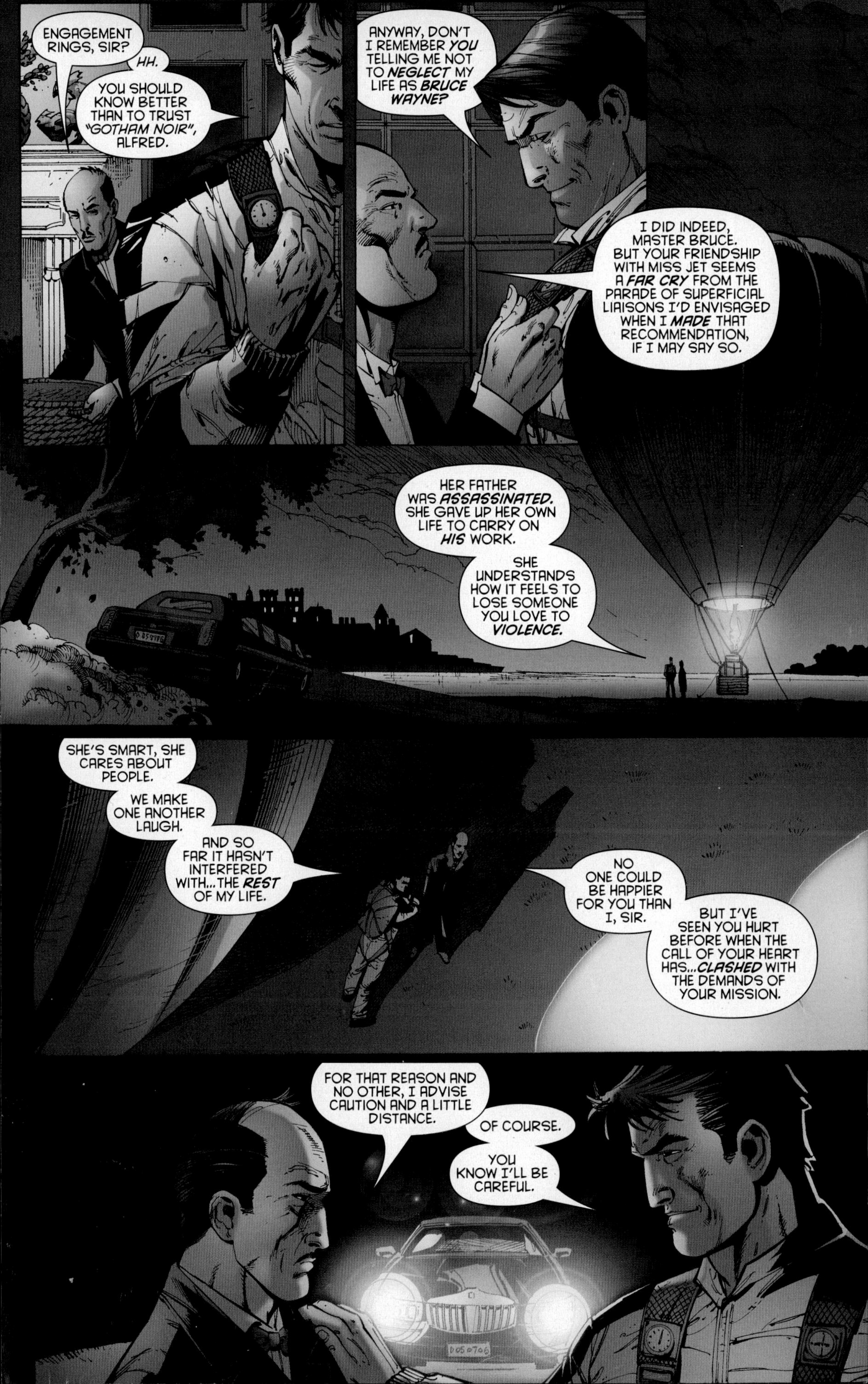
ENGAGEMENT RINGS, SIR?
HH.
YOU SHOULD KNOW BETTER THAN TO TRUST "GOTHAM NOIR", ALFRED.
ANYWAY, DON'T I REMEMBER *YOU* TELLING ME NOT TO *NEGLECT* MY LIFE AS *BRUCE WAYNE?*
I DID INDEED, MASTER BRUCE. BUT YOUR FRIENDSHIP WITH MISS JET SEEMS A *FAR CRY* FROM THE PARADE OF SUPERFICIAL LIAISONS I'D ENVISAGED WHEN I *MADE* THAT RECOMMENDATION, IF I MAY SAY SO.
HER FATHER WAS *ASSASSINATED.* SHE GAVE UP HER OWN LIFE TO CARRY ON *HIS* WORK.
SHE UNDERSTANDS HOW IT FEELS TO LOSE SOMEONE YOU LOVE TO *VIOLENCE.*
SHE'S SMART, SHE CARES ABOUT PEOPLE.
WE MAKE ONE ANOTHER LAUGH.
AND SO FAR IT HASN'T INTERFERED WITH... THE *REST* OF MY LIFE.
NO ONE COULD BE HAPPIER FOR YOU THAN I, SIR.
BUT I'VE SEEN YOU HURT BEFORE WHEN THE CALL OF YOUR HEART HAS... *CLASHED* WITH THE DEMANDS OF YOUR MISSION.
FOR THAT REASON AND NO OTHER, I ADVISE CAUTION AND A LITTLE DISTANCE.
OF COURSE.
YOU KNOW I'LL BE CAREFUL.

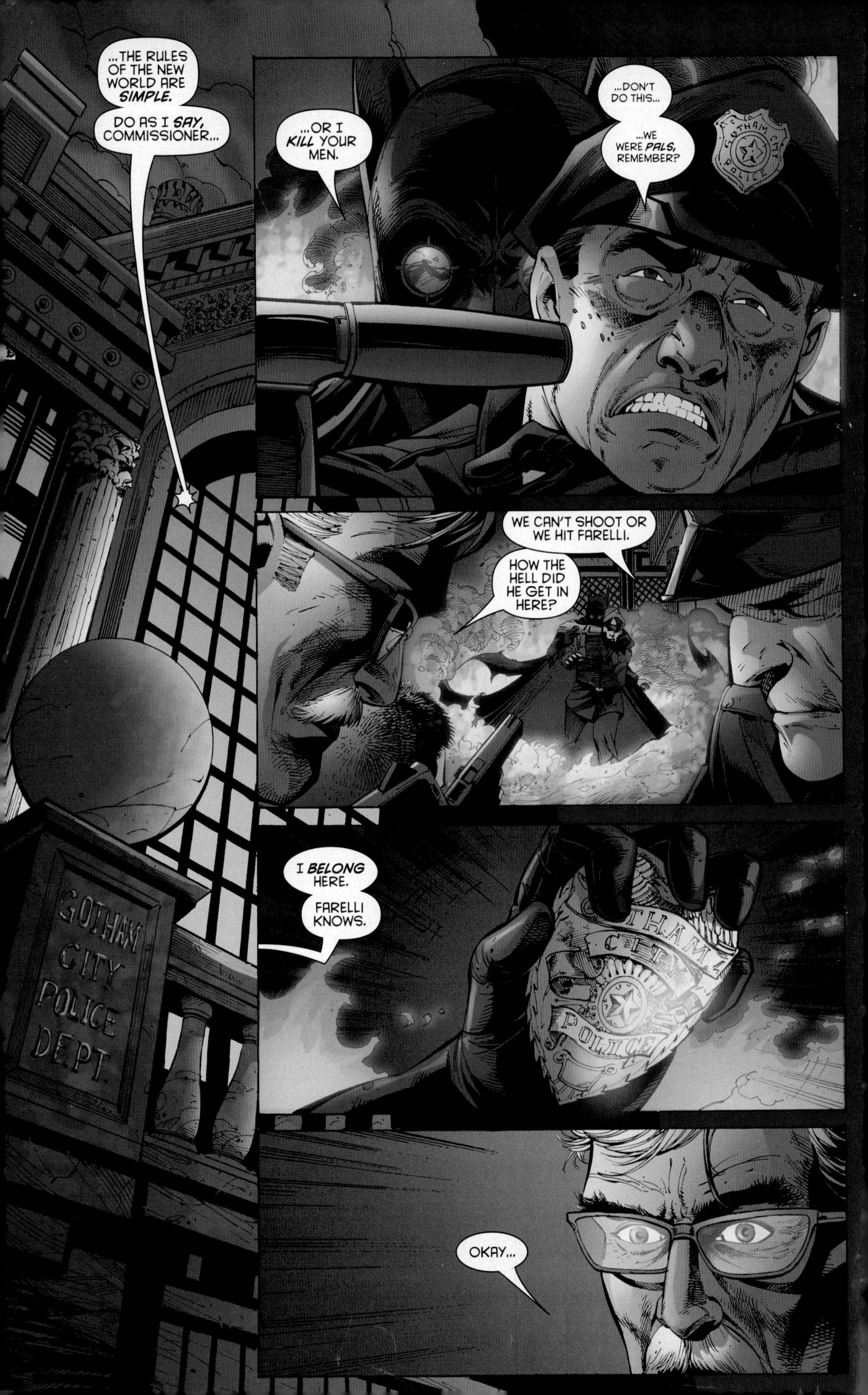
...THE RULES OF THE NEW WORLD ARE SIMPLE.
DO AS I SAY, COMMISSIONER...
...OR I KILL YOUR MEN.
...DON'T DO THIS...
...WE WERE PALS, REMEMBER?
GOTHAM CITY POLICE
WE CAN'T SHOOT OR WE HIT FARELLI.
HOW THE HELL DID HE GET IN HERE?
I BELONG HERE.
FARELLI KNOWS.
GOTHAM CITY POLICE
GOTHAM CITY POLICE DEPT
OKAY...

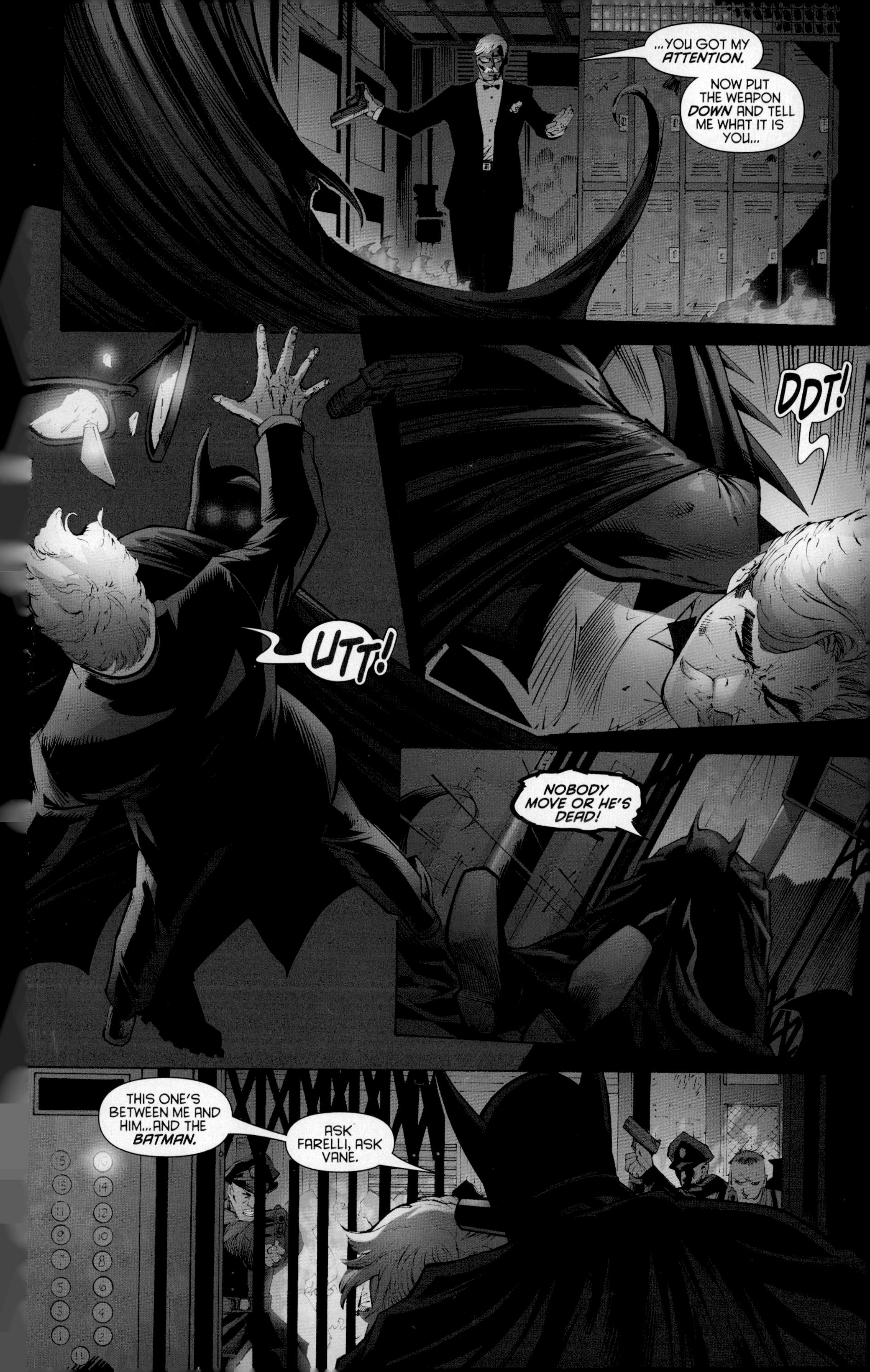
...YOU GOT MY ATTENTION.
NOW PUT THE WEAPON DOWN AND TELL ME WHAT IT IS YOU...
DDT!
UTT!
NOBODY MOVE OR HE'S DEAD!
THIS ONE'S BETWEEN ME AND HIM...AND THE BATMAN.
ASK FARELLI, ASK VANE.

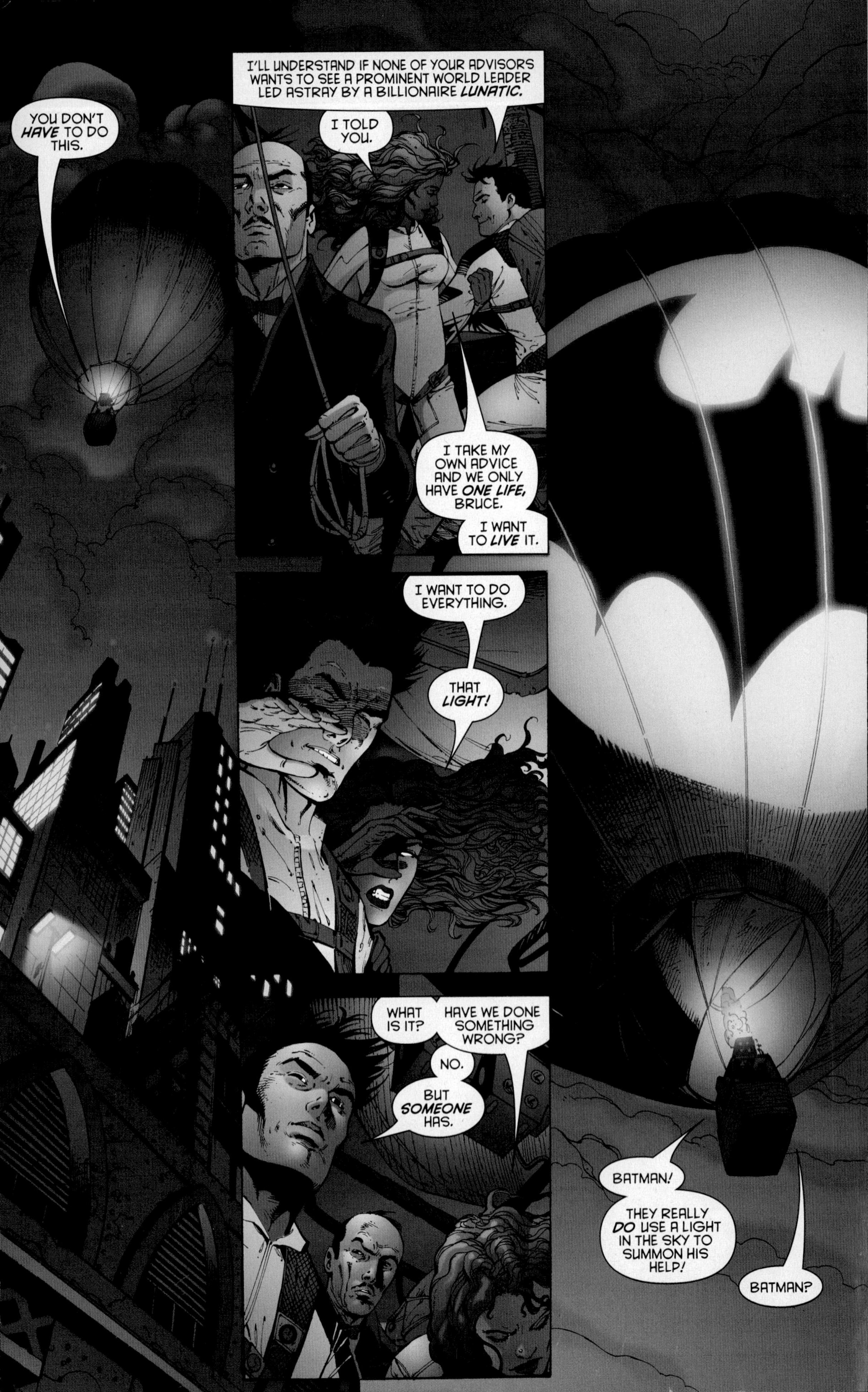
YOU DON'T HAVE TO DO THIS.
I'LL UNDERSTAND IF NONE OF YOUR ADVISORS WANTS TO SEE A PROMINENT WORLD LEADER LED ASTRAY BY A BILLIONAIRE LUNATIC.
I TOLD YOU.
I TAKE MY OWN ADVICE AND WE ONLY HAVE ONE LIFE, BRUCE.
I WANT TO LIVE IT.
I WANT TO DO EVERYTHING.
THAT LIGHT!
WHAT IS IT?
HAVE WE DONE SOMETHING WRONG?
NO.
BUT SOMEONE HAS.
BATMAN!
THEY REALLY DO USE A LIGHT IN THE SKY TO SUMMON HIS HELP!
BATMAN?

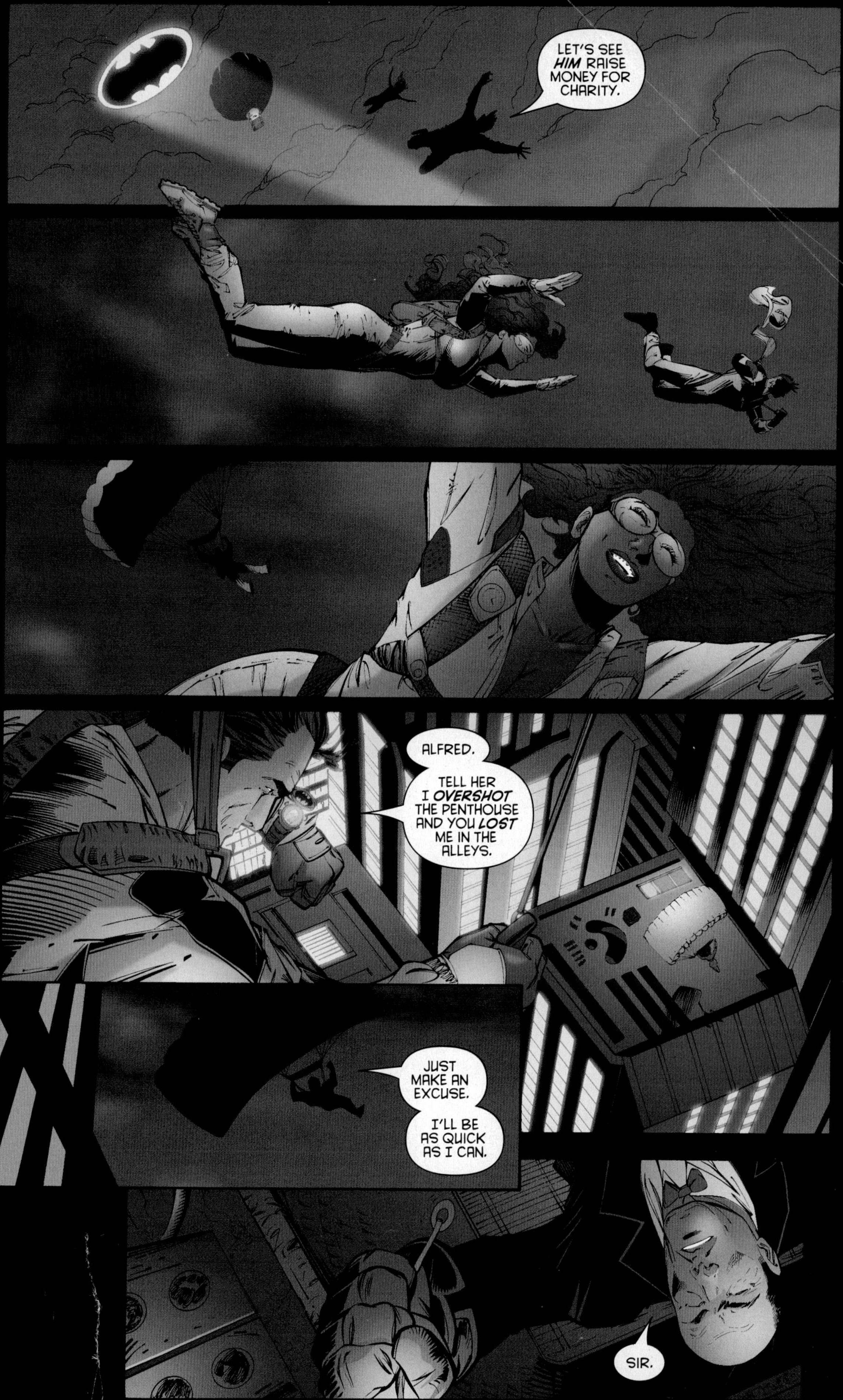
LET'S SEE *HIM* RAISE MONEY FOR CHARITY.
ALFRED.
TELL HER I *OVERSHOT* THE PENTHOUSE AND YOU *LOST* ME IN THE ALLEYS.
JUST MAKE AN EXCUSE.
I'LL BE AS QUICK AS I CAN.
SIR.

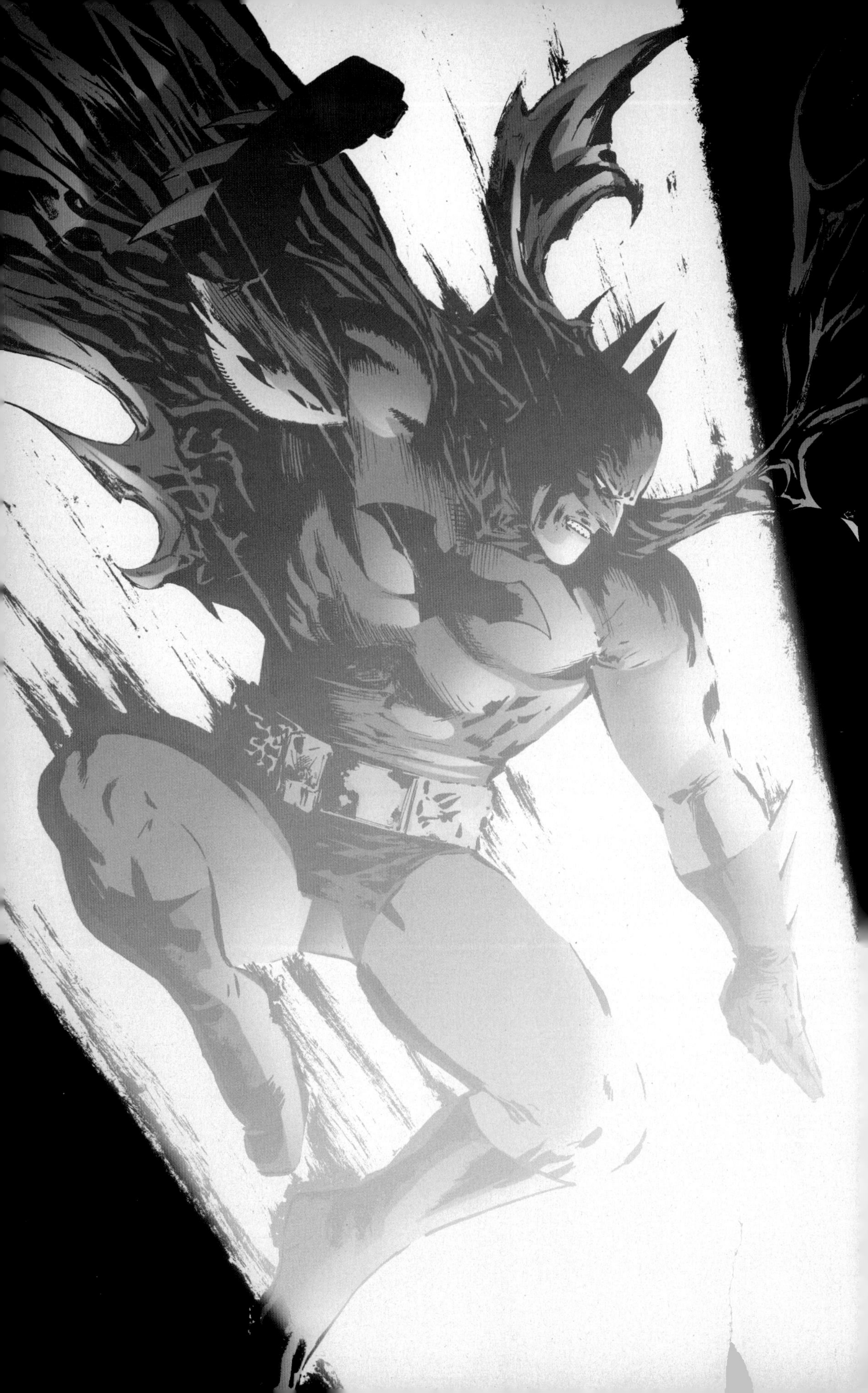

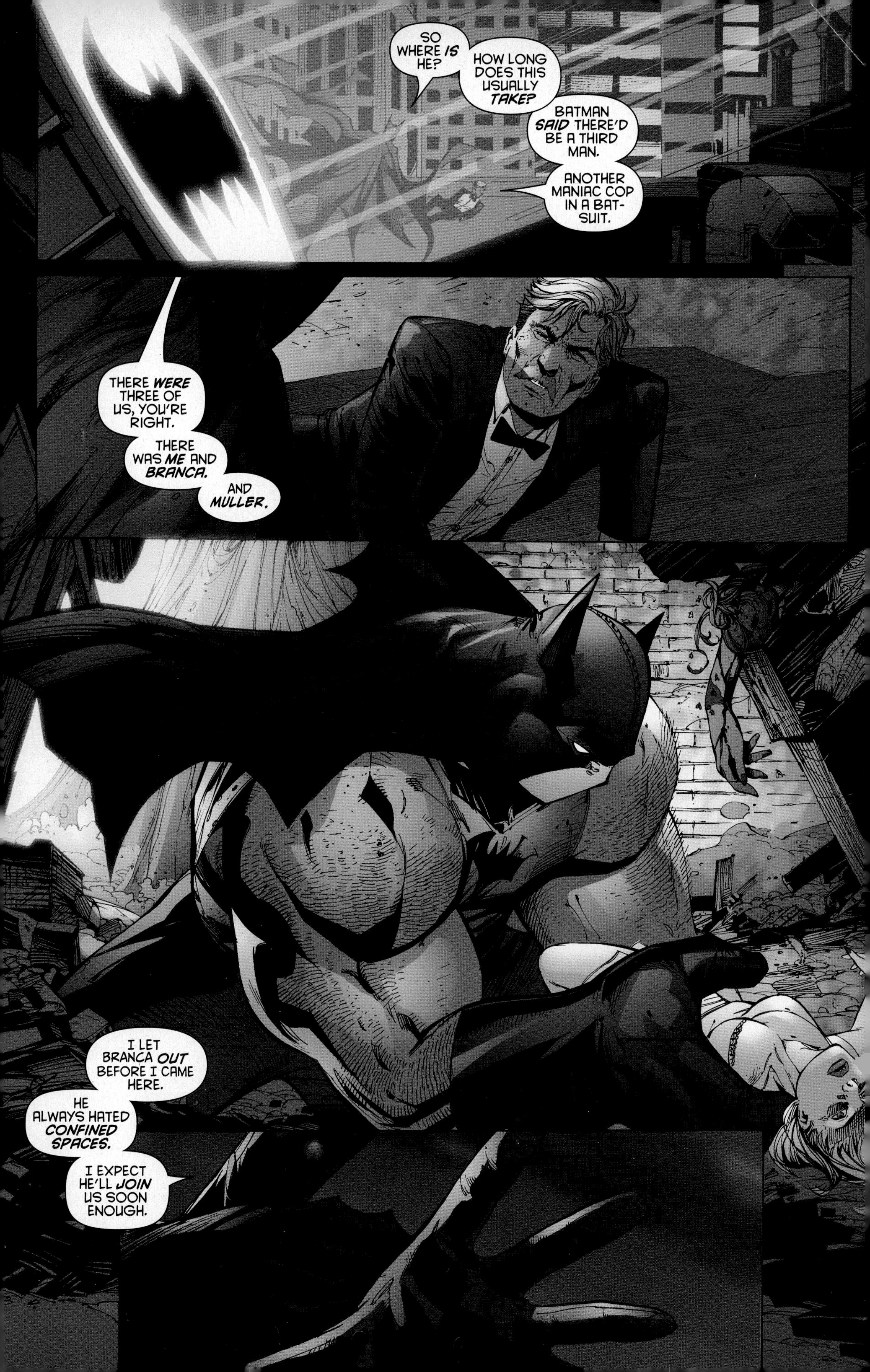

SO WHERE *IS* HE?
HOW LONG DOES THIS USUALLY *TAKE?*
BATMAN *SAID* THERE'D BE A THIRD MAN.
ANOTHER MANIAC COP IN A BAT-SUIT.
THERE *WERE* THREE OF US, YOU'RE RIGHT.
THERE WAS *ME* AND *BRANCA.*
AND *MULLER.*
I LET BRANCA *OUT* BEFORE I CAME HERE.
HE ALWAYS HATED *CONFINED SPACES.*
I EXPECT HE'LL *JOIN* US SOON ENOUGH.

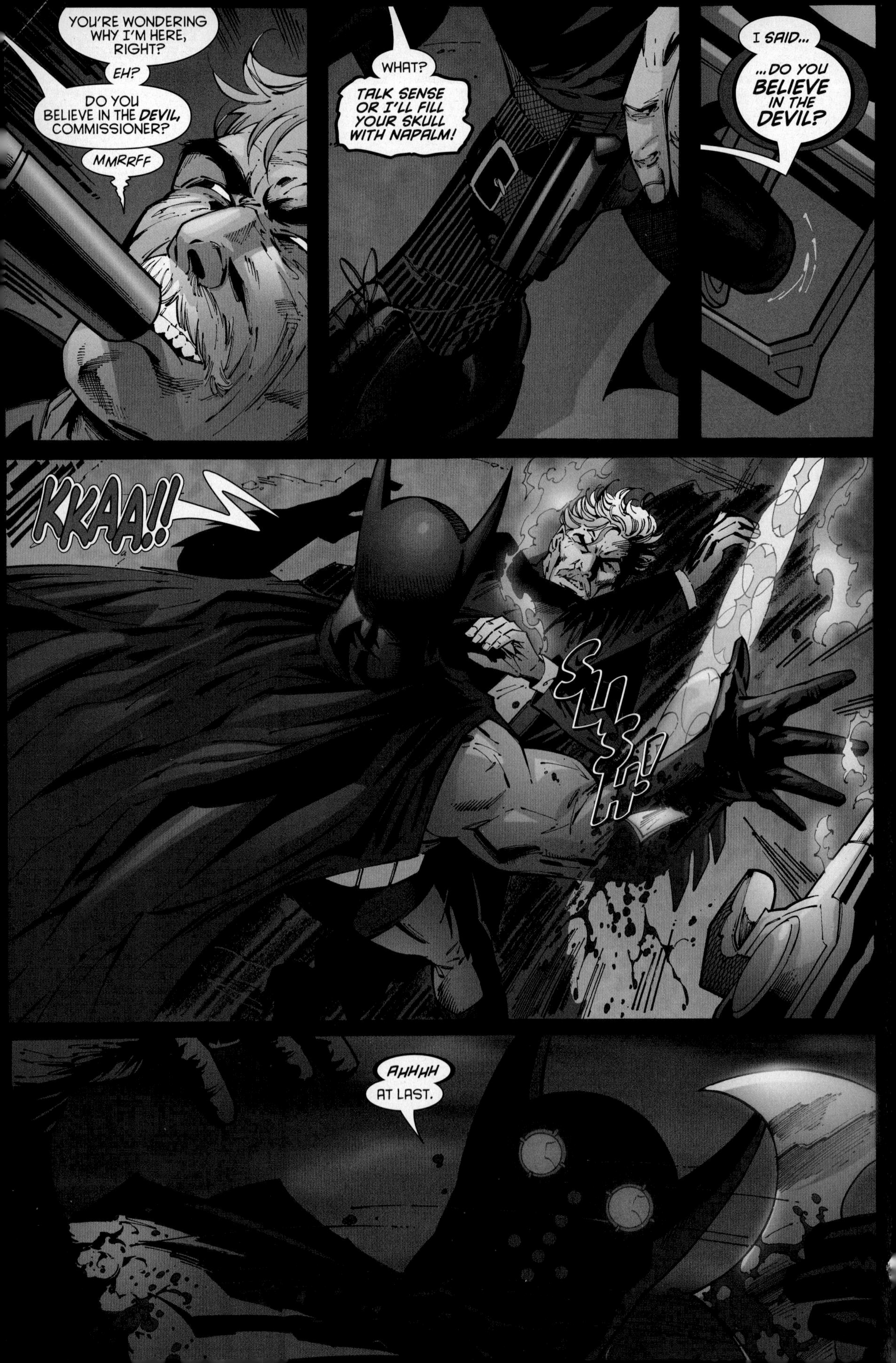
YOU'RE WONDERING WHY I'M HERE, RIGHT?
EH?
DO YOU BELIEVE IN THE DEVIL, COMMISSIONER?
MMRRFF
WHAT?
TALK SENSE OR I'LL FILL YOUR SKULL WITH NAPALM!
I SAID...
...DO YOU BELIEVE IN THE DEVIL?
KKAA!!
AHHHH
AT LAST.

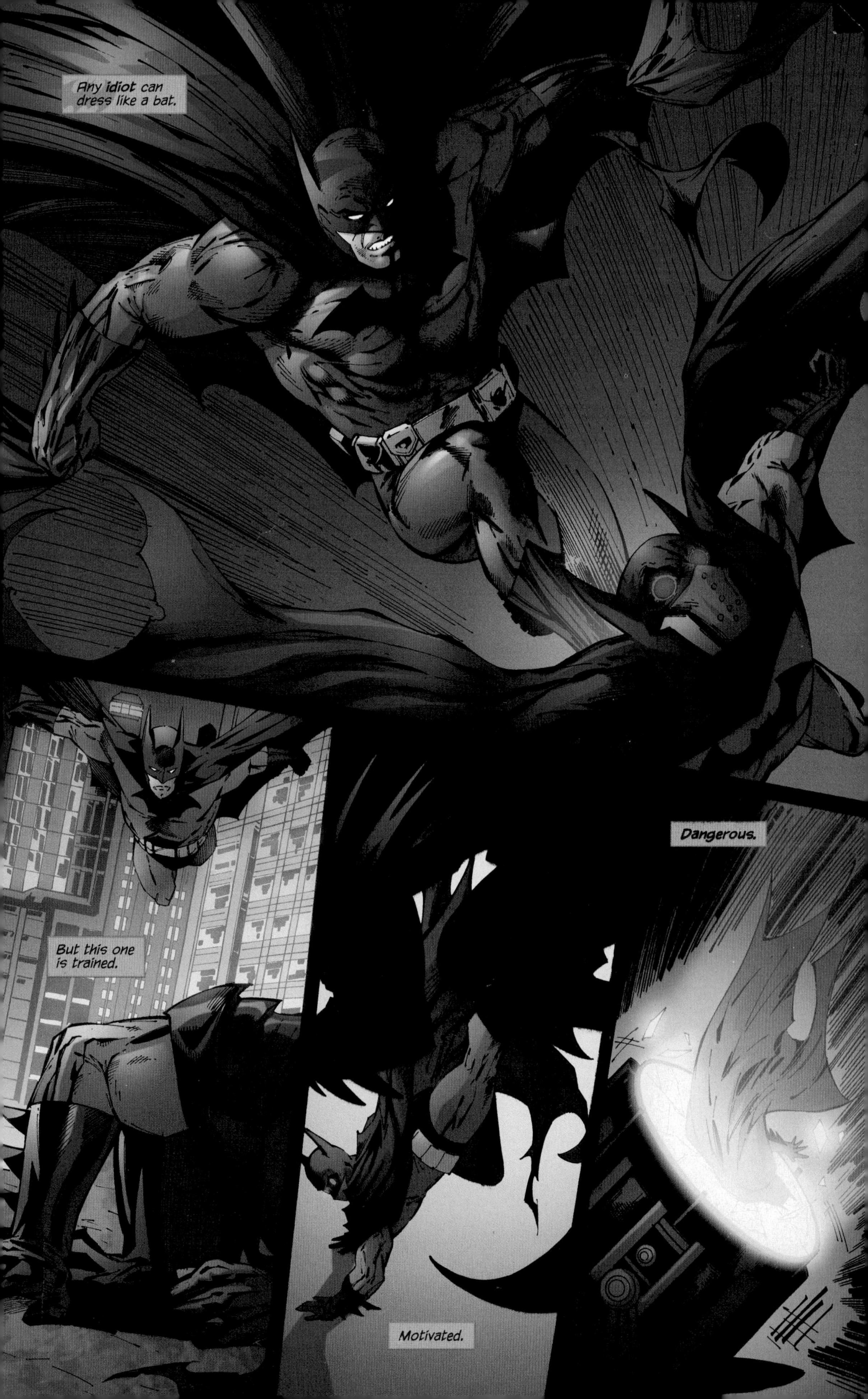

Any idiot can dress like a bat.
But this one is trained.
Dangerous.
Motivated.

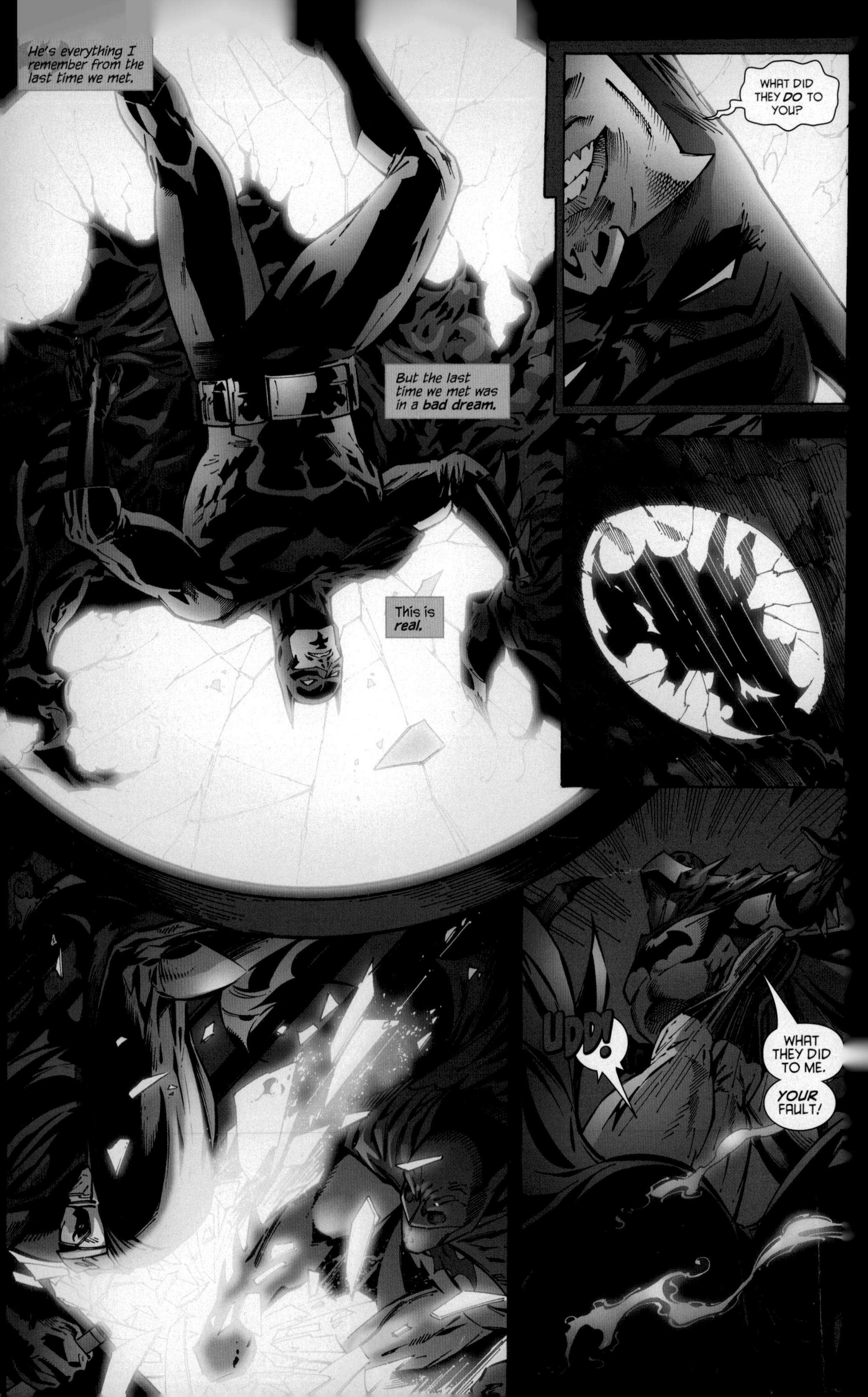
He's everything I remember from the last time we met.
WHAT DID THEY DO TO YOU?
But the last time we met was in a bad dream.
This is real.
UDD!
WHAT THEY DID TO ME. YOUR FAULT!

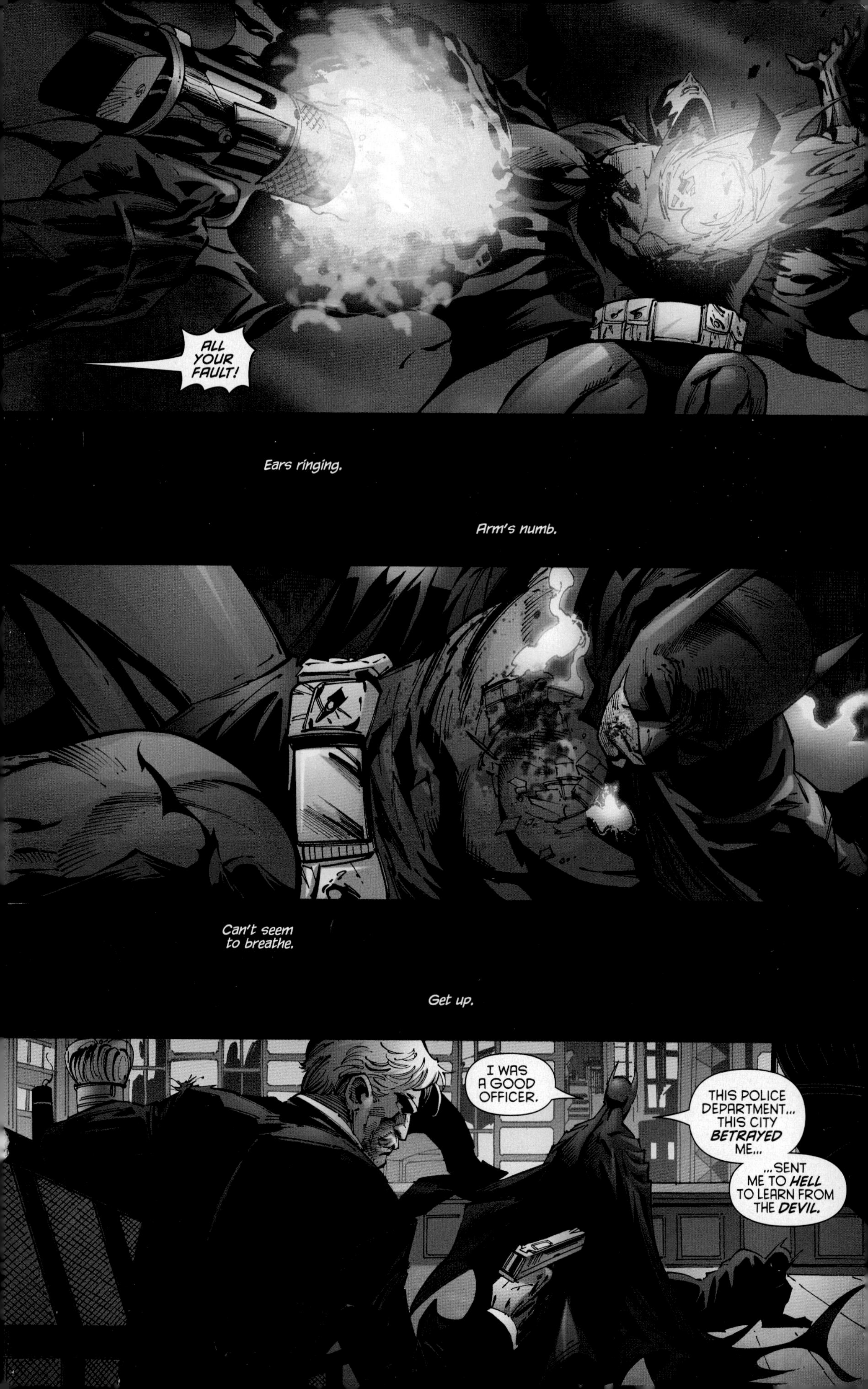
ALL YOUR FAULT!
Ears ringing.
Arm's numb.
Can't seem to breathe.
Get up.
I WAS A GOOD OFFICER.
THIS POLICE DEPARTMENT... THIS CITY BETRAYED ME...
...SENT ME TO HELL TO LEARN FROM THE DEVIL.

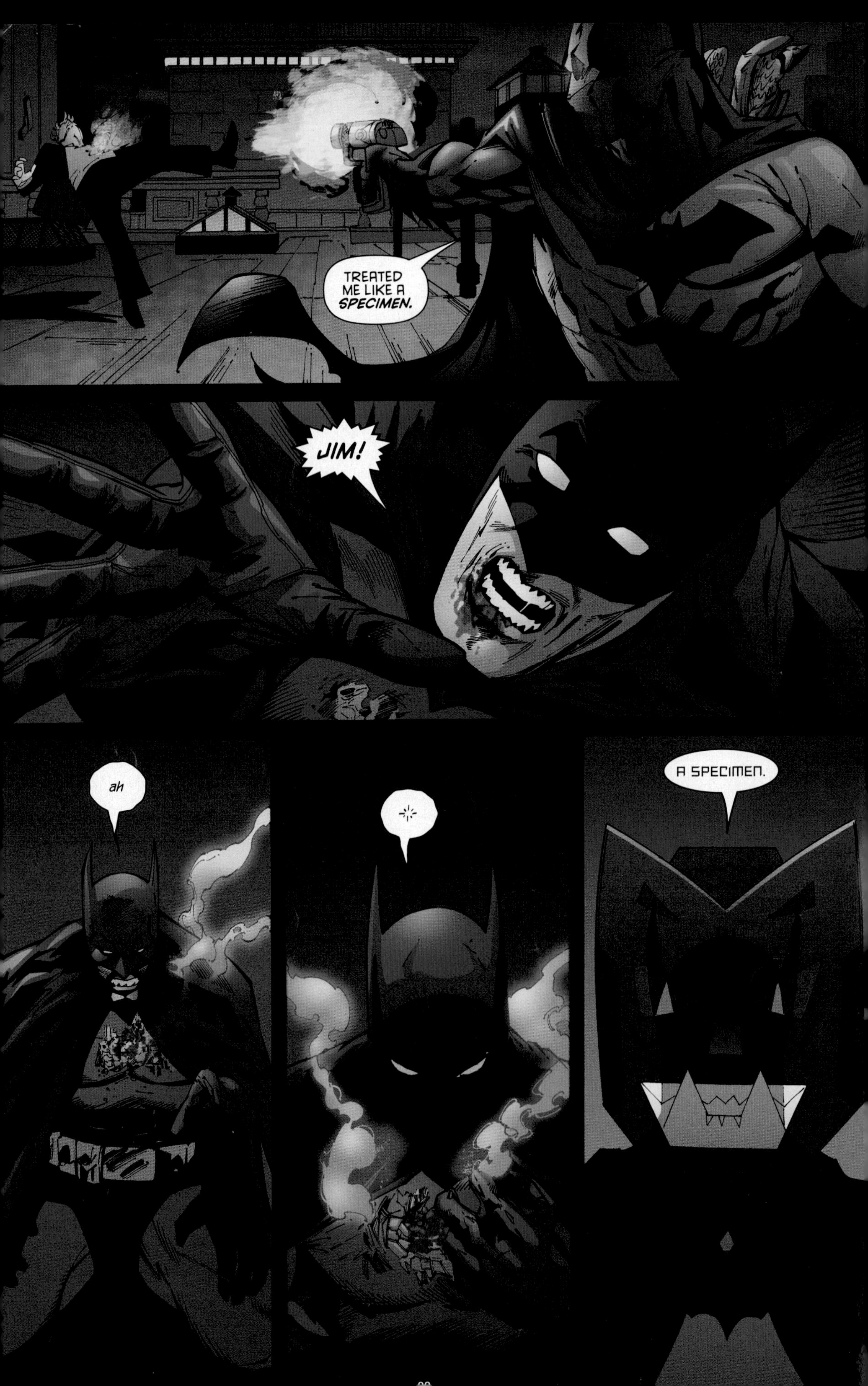
TREATED ME LIKE A *SPECIMEN.*
JIM!
ah
A SPECIMEN.

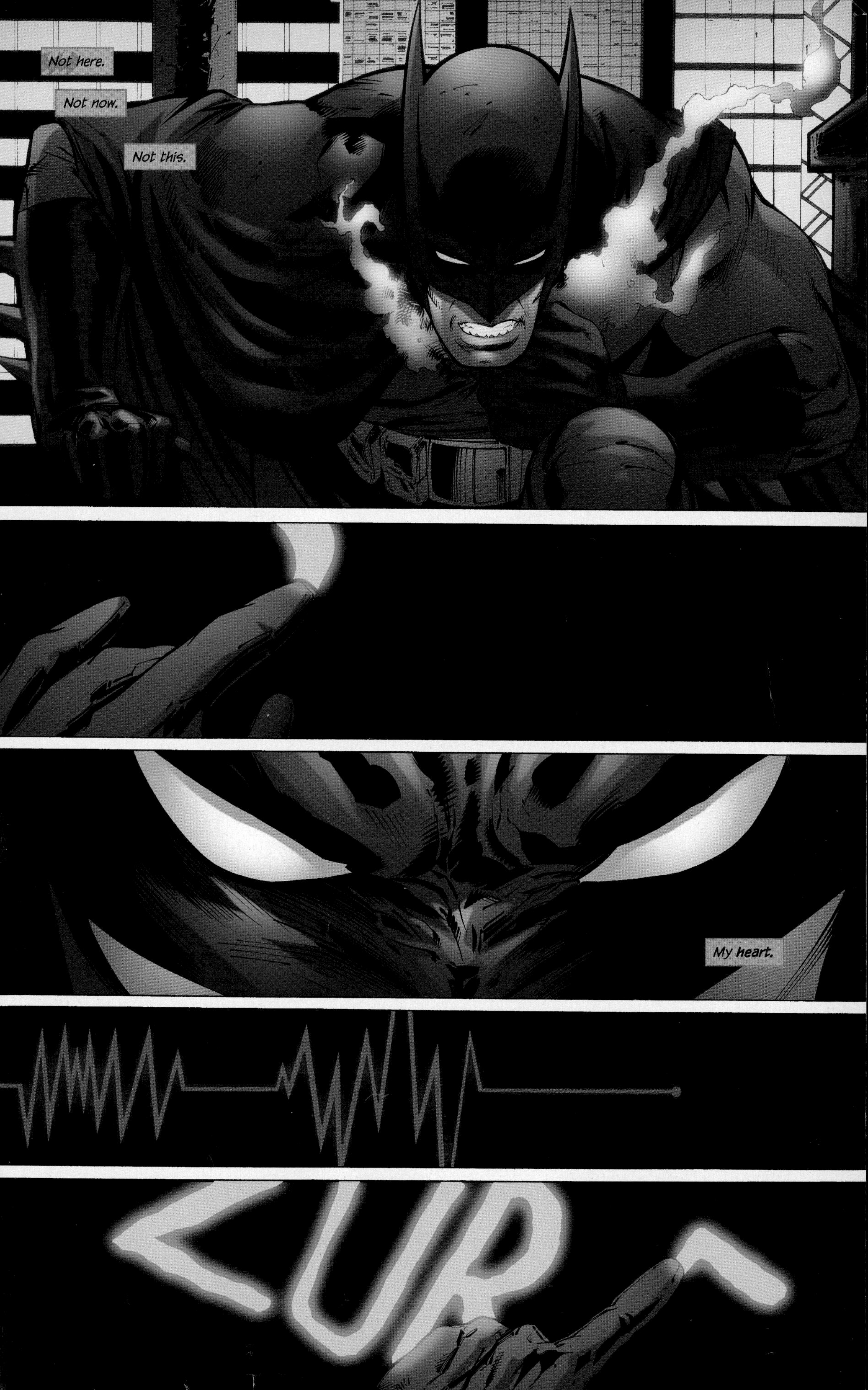
Not here.
Not now.
Not this.
My heart.
KUR

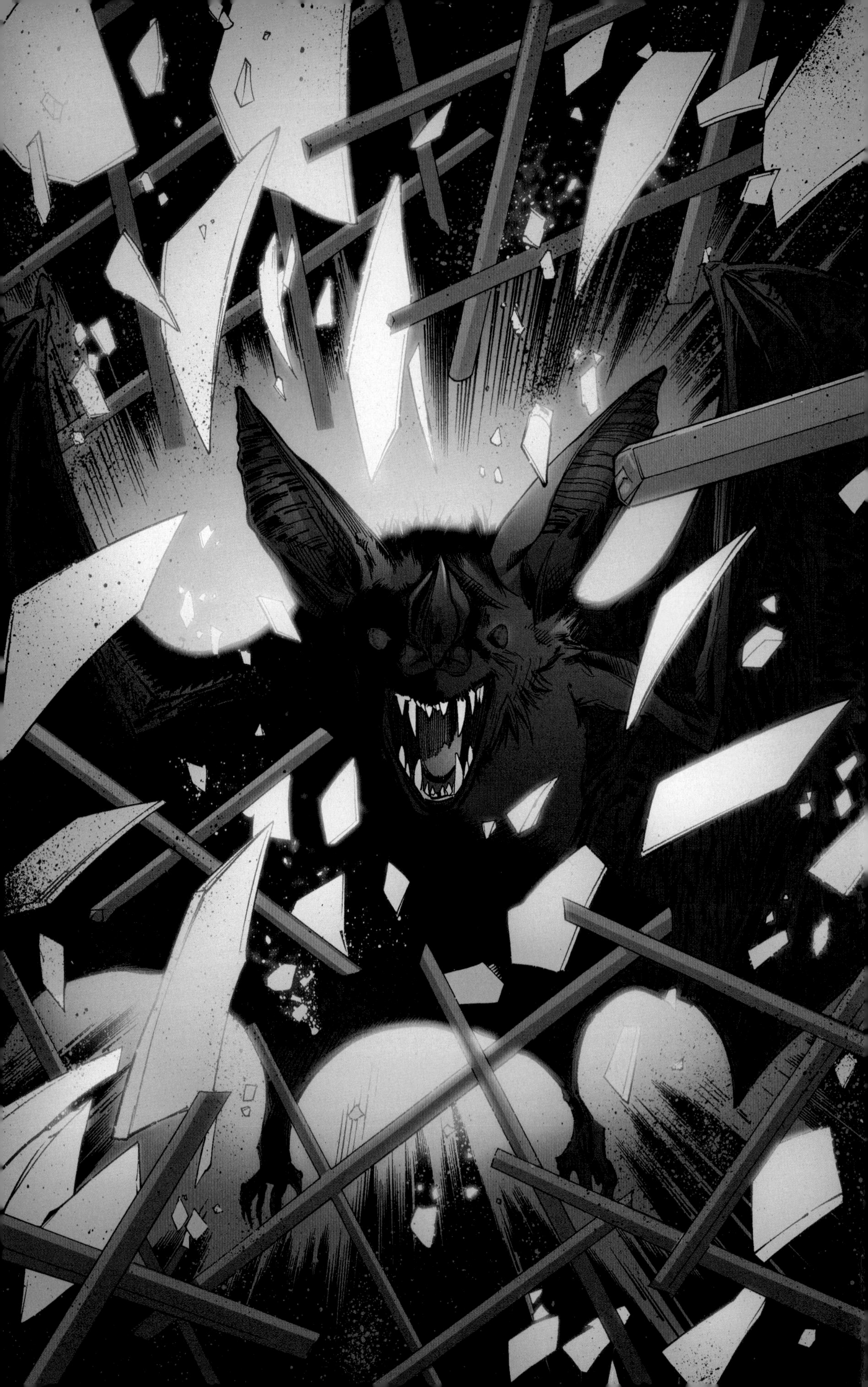

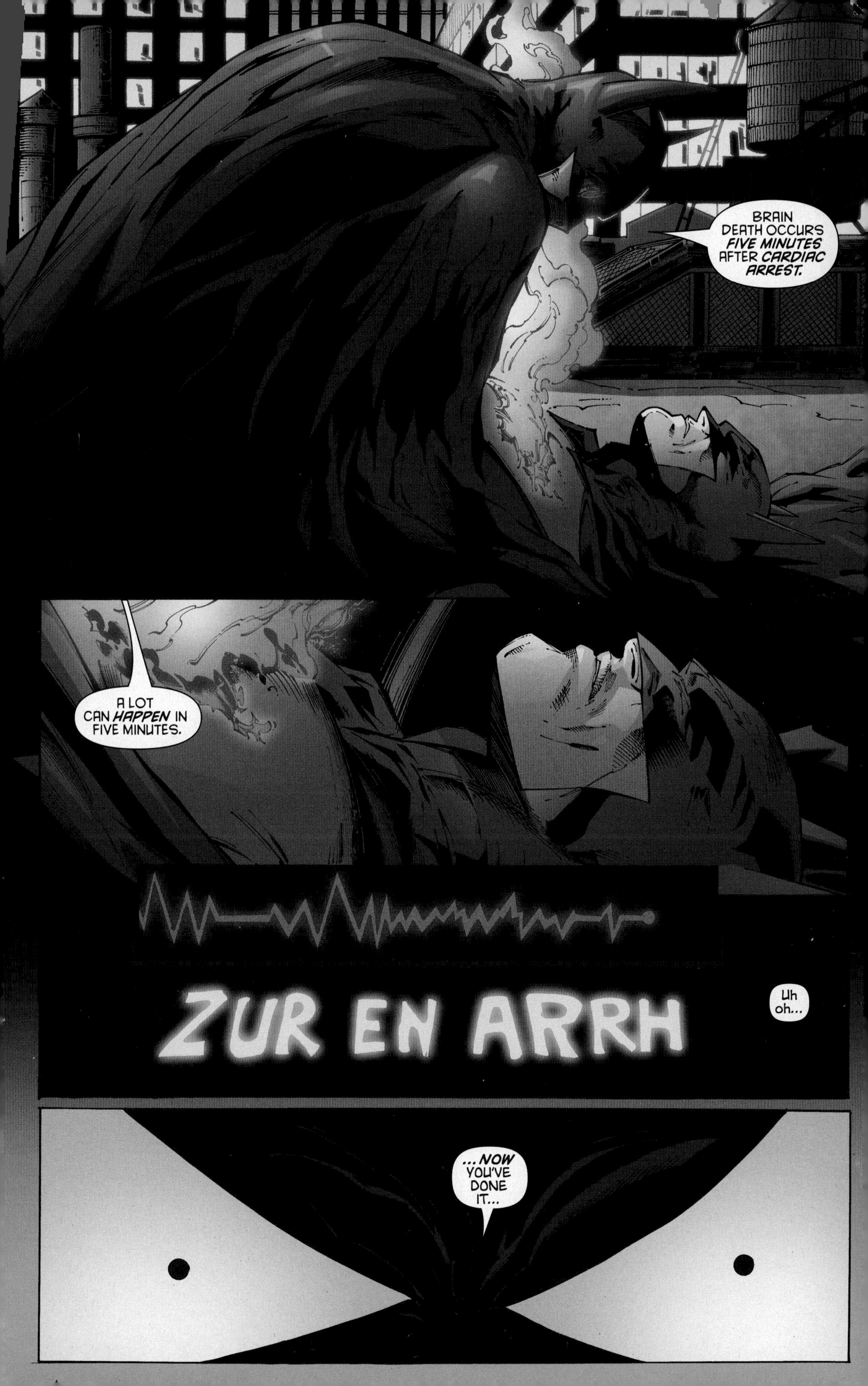
BRAIN DEATH OCCURS *FIVE MINUTES* AFTER *CARDIAC ARREST.*
A LOT CAN *HAPPEN* IN FIVE MINUTES.
ZUR EN ARRH
Uh oh...
...*NOW* YOU'VE DONE IT...

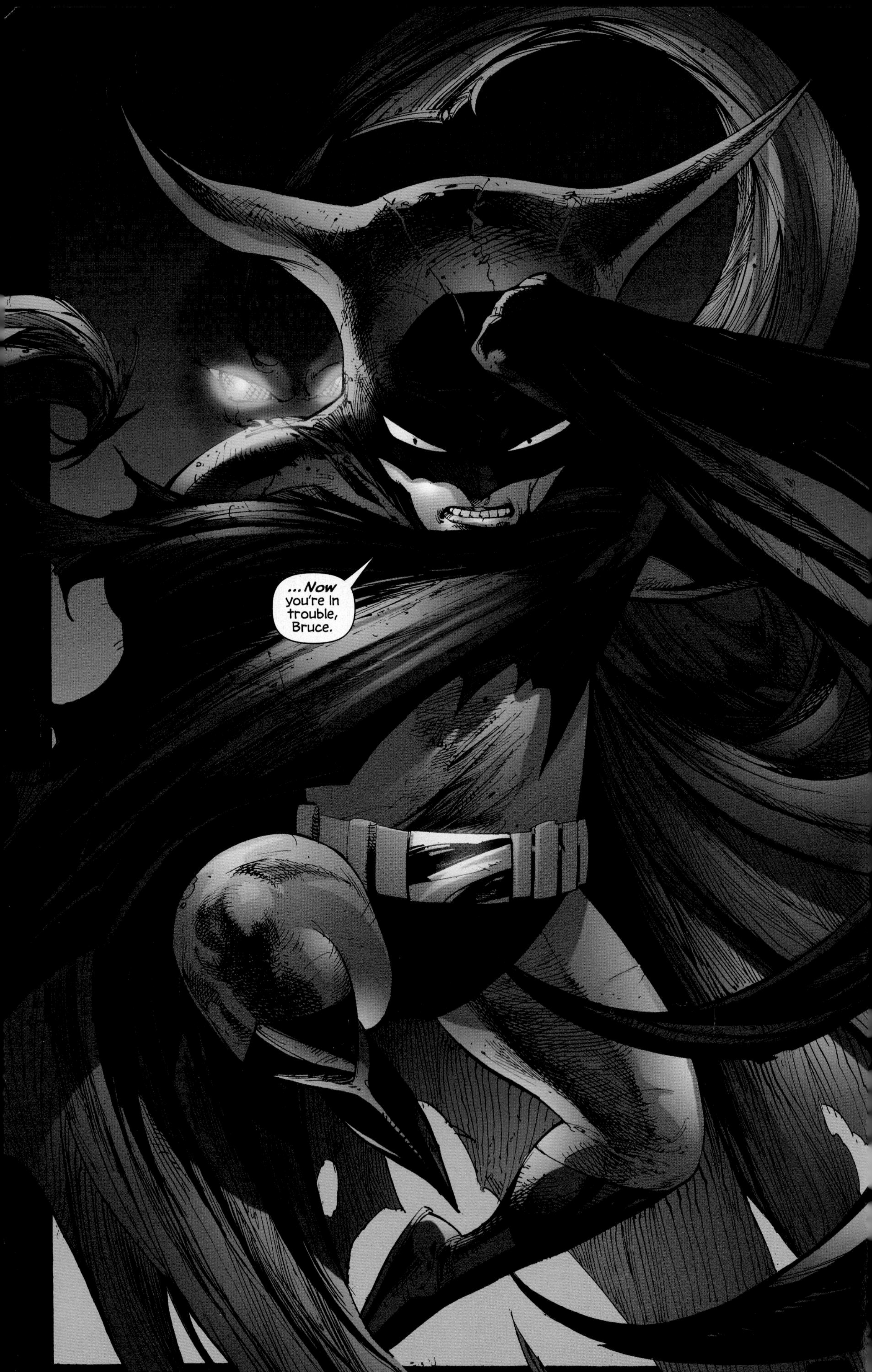
...Now you're in trouble, Bruce.

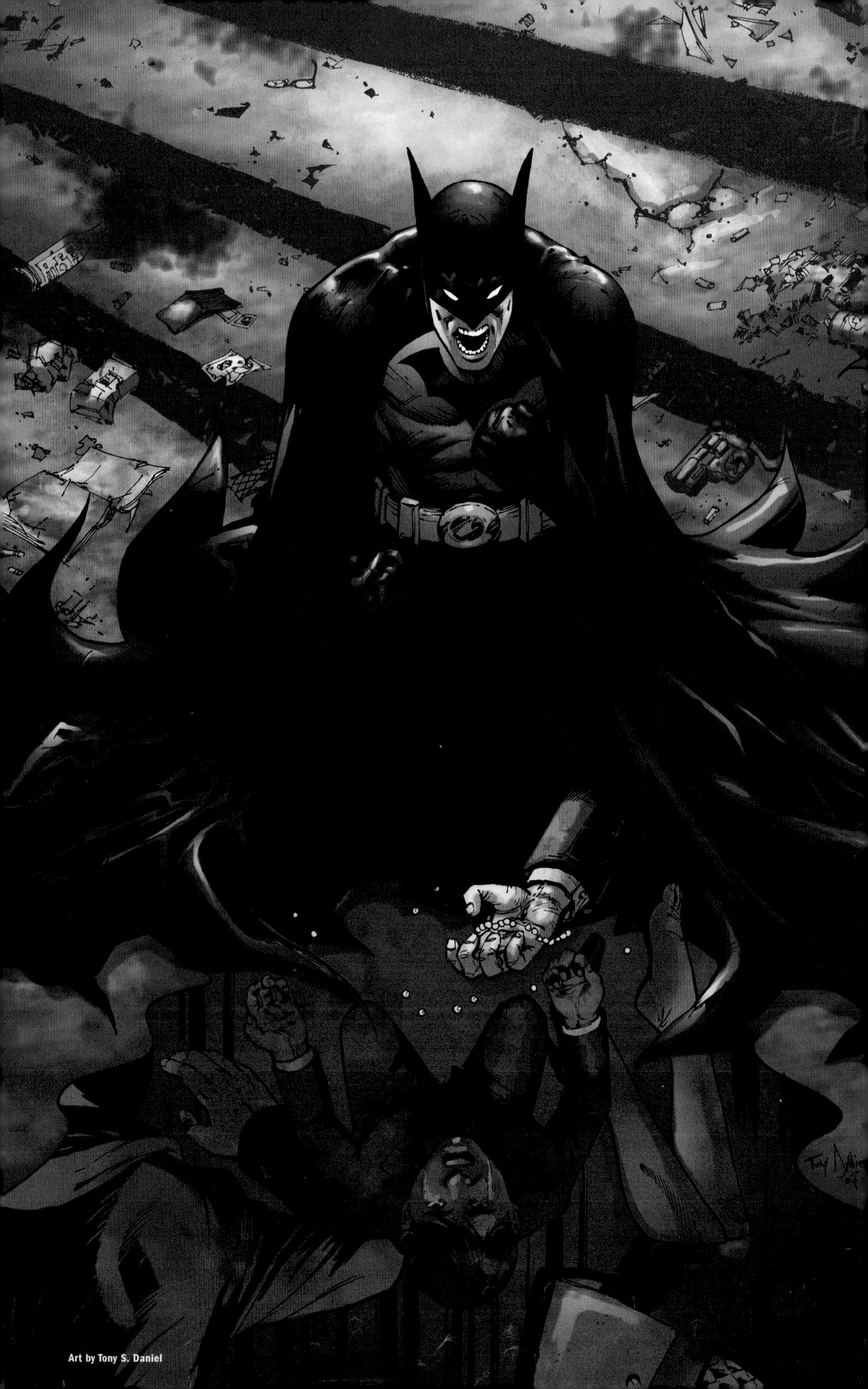

Art by Tony S. Daniel

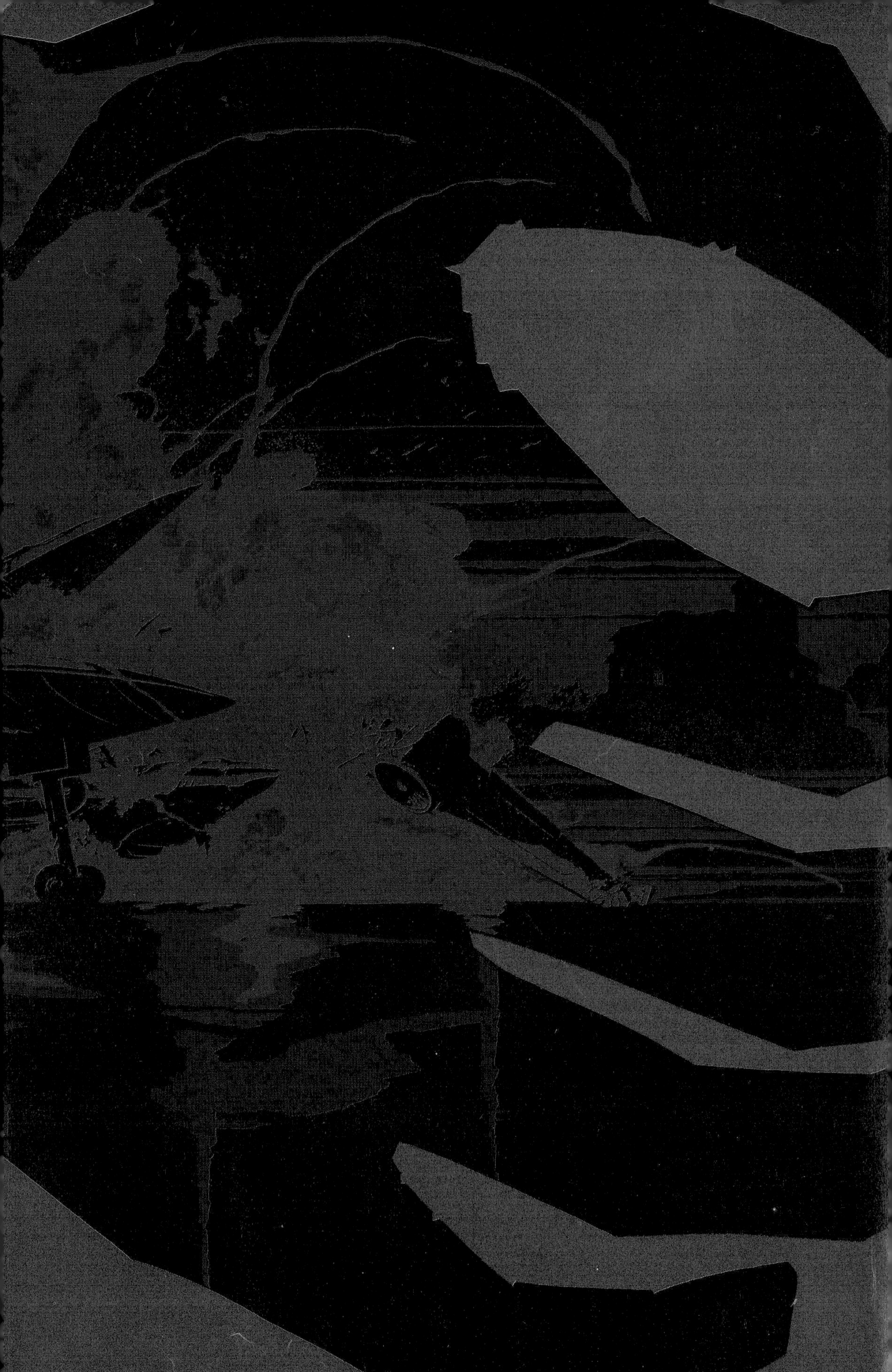

Chapter pencils by Tony S. Daniel
Chapter inks by Jonathan Glapion and Sandu Florea

NO ONE CAN *GET IN*, RIGHT?

The *Thögal Ritual* is one of the most highly advanced and dangerous forms of meditation.

During a seven-week retreat known as *Yangti*, the practitioner undergoes an experience designed to simulate *death* and *after-death*.

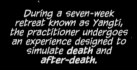

And *rebirth*, too.

HE CAN'T GET TO ME, RIGHT?

I'M *SAFE* HERE?

HE CAN'T GET *NEAR* ME?

1st day...

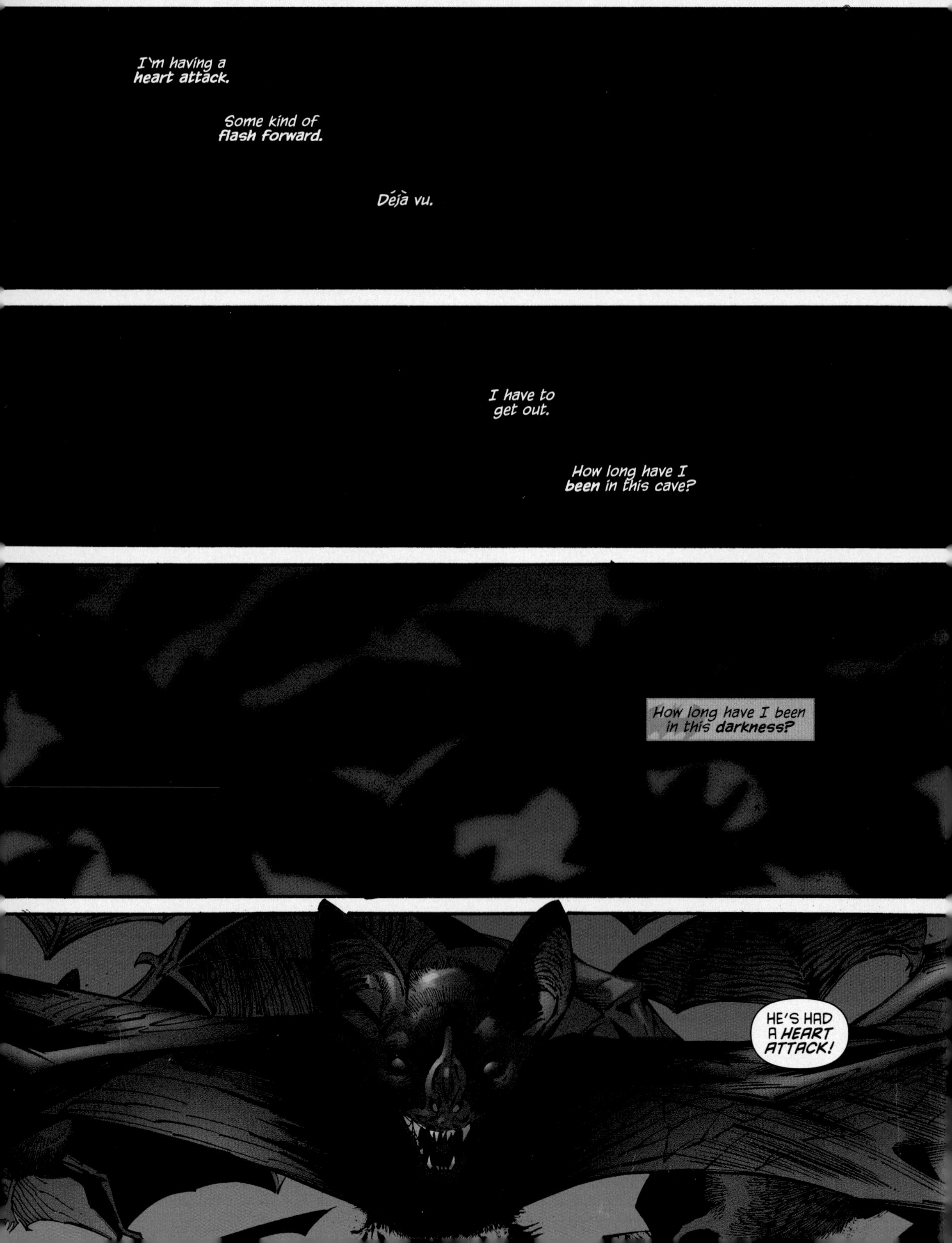

I'm having a heart attack.
Some kind of flash forward.
Déjà vu.
I have to get out.
How long have I been in this cave?
How long have I been in this darkness?
HE'S HAD A HEART ATTACK!

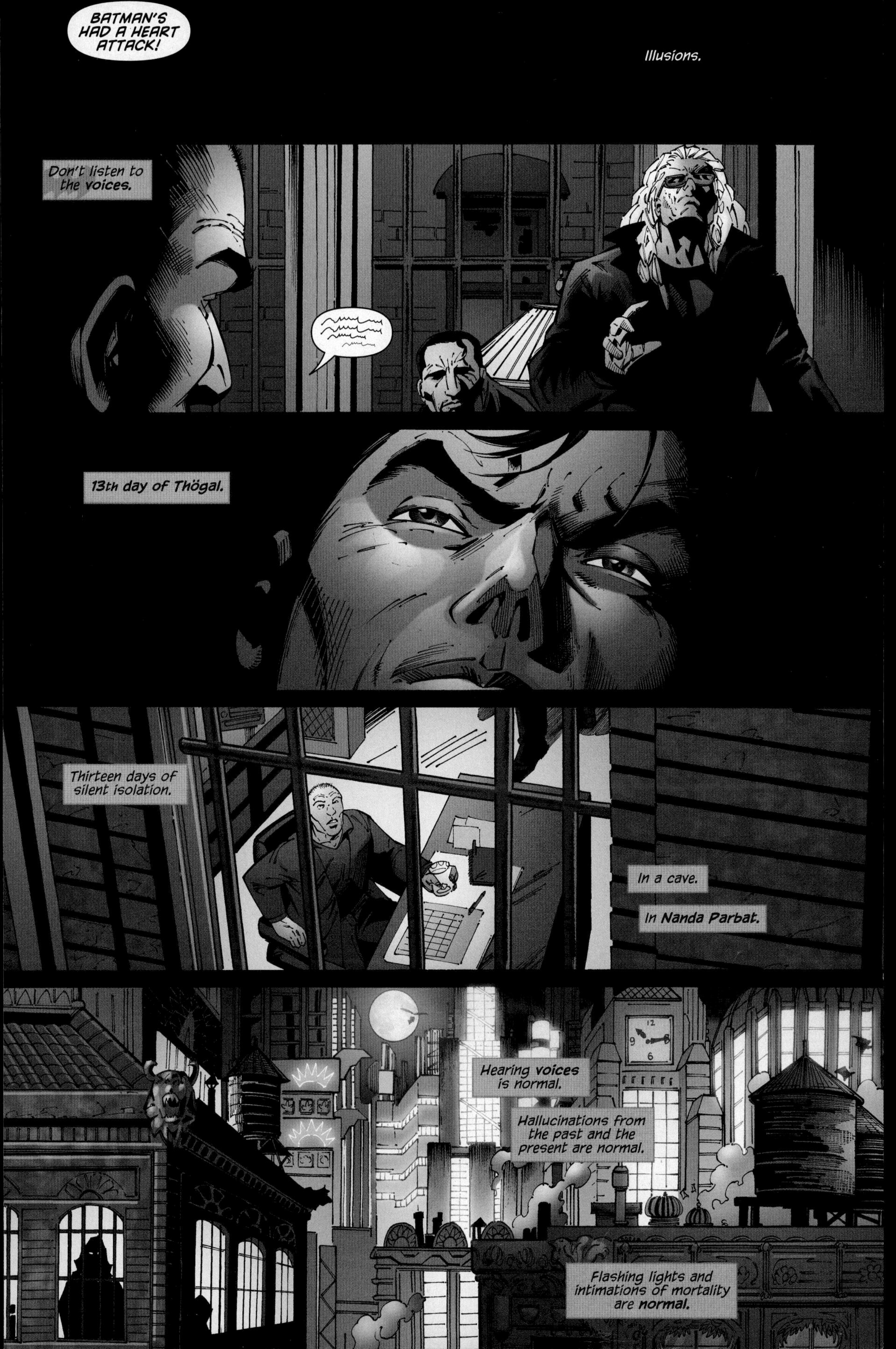
BATMAN'S HAD A HEART ATTACK!
Illusions.
Don't listen to the voices.
13th day of Thögal.
Thirteen days of silent isolation.
In a cave.
In Nanda Parbat.
Hearing voices is normal.
Hallucinations from the past and the present are normal.
Flashing lights and intimations of mortality are normal.

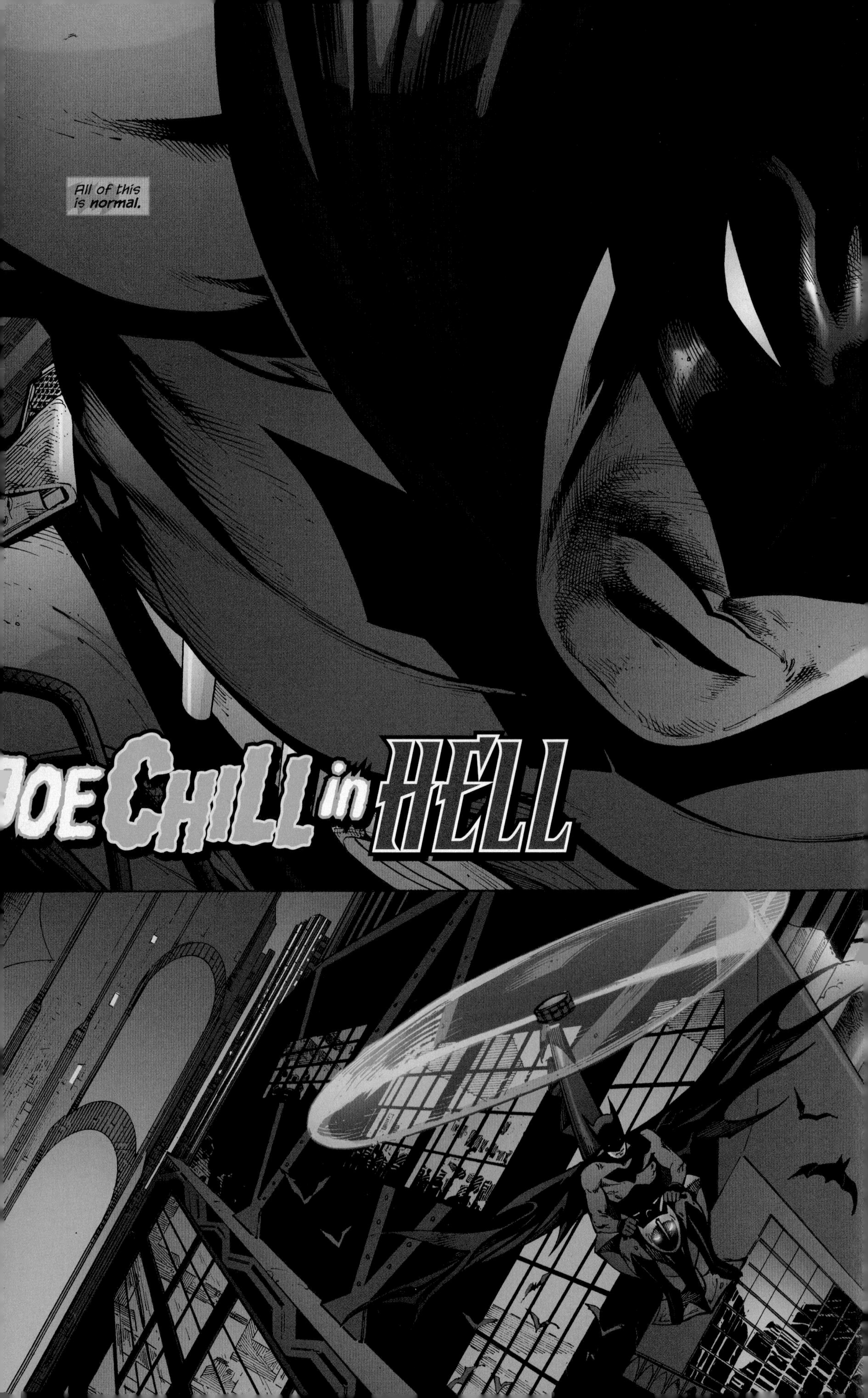
All of this is normal.
JOE CHILL in HELL

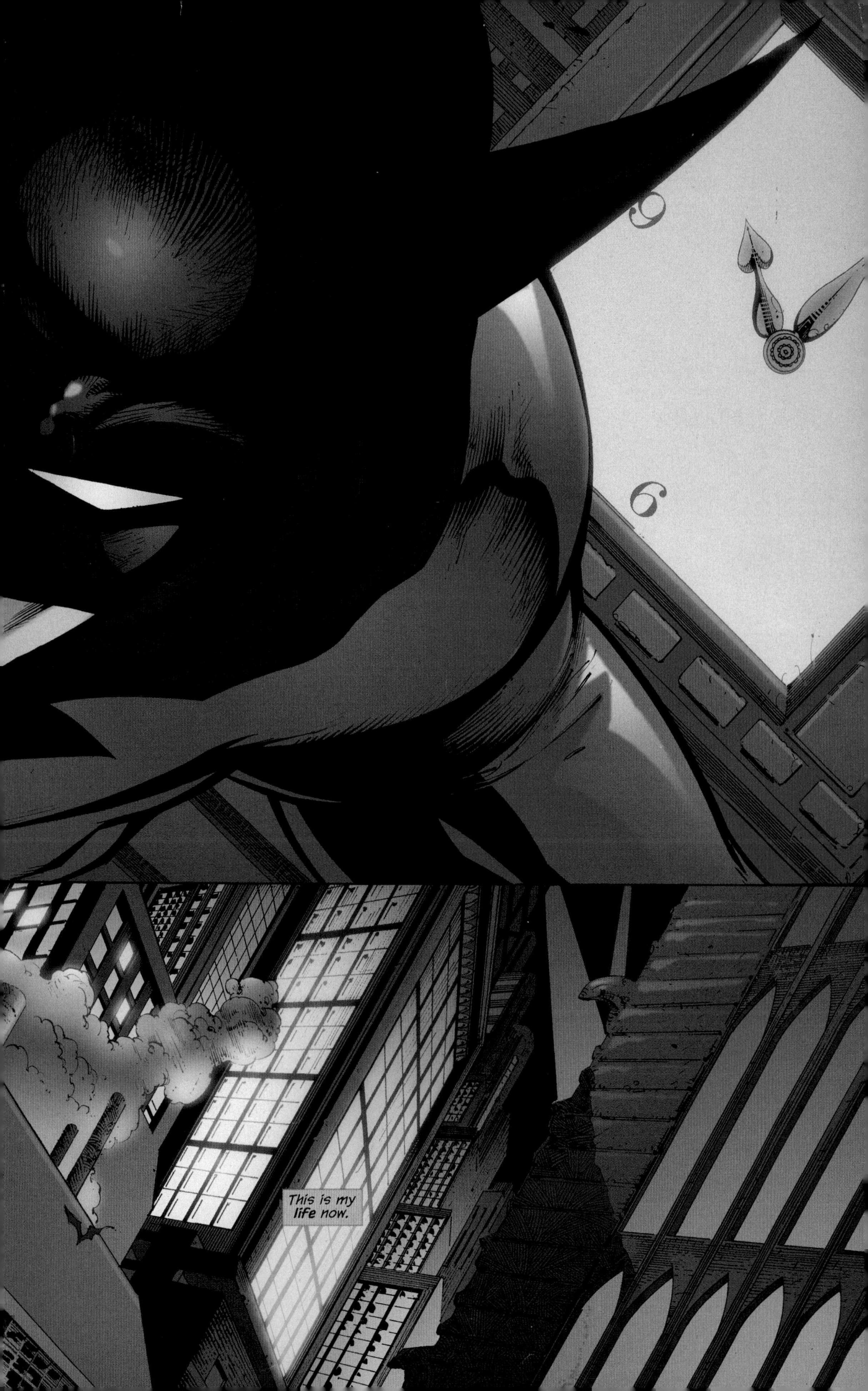
This is my life now.

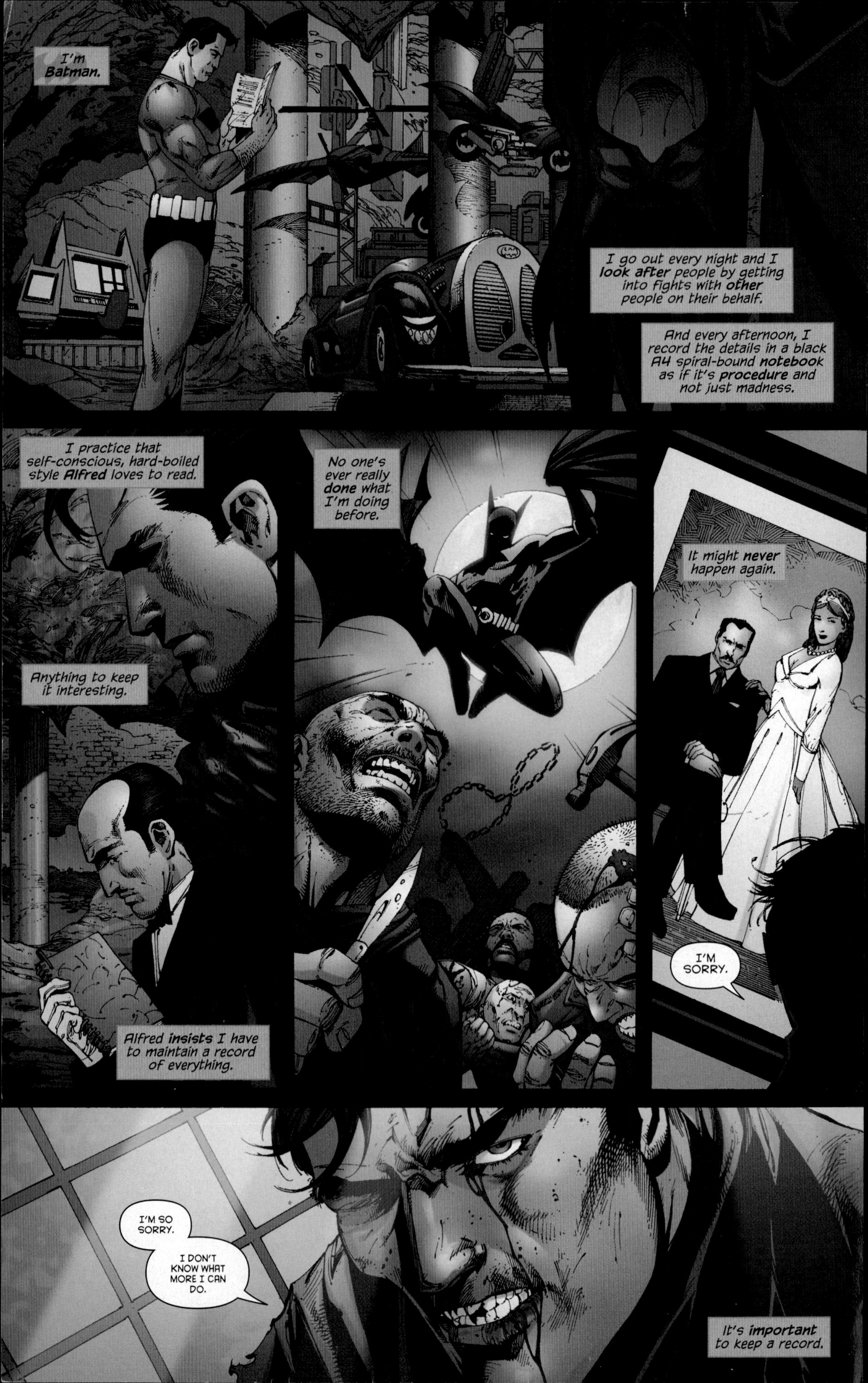
I'm Batman.
I go out every night and I look after people by getting into fights with other people on their behalf.
And every afternoon, I record the details in a black A4 spiral-bound notebook as if it's procedure and not just madness.
I practice that self-conscious, hard-boiled style Alfred loves to read.
Anything to keep it interesting.
Alfred insists I have to maintain a record of everything.
No one's ever really done what I'm doing before.
It might never happen again.
I'M SORRY.
I'M SO SORRY.
I DON'T KNOW WHAT MORE I CAN DO.
It's important to keep a record.

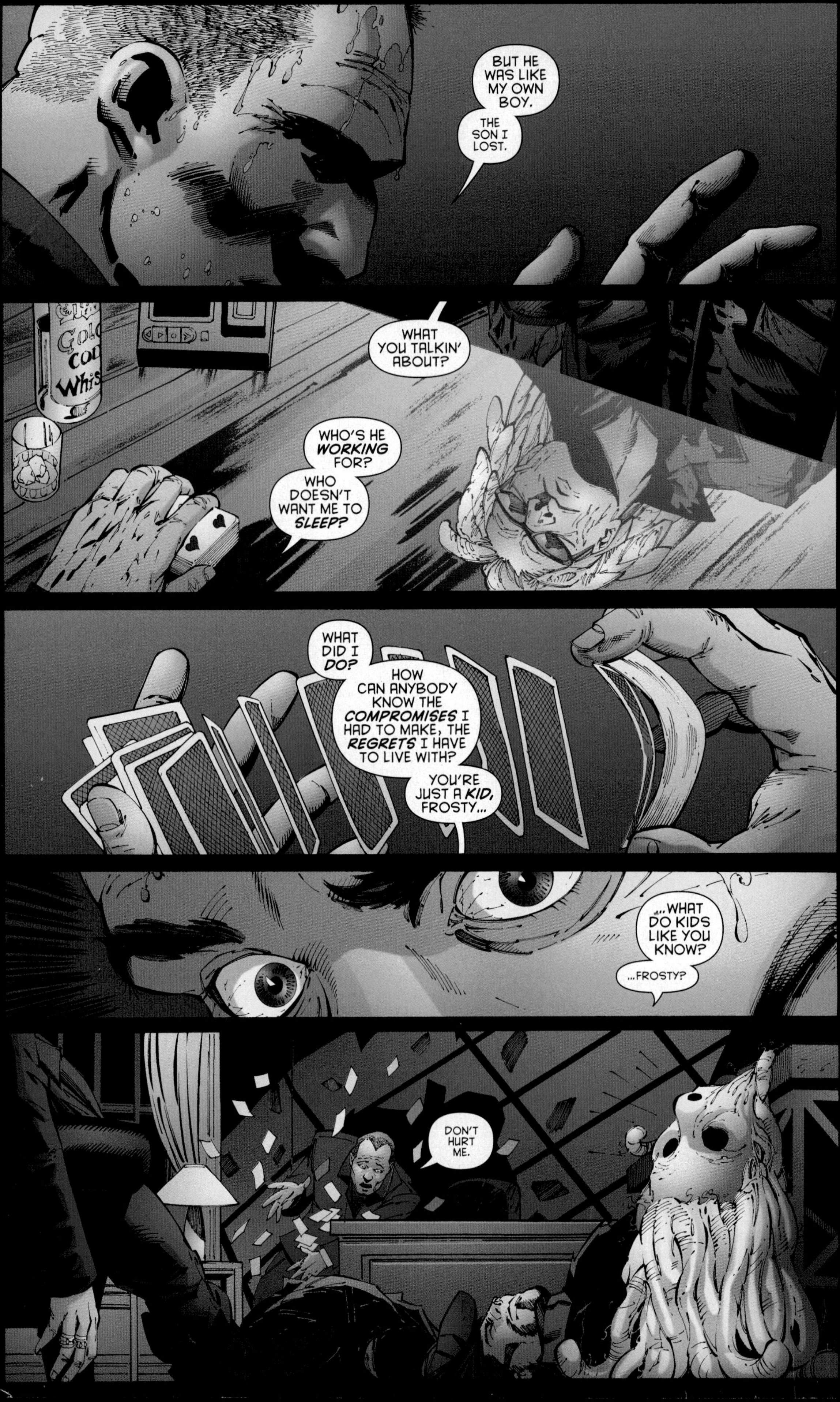
BUT HE WAS LIKE MY OWN BOY.
THE SON I LOST.
WHAT YOU TALKIN' ABOUT?
WHO'S HE WORKING FOR?
WHO DOESN'T WANT ME TO SLEEP?
WHAT DID I DO?
HOW CAN ANYBODY KNOW THE COMPROMISES I HAD TO MAKE, THE REGRETS I HAVE TO LIVE WITH?
YOU'RE JUST A KID, FROSTY...
...WHAT DO KIDS LIKE YOU KNOW?
...FROSTY?
DON'T HURT ME.

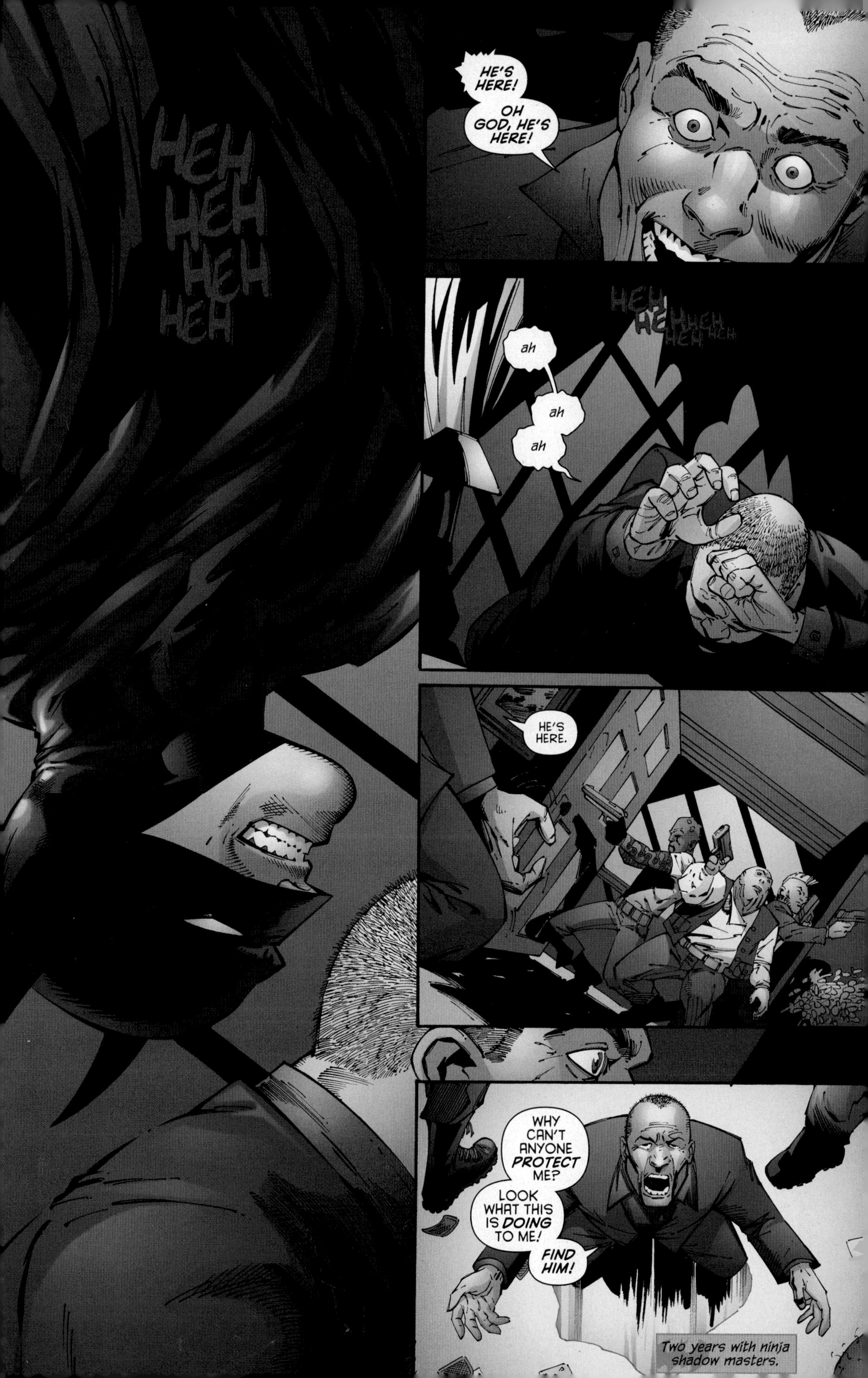
HEH HEH HEH HEH
HE'S HERE!
OH GOD, HE'S HERE!
HEH HEH HEH HEH HEH
ah
ah
ah
HE'S HERE.
WHY CAN'T ANYONE PROTECT ME?
LOOK WHAT THIS IS DOING TO ME!
FIND HIM!
Two years with ninja shadow masters.

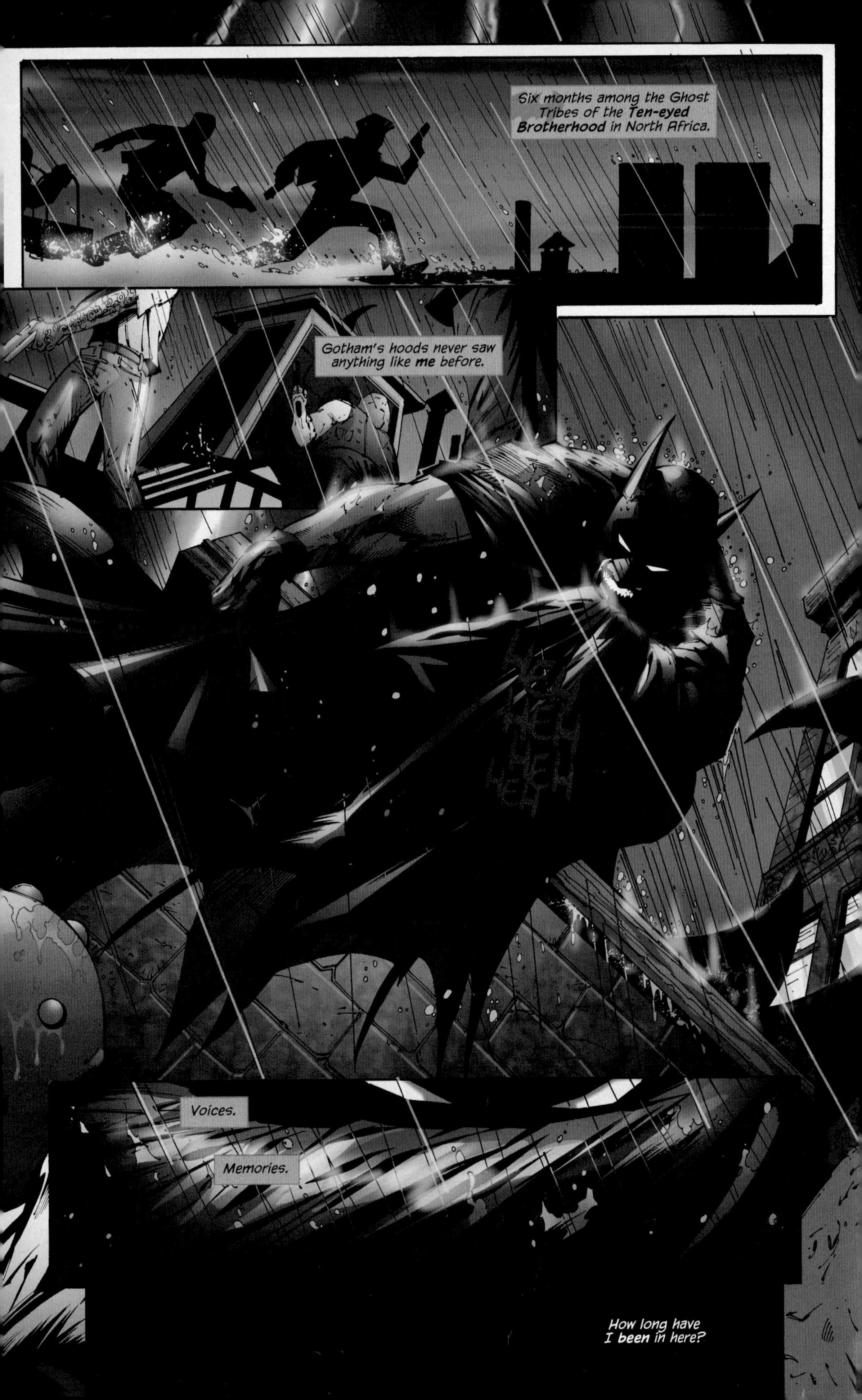
Six months among the Ghost Tribes of the Ten-eyed Brotherhood in North Africa.
Gotham's hoods never saw anything like me before.
Voices.
Memories.
How long have I been in here?

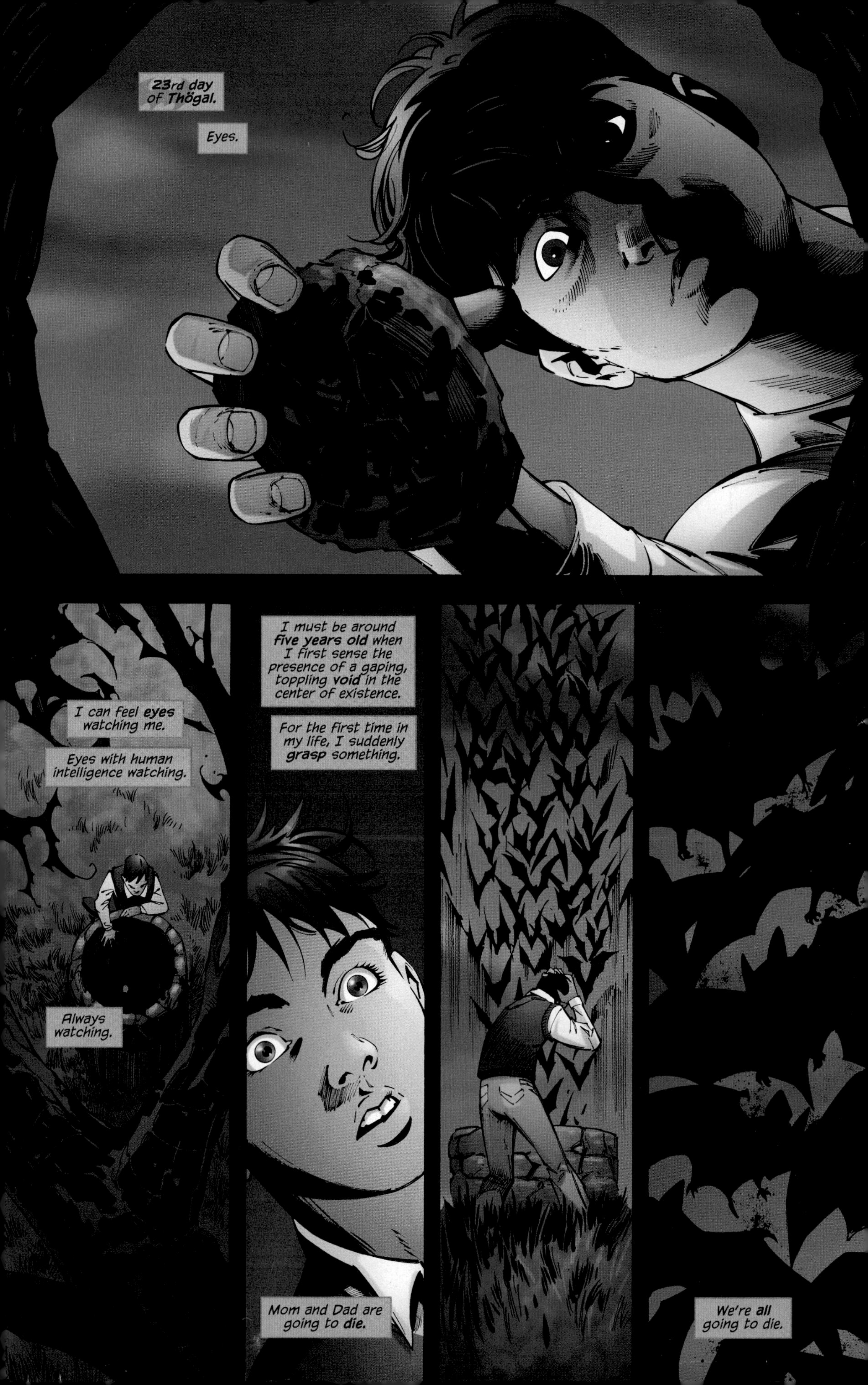
23rd day of Thögal.
Eyes.
I can feel eyes watching me.
Eyes with human intelligence watching.
Always watching.
I must be around five years old when I first sense the presence of a gaping, toppling void in the center of existence.
For the first time in my life, I suddenly grasp something.
Mom and Dad are going to die.
We're all going to die.

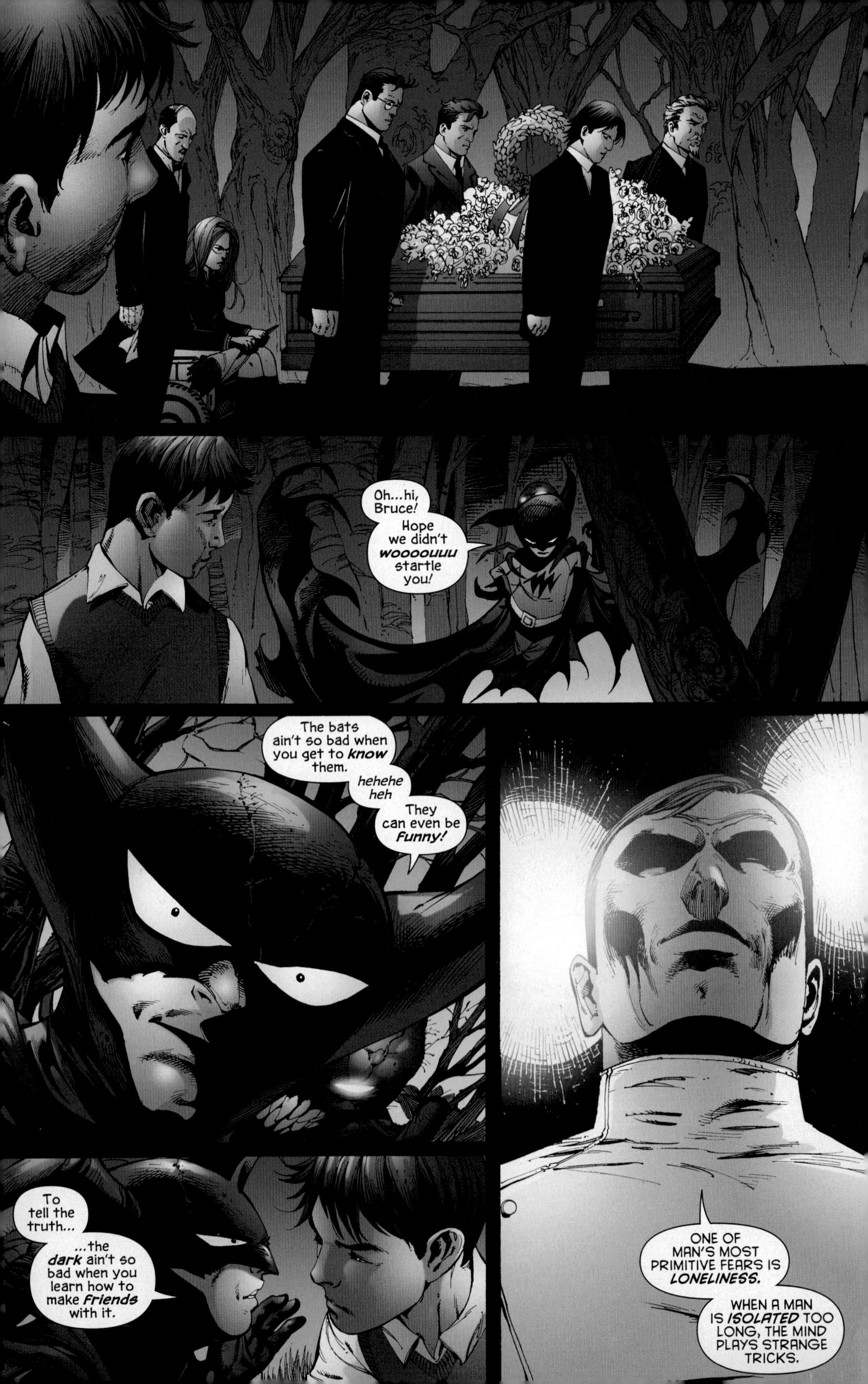
Oh...hi, Bruce! Hope we didn't wooooouuu startle you!
The bats ain't so bad when you get to know them.
hehehe heh
They can even be funny!
To tell the truth...
...the dark ain't so bad when you learn how to make friends with it.
ONE OF MAN'S MOST PRIMITIVE FEARS IS LONELINESS.
WHEN A MAN IS ISOLATED TOO LONG, THE MIND PLAYS STRANGE TRICKS.

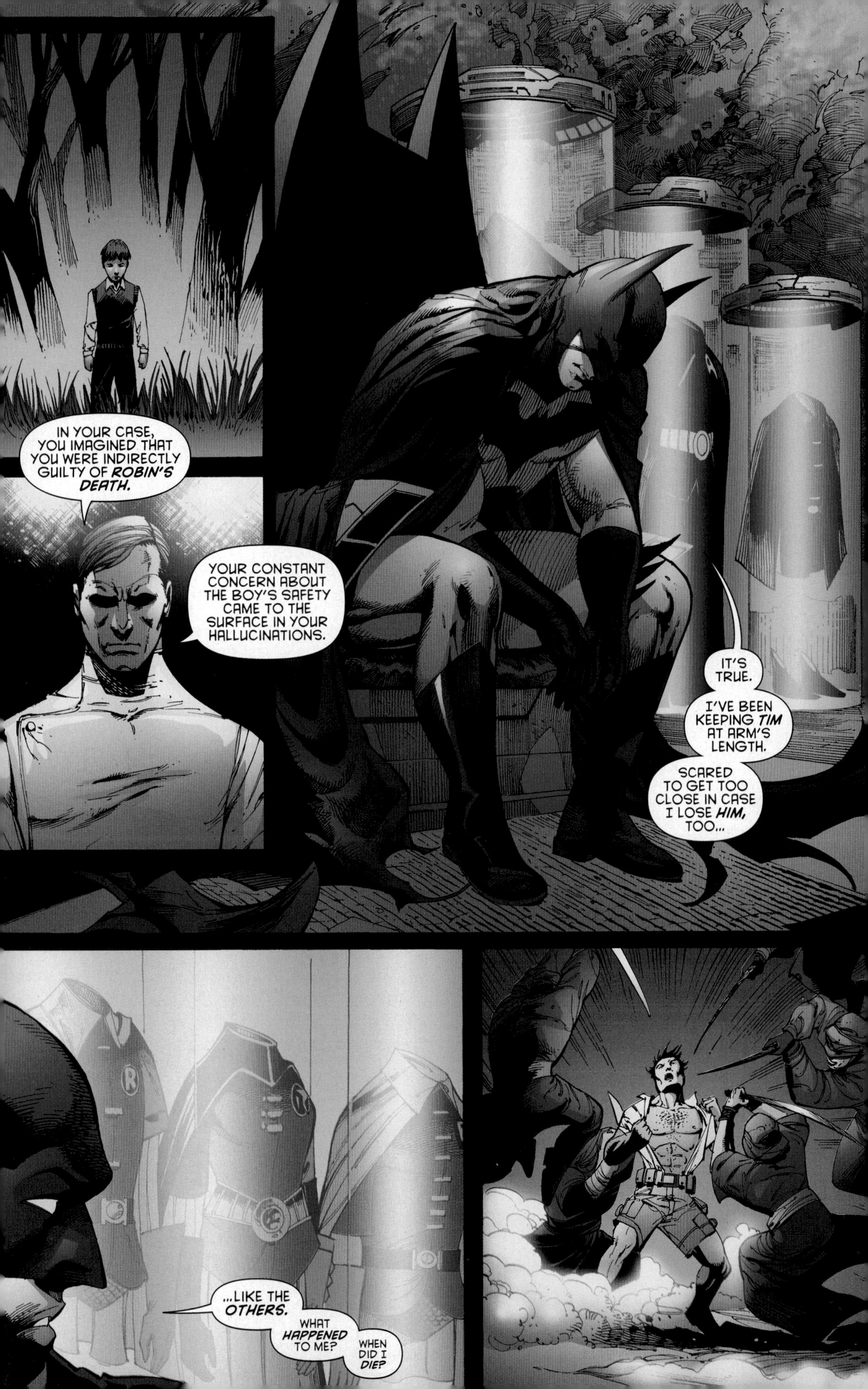
IN YOUR CASE, YOU IMAGINED THAT YOU WERE INDIRECTLY GUILTY OF *ROBIN'S DEATH.*
YOUR CONSTANT CONCERN ABOUT THE BOY'S SAFETY CAME TO THE SURFACE IN YOUR HALLUCINATIONS.
IT'S TRUE.
I'VE BEEN KEEPING *TIM* AT ARM'S LENGTH.
SCARED TO GET TOO CLOSE IN CASE I LOSE *HIM,* TOO...
...LIKE THE *OTHERS.*
WHAT *HAPPENED* TO ME?
WHEN DID I *DIE?*

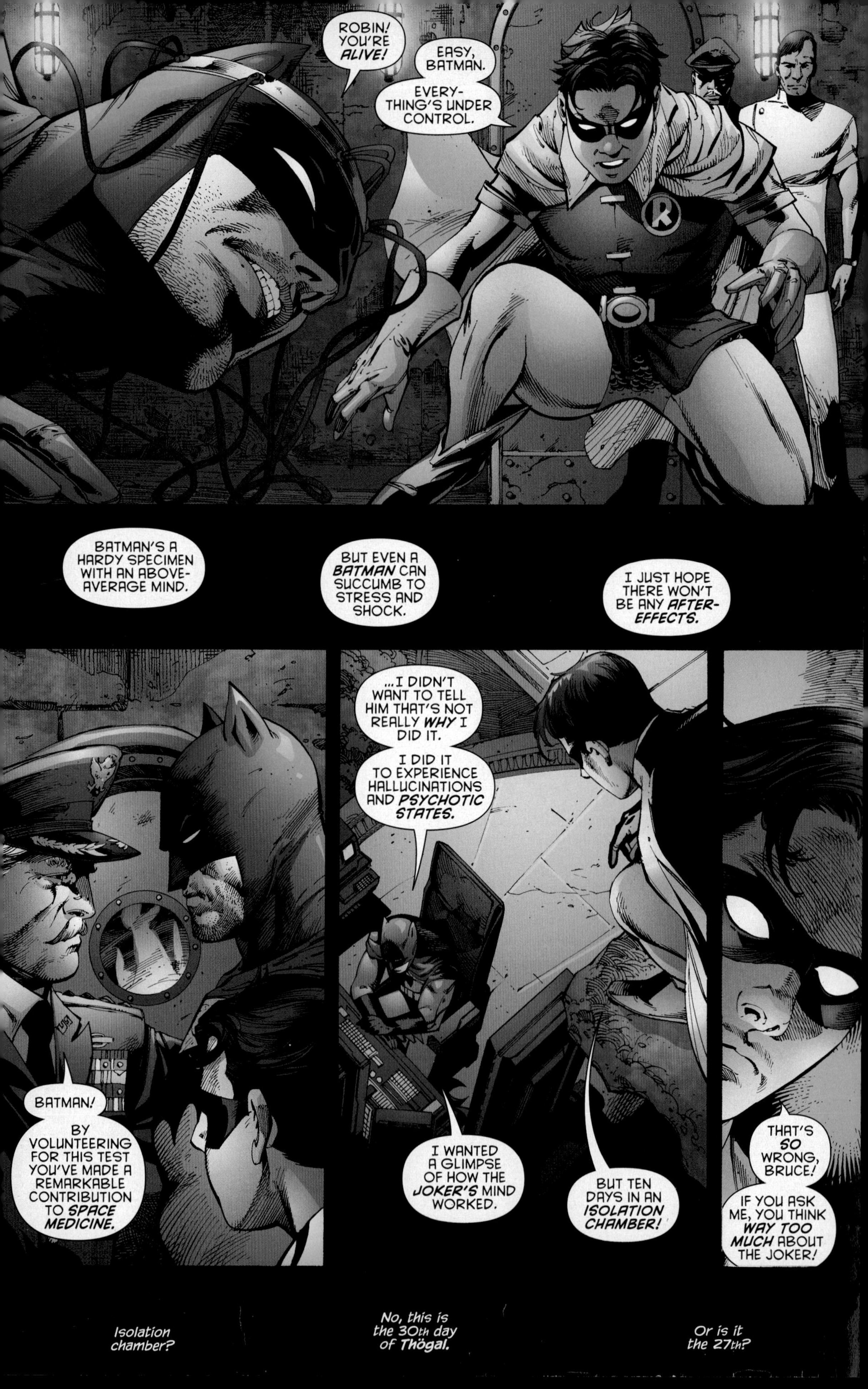
ROBIN! YOU'RE *ALIVE!*
EASY, BATMAN.
EVERY-THING'S UNDER CONTROL.
BATMAN'S A HARDY SPECIMEN WITH AN ABOVE-AVERAGE MIND.
BUT EVEN A *BATMAN* CAN SUCCUMB TO STRESS AND SHOCK.
I JUST HOPE THERE WON'T BE ANY *AFTER-EFFECTS.*
BATMAN!
BY VOLUNTEERING FOR THIS TEST YOU'VE MADE A REMARKABLE CONTRIBUTION TO *SPACE MEDICINE.*
...I DIDN'T WANT TO TELL HIM THAT'S NOT REALLY *WHY* I DID IT.
I DID IT TO EXPERIENCE HALLUCINATIONS AND *PSYCHOTIC STATES.*
I WANTED A GLIMPSE OF HOW THE *JOKER'S* MIND WORKED.
BUT TEN DAYS IN AN *ISOLATION CHAMBER!*
THAT'S *SO* WRONG, BRUCE!
IF YOU ASK ME, YOU THINK *WAY TOO MUCH* ABOUT THE JOKER!
Isolation chamber?
No, this is the 30th day of Thögal.
Or is it the 27th?

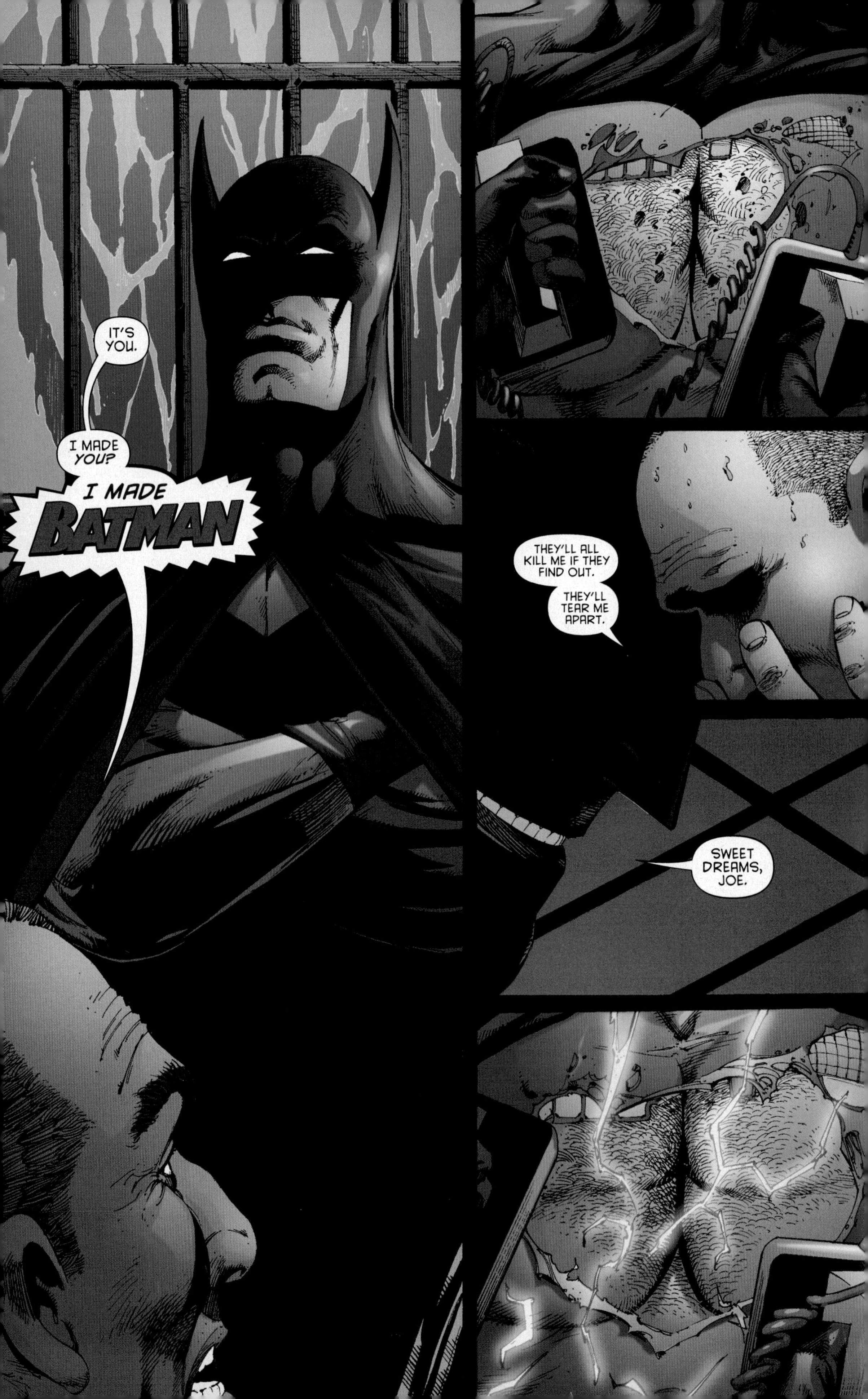
IT'S YOU.
I MADE YOU?
I MADE BATMAN
THEY'LL ALL KILL ME IF THEY FIND OUT.
THEY'LL TEAR ME APART.
SWEET DREAMS, JOE.

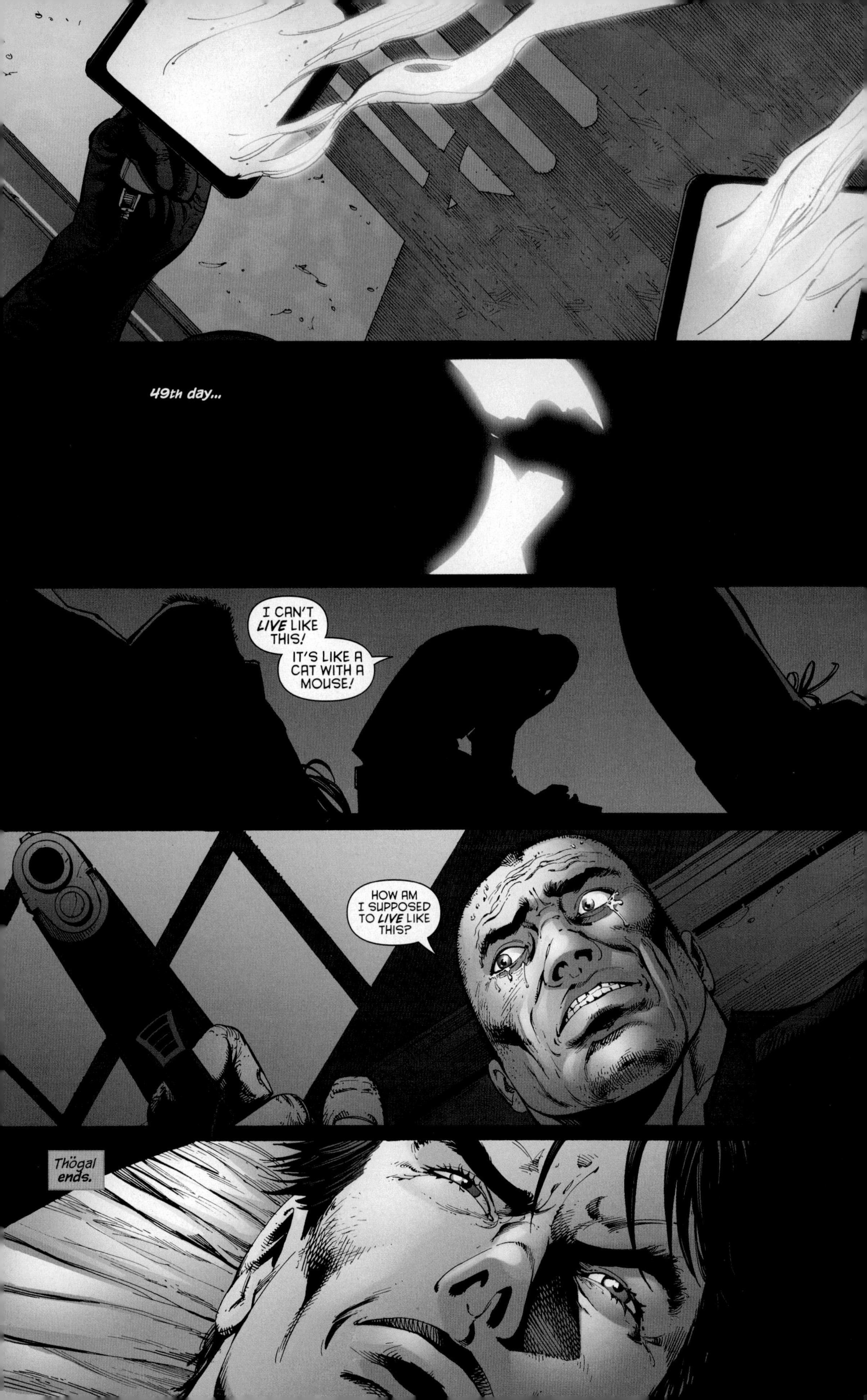
49th day...
I CAN'T LIVE LIKE THIS!
IT'S LIKE A CAT WITH A MOUSE!
HOW AM I SUPPOSED TO LIVE LIKE THIS?
Thögal ends.

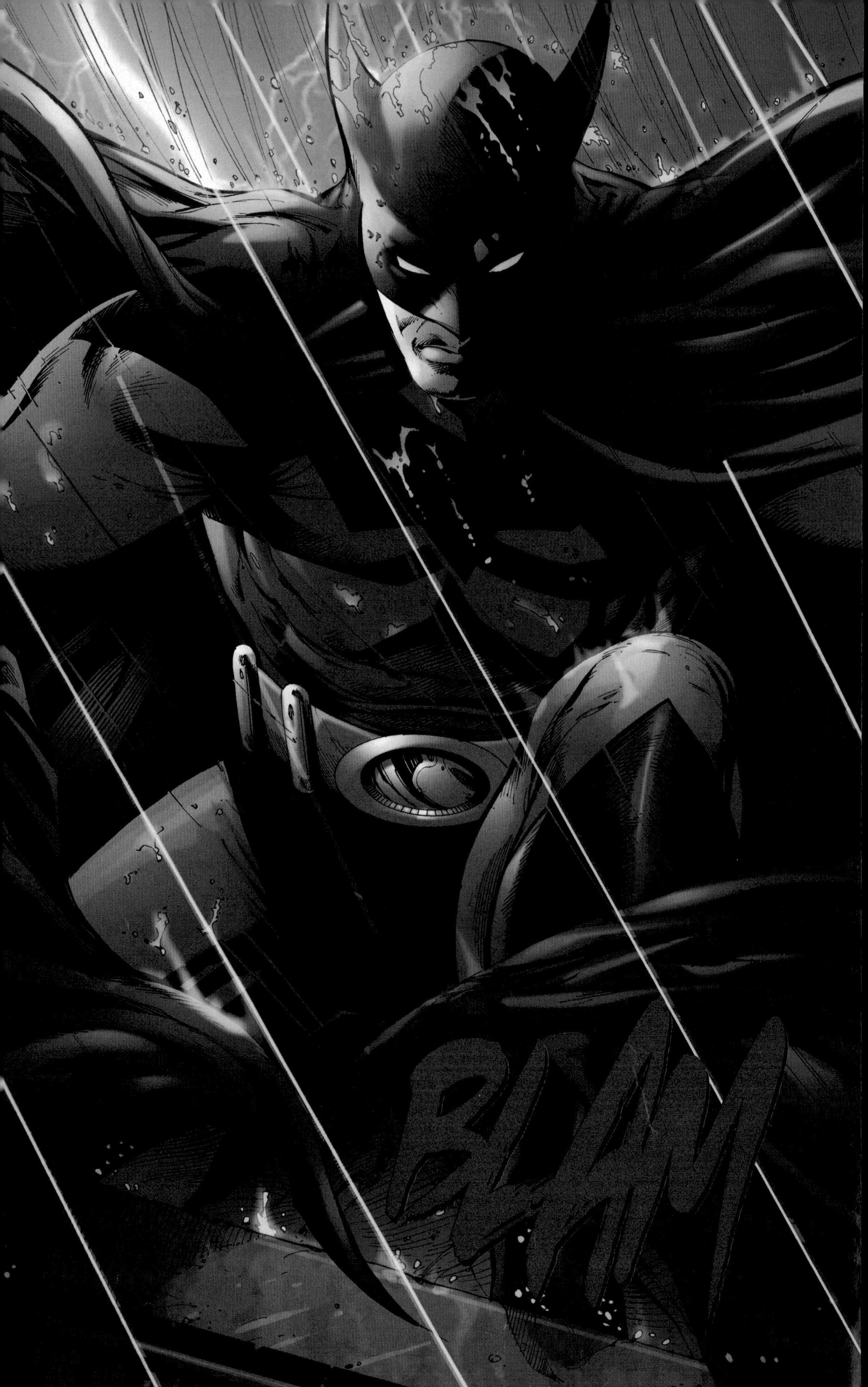
BLAM

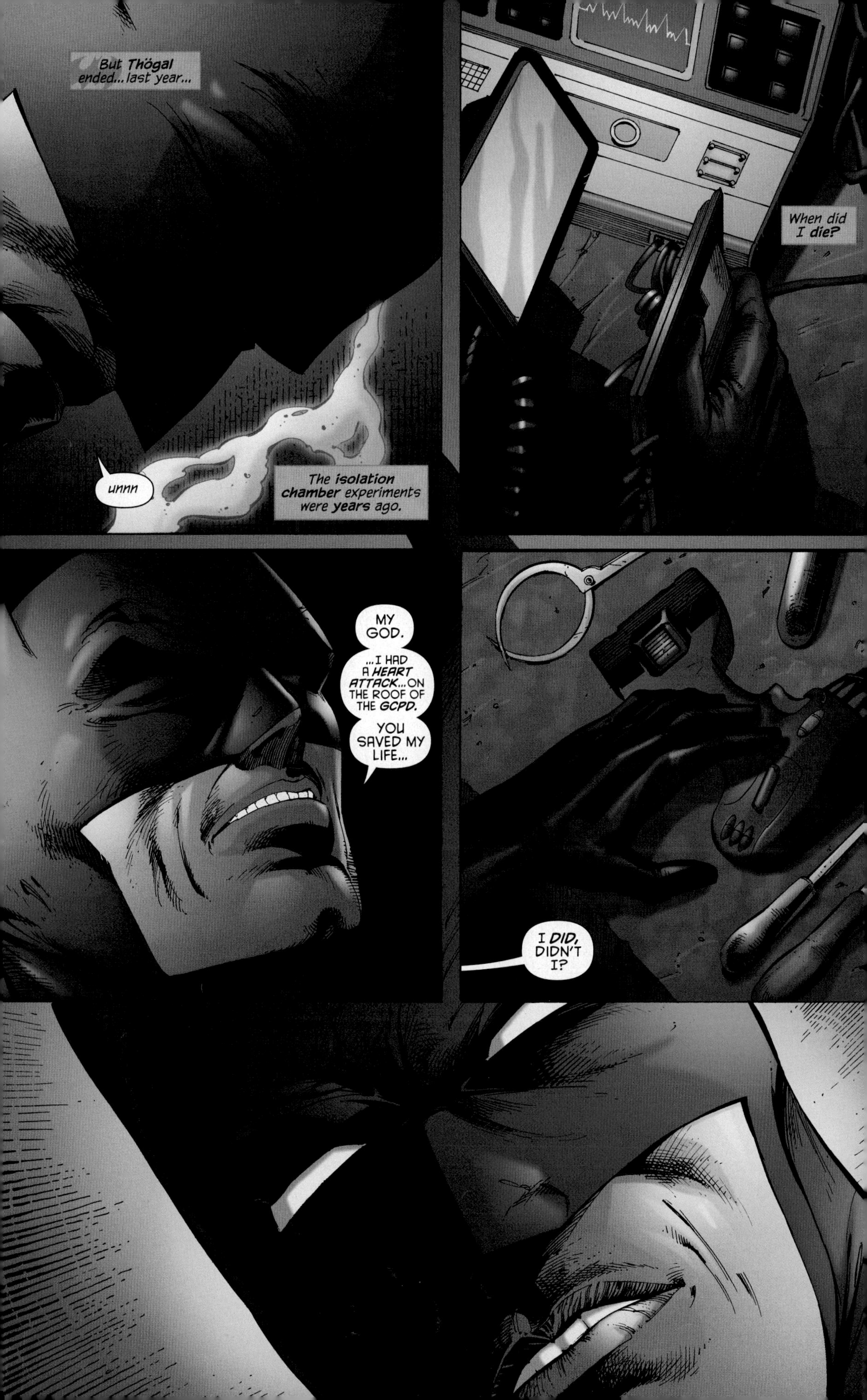

But Thögal ended...last year...
unnn
The isolation chamber experiments were years ago.
When did I die?
MY GOD.
...I HAD A HEART ATTACK...ON THE ROOF OF THE GCPD.
YOU SAVED MY LIFE...
I DID, DIDN'T I?

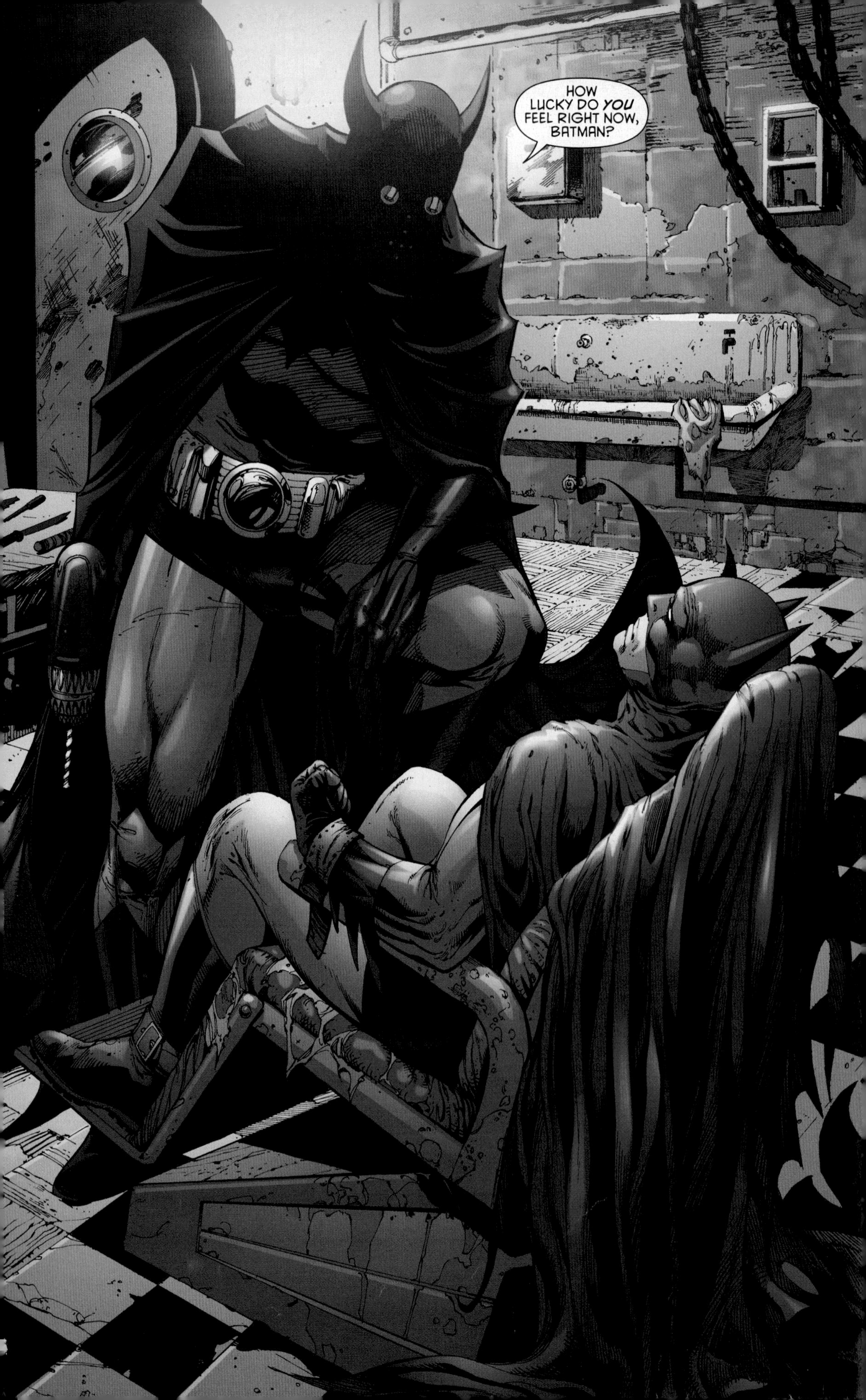
HOW LUCKY DO YOU FEEL RIGHT NOW, BATMAN?

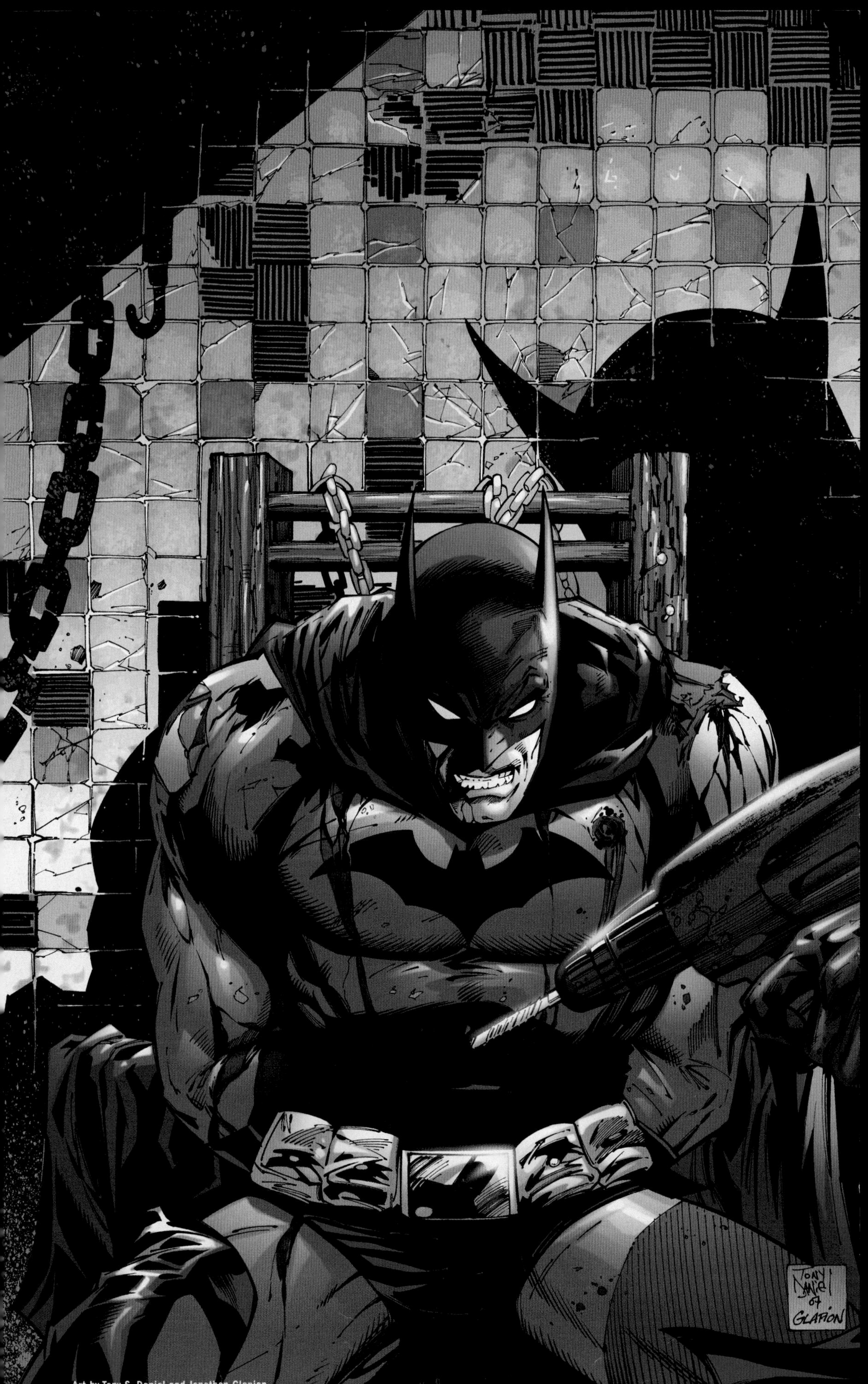
TONY DANIEL 07
GLAPION

Art by Tony S. Daniel and Jonathan Glapion

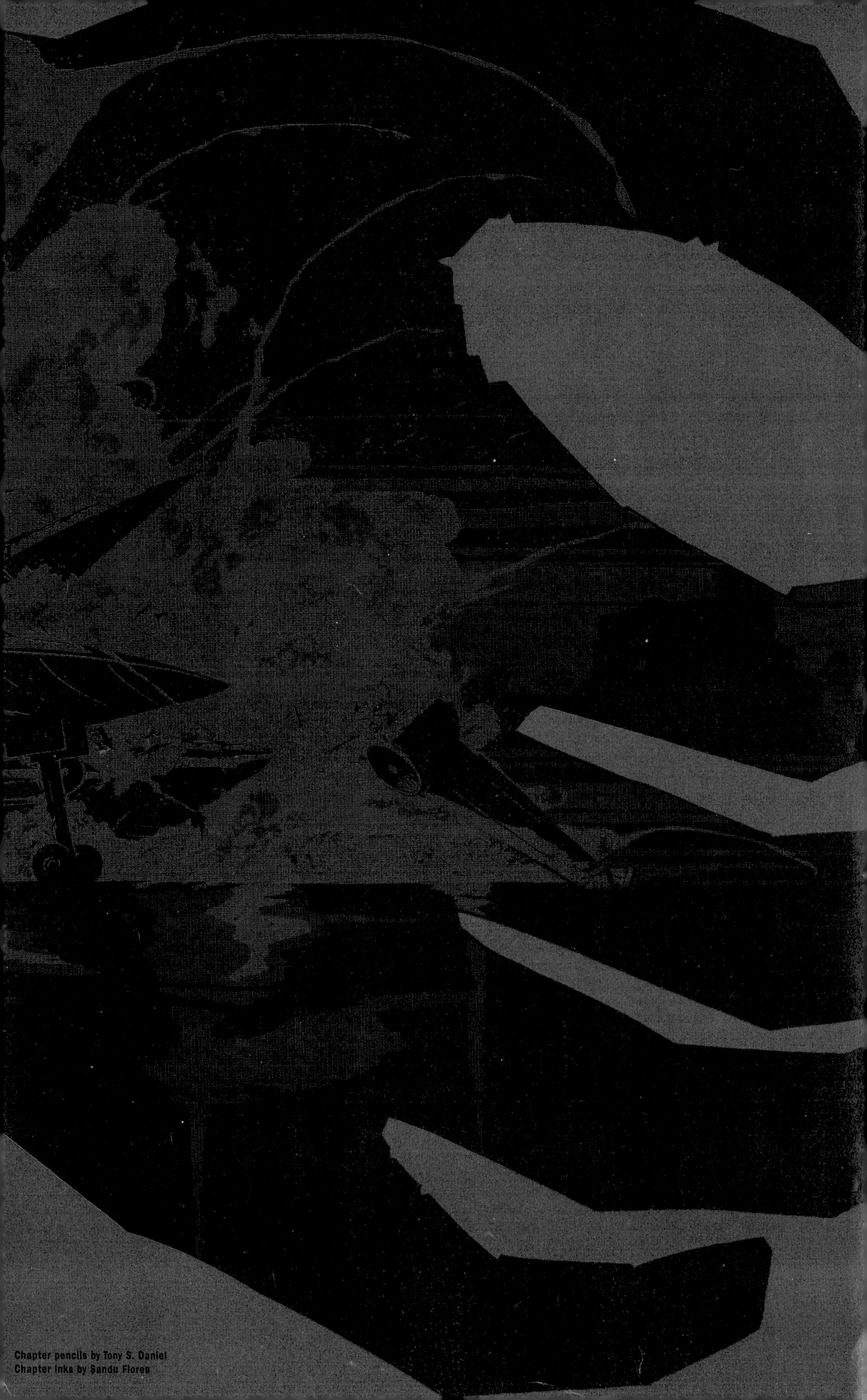

Chapter pencils by Tony S. Daniel
Chapter inks by Sandu Florea

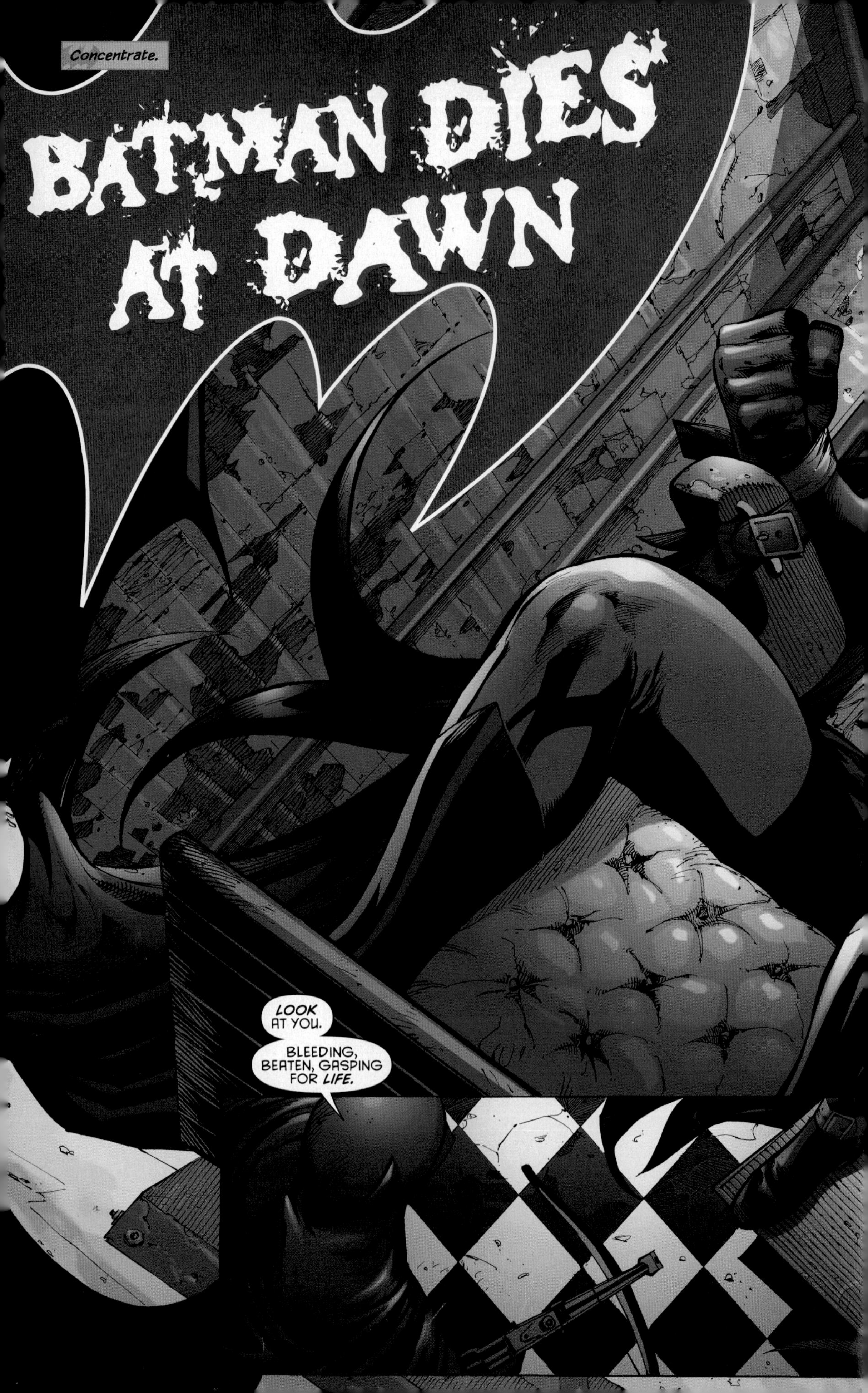
Concentrate.
BATMAN DIES AT DAWN
LOOK AT YOU.
BLEEDING, BEATEN, GASPING FOR LIFE.

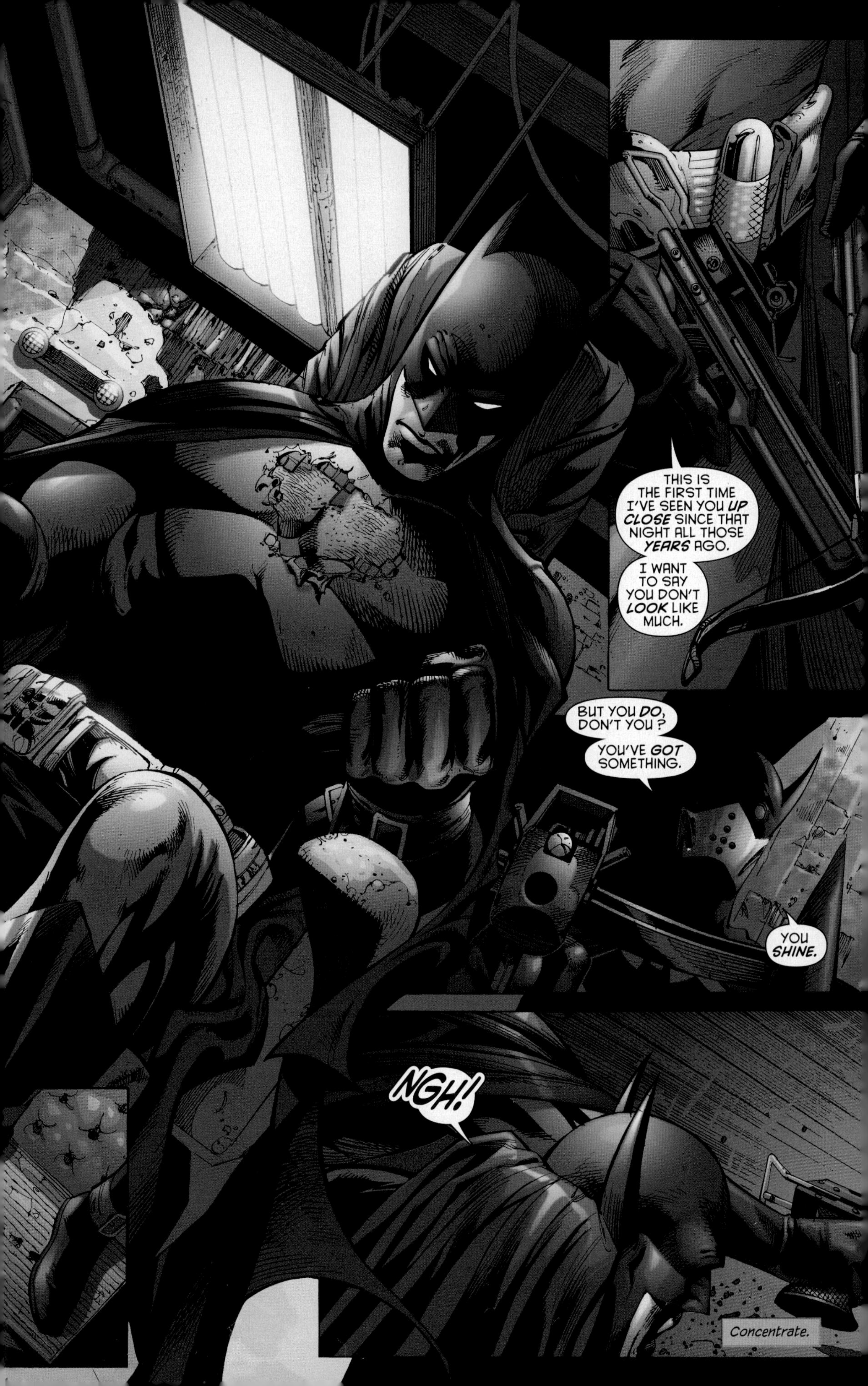
THIS IS THE FIRST TIME I'VE SEEN YOU *UP CLOSE* SINCE THAT NIGHT ALL THOSE *YEARS* AGO.
I WANT TO SAY YOU DON'T *LOOK* LIKE MUCH.
BUT YOU *DO*, DON'T YOU?
YOU'VE *GOT* SOMETHING.
YOU *SHINE.*
NGH!
Concentrate.

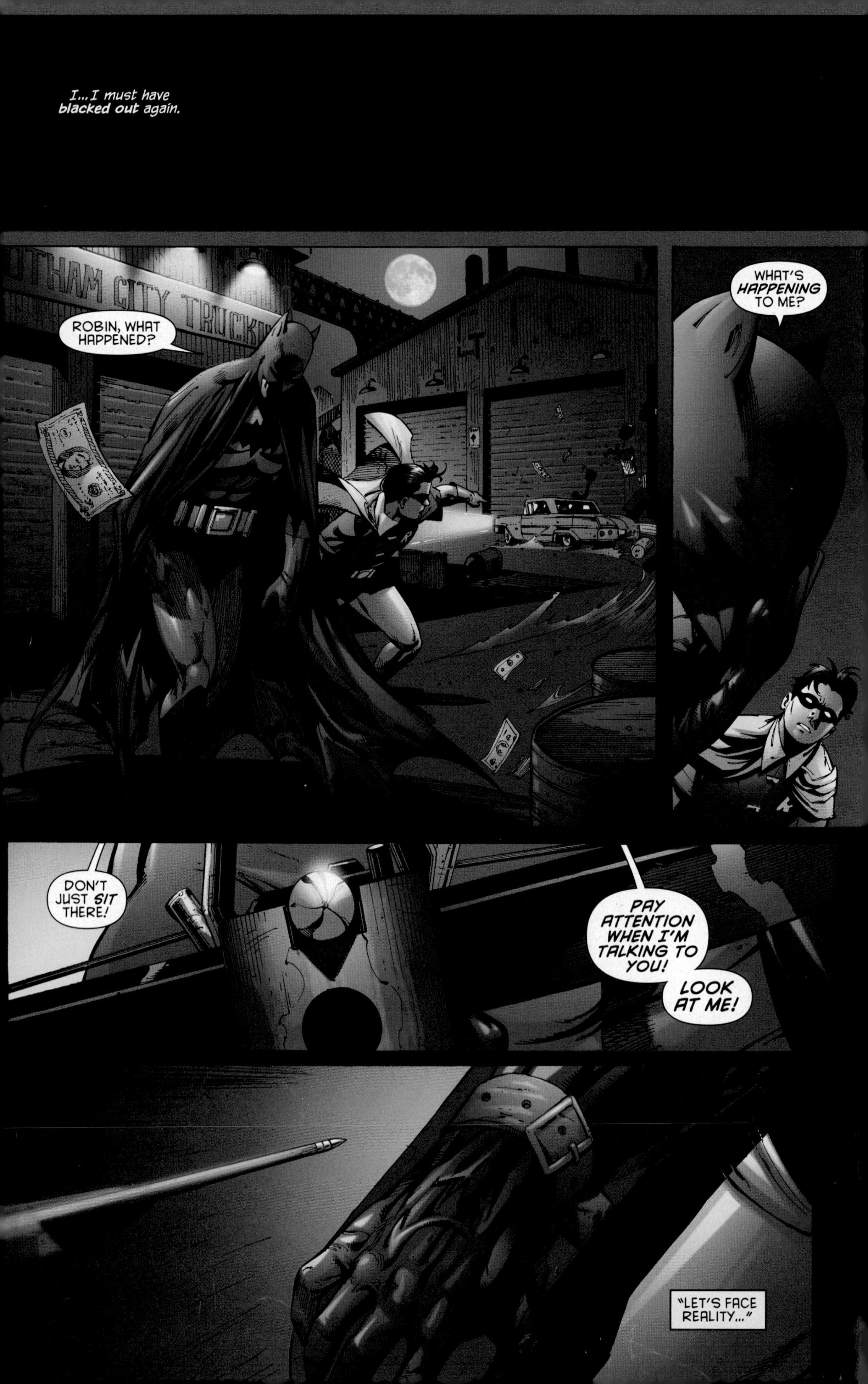

I... I must have blacked out again.
ROBIN, WHAT HAPPENED?
WHAT'S *HAPPENING* TO ME?
DON'T JUST *SIT* THERE!
PAY ATTENTION WHEN I'M TALKING TO YOU!
LOOK AT ME!
"LET'S FACE REALITY..."

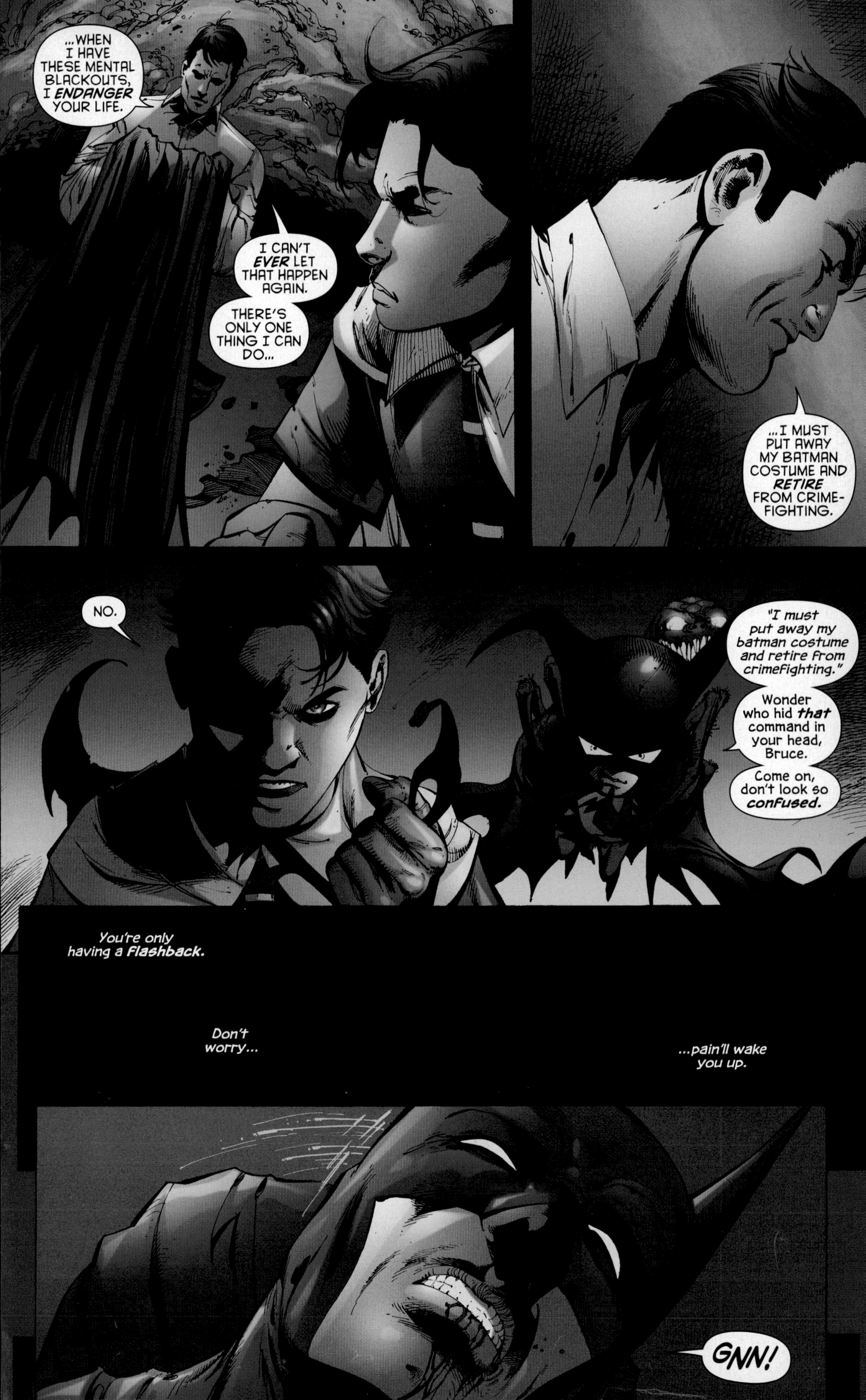
...WHEN I HAVE THESE MENTAL BLACKOUTS, I ENDANGER YOUR LIFE.
I CAN'T EVER LET THAT HAPPEN AGAIN.
THERE'S ONLY ONE THING I CAN DO...
...I MUST PUT AWAY MY BATMAN COSTUME AND RETIRE FROM CRIME-FIGHTING.
NO.
"I must put away my batman costume and retire from crimefighting."
Wonder who hid that command in your head, Bruce.
Come on, don't look so confused.
You're only having a flashback.
Don't worry...
...pain'll wake you up.
GNN!

I SCORED A DIRECT HIT TO YOUR CHEST WITH AN EXPLOSIVE SHELL.
EVEN YOUR ARMOR COULDN'T PROTECT YOU FROM THAT KIND OF IMPACT.
YOUR HEART ACTUALLY STOPPED.
THAT'S FOR WHAT YOU DID TO MY ARM WITH YOUR BATARANG.
Four minutes.
Years ago, I took part in a ten-day isolation experiment.
I hallucinated the death of Robin.
I felt so guilty I almost gave up being Batman.
Can't be far from the roof of police HQ.
We're all rooting for ya, Bruce.
Heh heh heh
Every word he says, every move he makes...
It happened here.

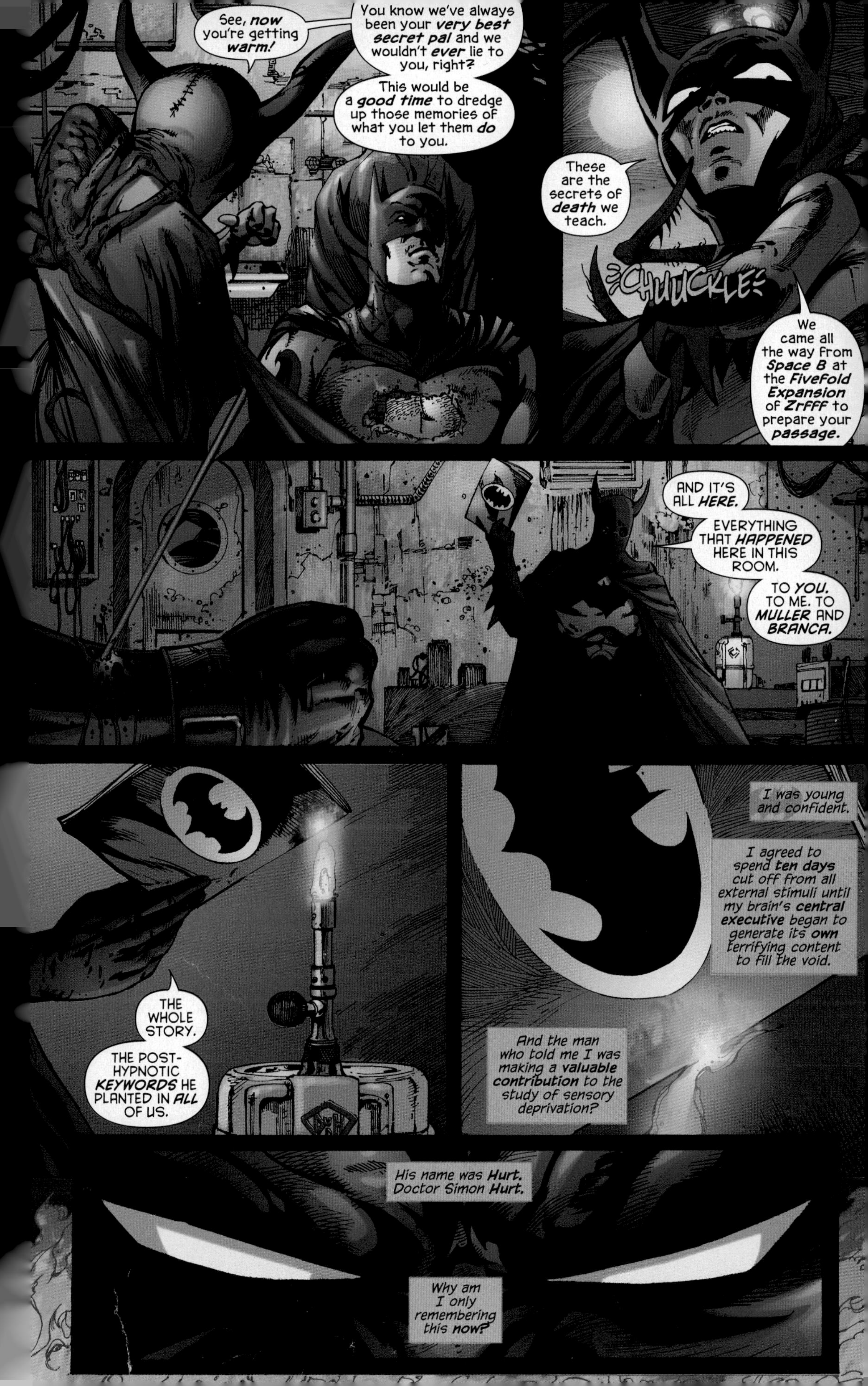
See, **now** you're getting **warm!**
You know we've always been your **very best secret pal** and we wouldn't **ever** lie to you, right?
This would be a **good time** to dredge up those memories of what you let them **do** to you.
These are the secrets of **death** we teach.
CHUUCKLE
We came all the way from **Space 8** at the **Fivefold Expansion** of **Zrfff** to prepare your **passage.**
AND IT'S ALL **HERE.**
EVERYTHING THAT **HAPPENED** HERE IN THIS ROOM.
TO **YOU.** TO ME. TO **MULLER** AND **BRANCA.**
THE WHOLE STORY.
THE POST-HYPNOTIC **KEYWORDS** HE PLANTED IN **ALL** OF US.
I was young and confident.
I agreed to spend **ten days** cut off from all external stimuli until my brain's **central executive** began to generate its **own** terrifying content to fill the void.
And the man who told me I was making a **valuable contribution** to the study of sensory deprivation?
His name was **Hurt.** Doctor Simon **Hurt.**
Why am I only remembering this **now?**

YOU DON'T *UNDERSTAND?* THIS AIN'T GOT *NOTHIN'* TO DO WITH POLICE CORRUPTION, NOR ANYTHING *ELSE* BATMAN TELLS YOU!

THIS IS ABOUT *LOYALTY!*

SIR.

THESE MEN AND ME, WE WERE *VOLUNTEERS* TOGETHER.

THEY WERE MY *BROTHERS* AND I MADE A PROMISE I'D TAKE CARE OF THEM, ESPECIALLY AFTER... AFTER WHAT *HAPPENED.*

YOU DON'T KNOW WHAT THEY *SUFFERED.*

SO *TELL* ME!

THIS IS OVER, FARELLI!

GCPD AND THE MILITARY WERE TRAINING MEN TO TAKE BATMAN'S *PLACE,* IN CASE ANYTHING EVER *HAPPENED* TO HIM... AND IT ALL WENT *WRONG.*

RIGHT HERE IN THE *BASEMENT* AT POLICE HEADQUARTERS.

PLACE HAS BEEN *SEALED OFF* FOR YEARS.

...THIS ALL HAPPENED BACK WHEN I GOT DEMOTED TO PATROLMAN...

BUT SIR, YOUR *LEG*—

I CAN LIMP *JUST FINE!*

GET ME *DOWN* TO THAT BASEMENT *NOW!*

MY GOD.

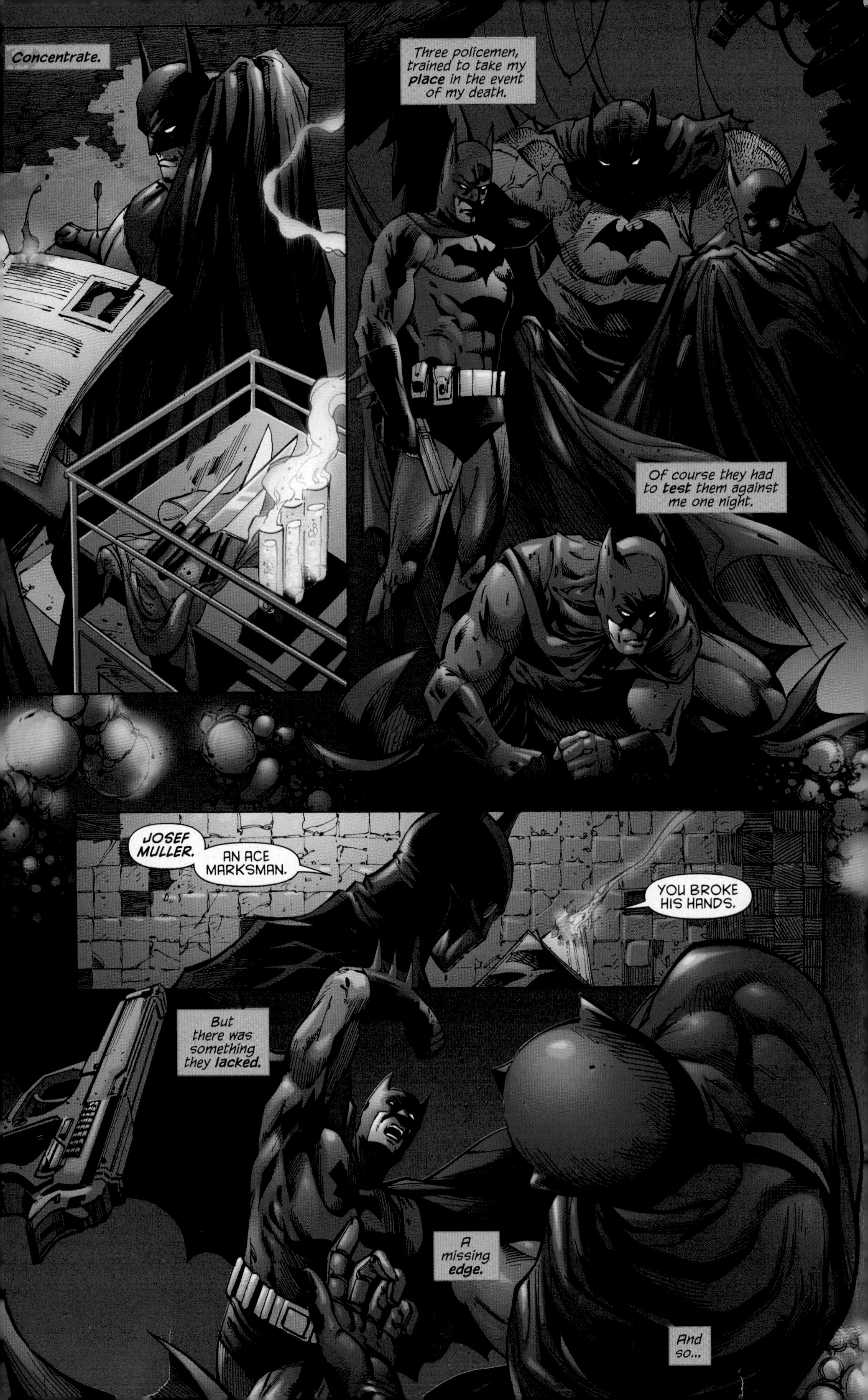

Concentrate.
Three policemen, trained to take my place in the event of my death.
Of course they had to test them against me one night.
JOSEF MULLER.
AN ACE MARKSMAN.
YOU BROKE HIS HANDS.
But there was something they lacked.
A missing edge.
And so...

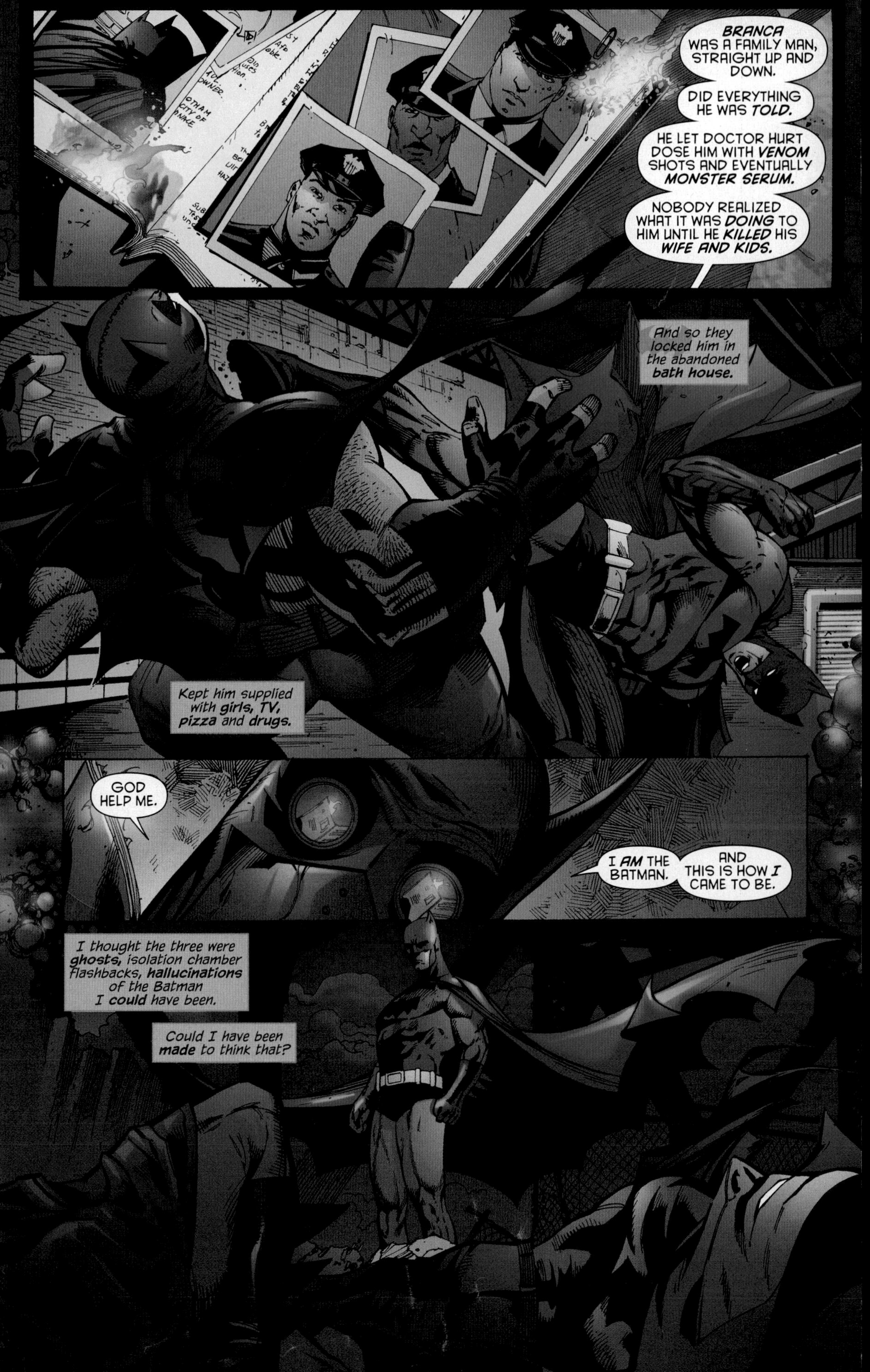

BRANCA WAS A FAMILY MAN, STRAIGHT UP AND DOWN.
DID EVERYTHING HE WAS TOLD.
HE LET DOCTOR HURT DOSE HIM WITH VENOM SHOTS AND EVENTUALLY MONSTER SERUM.
NOBODY REALIZED WHAT IT WAS DOING TO HIM UNTIL HE KILLED HIS WIFE AND KIDS.
And so they locked him in the abandoned bath house.
Kept him supplied with girls, TV, pizza and drugs.
GOD HELP ME.
I AM THE BATMAN.
AND THIS IS HOW I CAME TO BE.
I thought the three were ghosts, isolation chamber flashbacks, hallucinations of the Batman I could have been.
Could I have been made to think that?

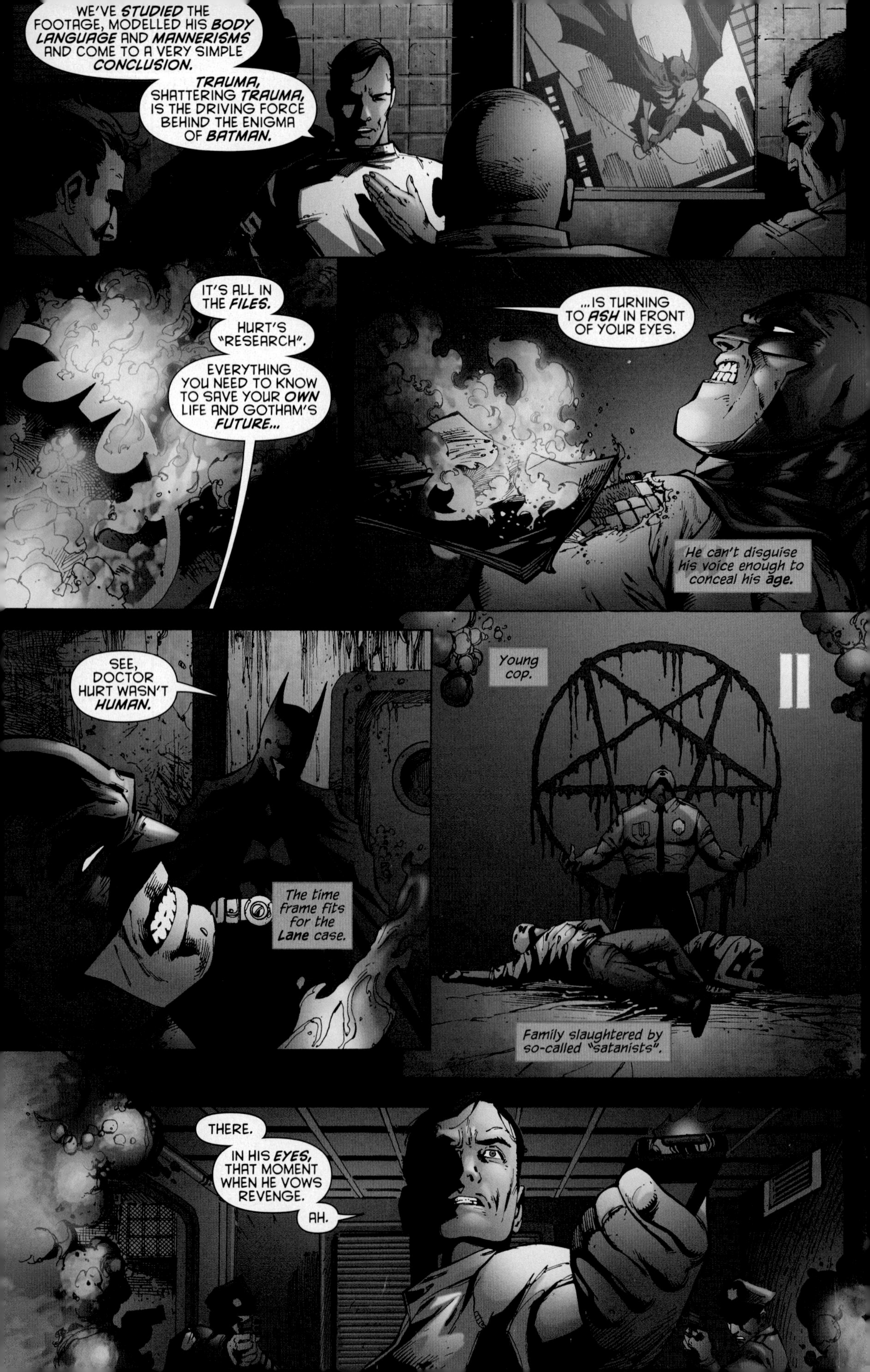

WE'VE STUDIED THE FOOTAGE, MODELLED HIS BODY LANGUAGE AND MANNERISMS AND COME TO A VERY SIMPLE CONCLUSION.
TRAUMA, SHATTERING TRAUMA, IS THE DRIVING FORCE BEHIND THE ENIGMA OF BATMAN.
IT'S ALL IN THE FILES.
HURT'S "RESEARCH".
EVERYTHING YOU NEED TO KNOW TO SAVE YOUR OWN LIFE AND GOTHAM'S FUTURE...
...IS TURNING TO ASH IN FRONT OF YOUR EYES.
He can't disguise his voice enough to conceal his age.
SEE, DOCTOR HURT WASN'T HUMAN.
The time frame fits for the Lane case.
Young cop.
Family slaughtered by so-called "satanists".
THERE.
IN HIS EYES, THAT MOMENT WHEN HE VOWS REVENGE.
AH.

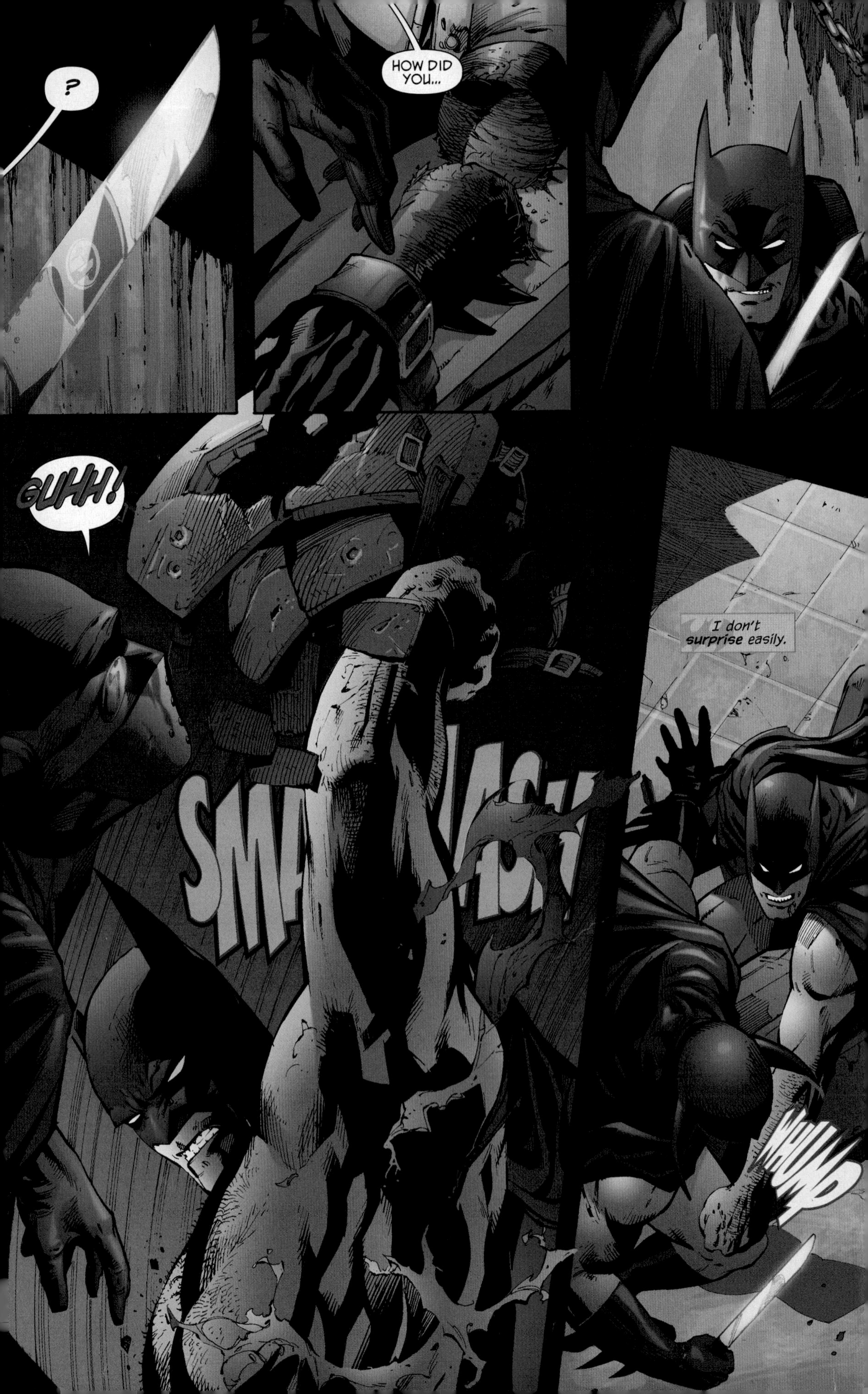

?
HOW DID YOU...
GUHH!
SMASH
I don't surprise easily.
WHUMP

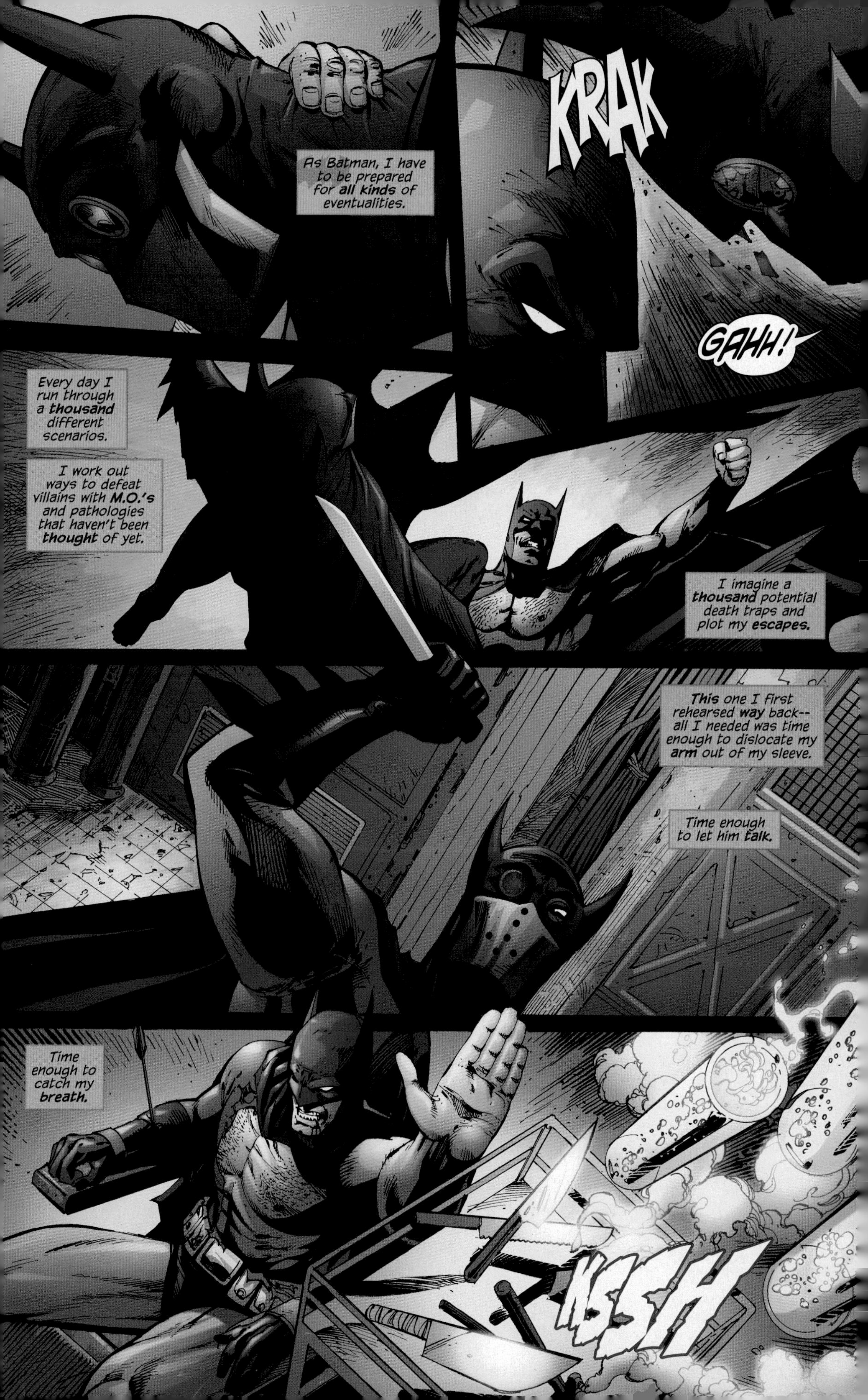

As Batman, I have to be prepared for all kinds of eventualities.
KRAK
GAHH!
Every day I run through a thousand different scenarios.
I work out ways to defeat villains with M.O.'s and pathologies that haven't been thought of yet.
I imagine a thousand potential death traps and plot my escapes.
This one I first rehearsed way back--all I needed was time enough to dislocate my arm out of my sleeve.
Time enough to let him talk.
Time enough to catch my breath.
KSSH

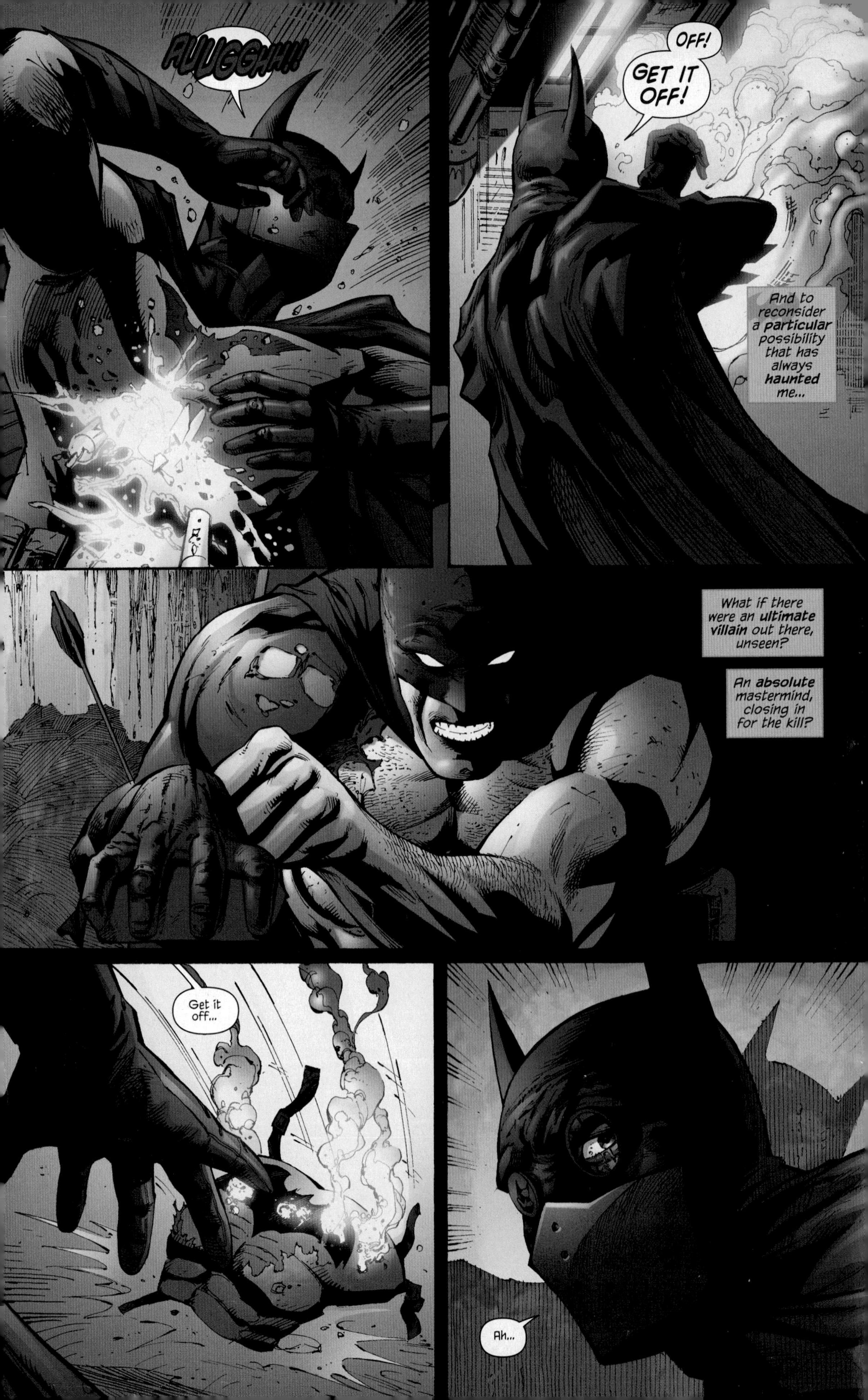
PUUGGHH!!!
OFF!
GET IT OFF!
And to reconsider a **particular** possibility that has always **haunted** me...
What if there were an **ultimate villain** out there, unseen?
An **absolute** mastermind, closing in for the kill?
Get it off...
Ah...

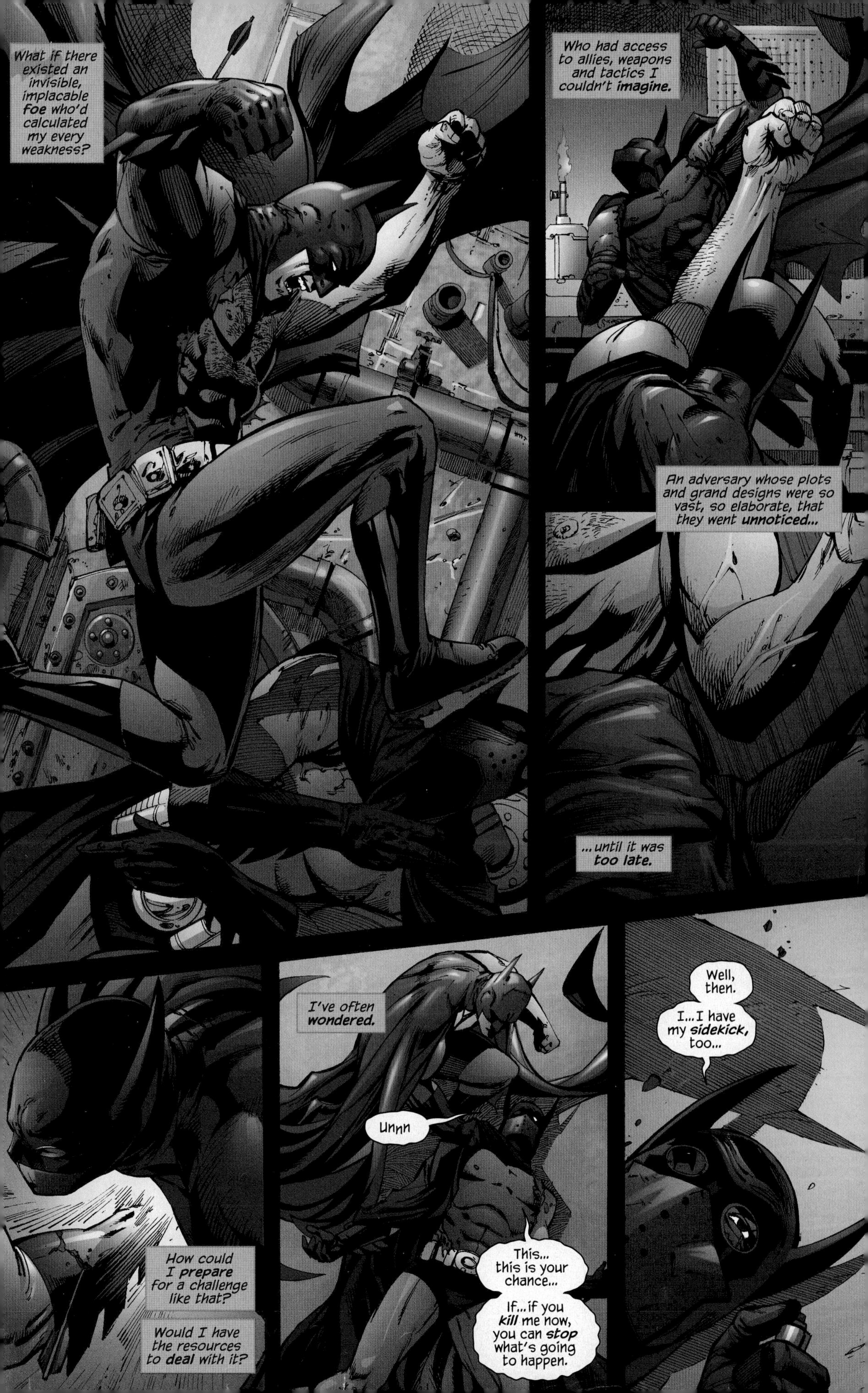
What if there existed an invisible, implacable foe who'd calculated my every weakness?
Who had access to allies, weapons and tactics I couldn't imagine.
An adversary whose plots and grand designs were so vast, so elaborate, that they went unnoticed...
...until it was too late.
How could I prepare for a challenge like that?
Would I have the resources to deal with it?
I've often wondered.
Unnn
This... this is your chance...
If... if you kill me now, you can stop what's going to happen.
Well, then.
I... I have my sidekick, too...

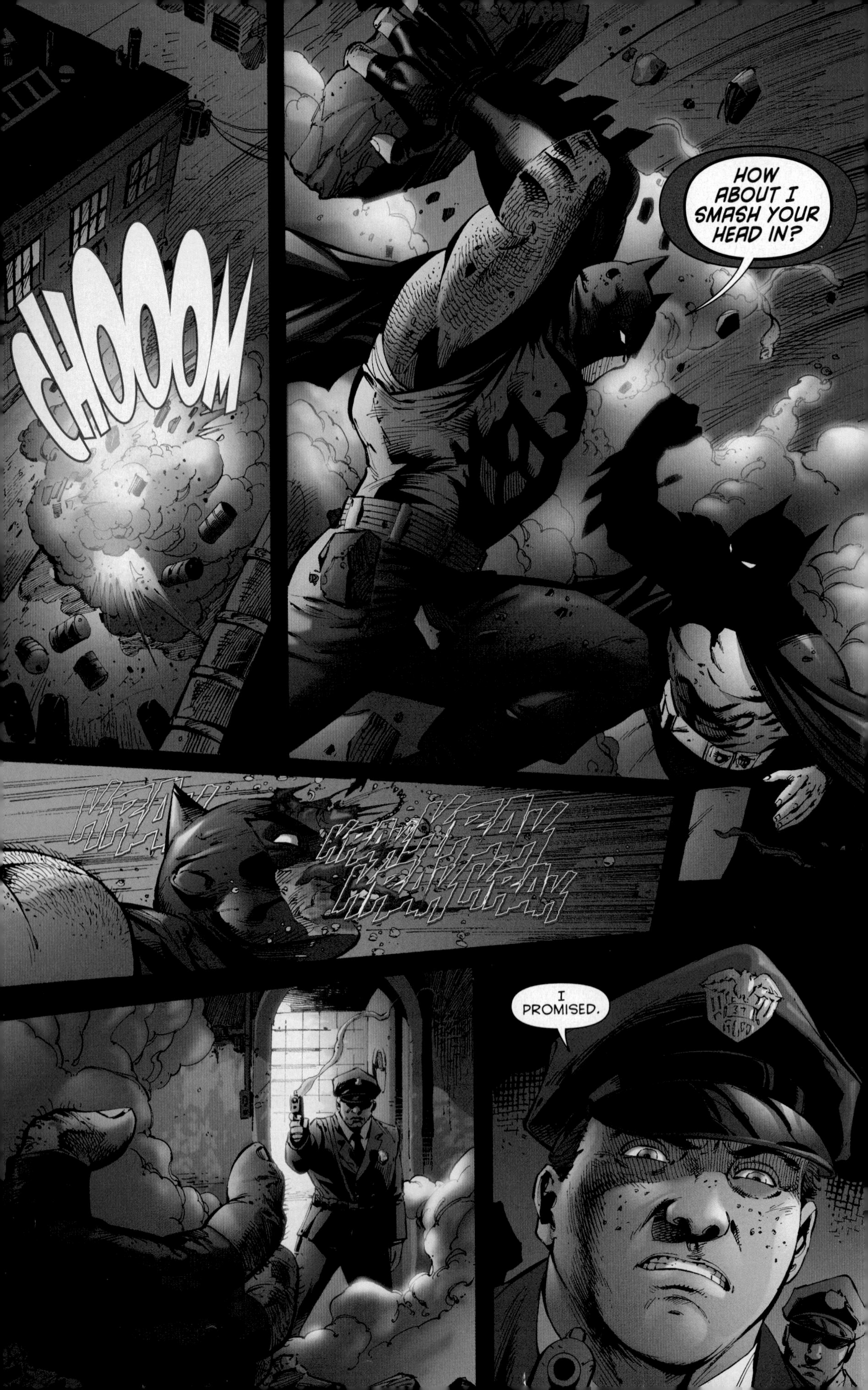
CHOOOM
HOW ABOUT I SMASH YOUR HEAD IN?
I PROMISED.

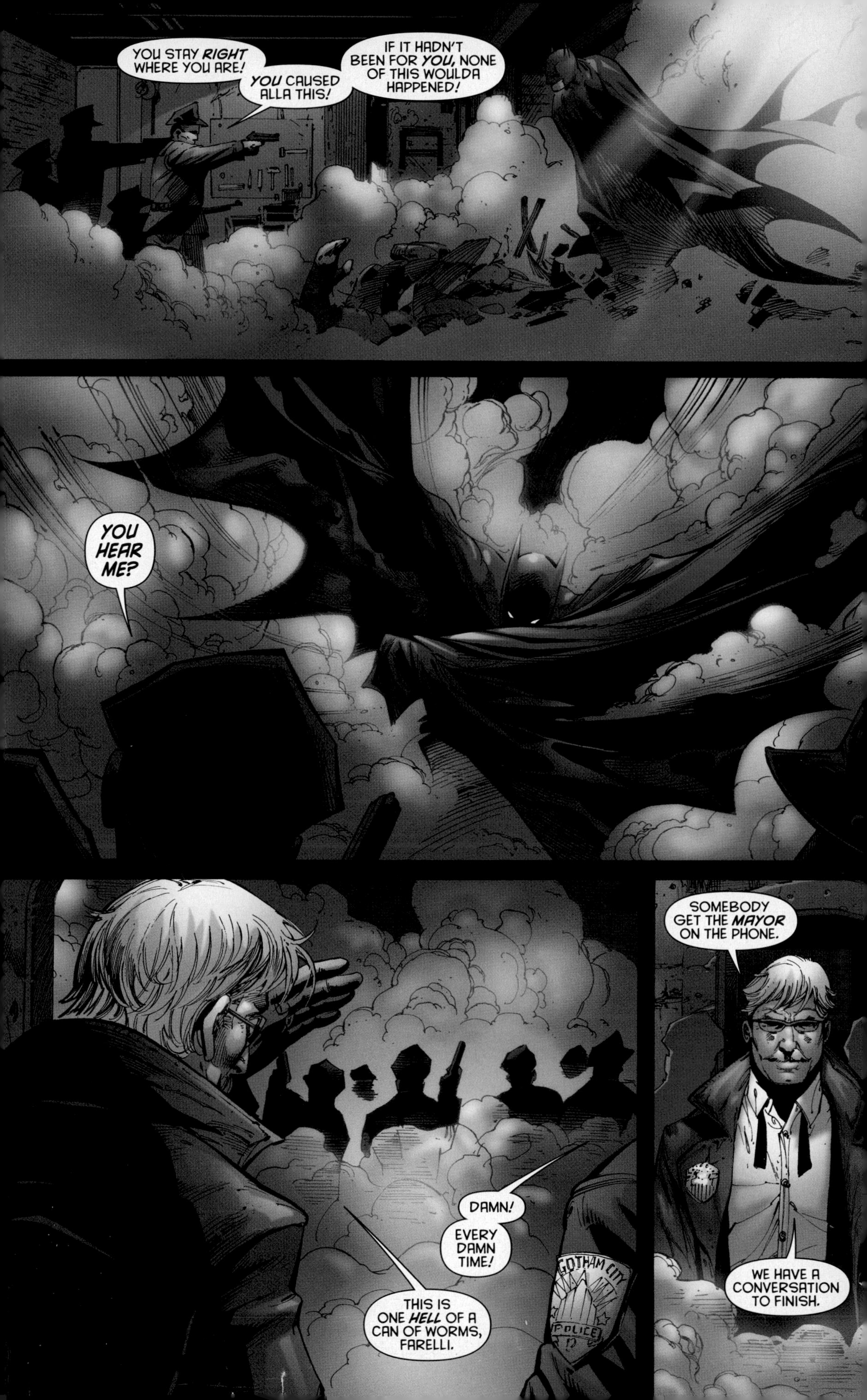

YOU STAY *RIGHT* WHERE YOU ARE!
YOU CAUSED ALLA THIS!
IF IT HADN'T BEEN FOR *YOU*, NONE OF THIS WOULDA HAPPENED!
YOU HEAR ME?
THIS IS ONE *HELL* OF A CAN OF WORMS, FARELLI.
DAMN!
EVERY DAMN TIME!
SOMEBODY GET THE *MAYOR* ON THE PHONE.
WE HAVE A CONVERSATION TO FINISH.

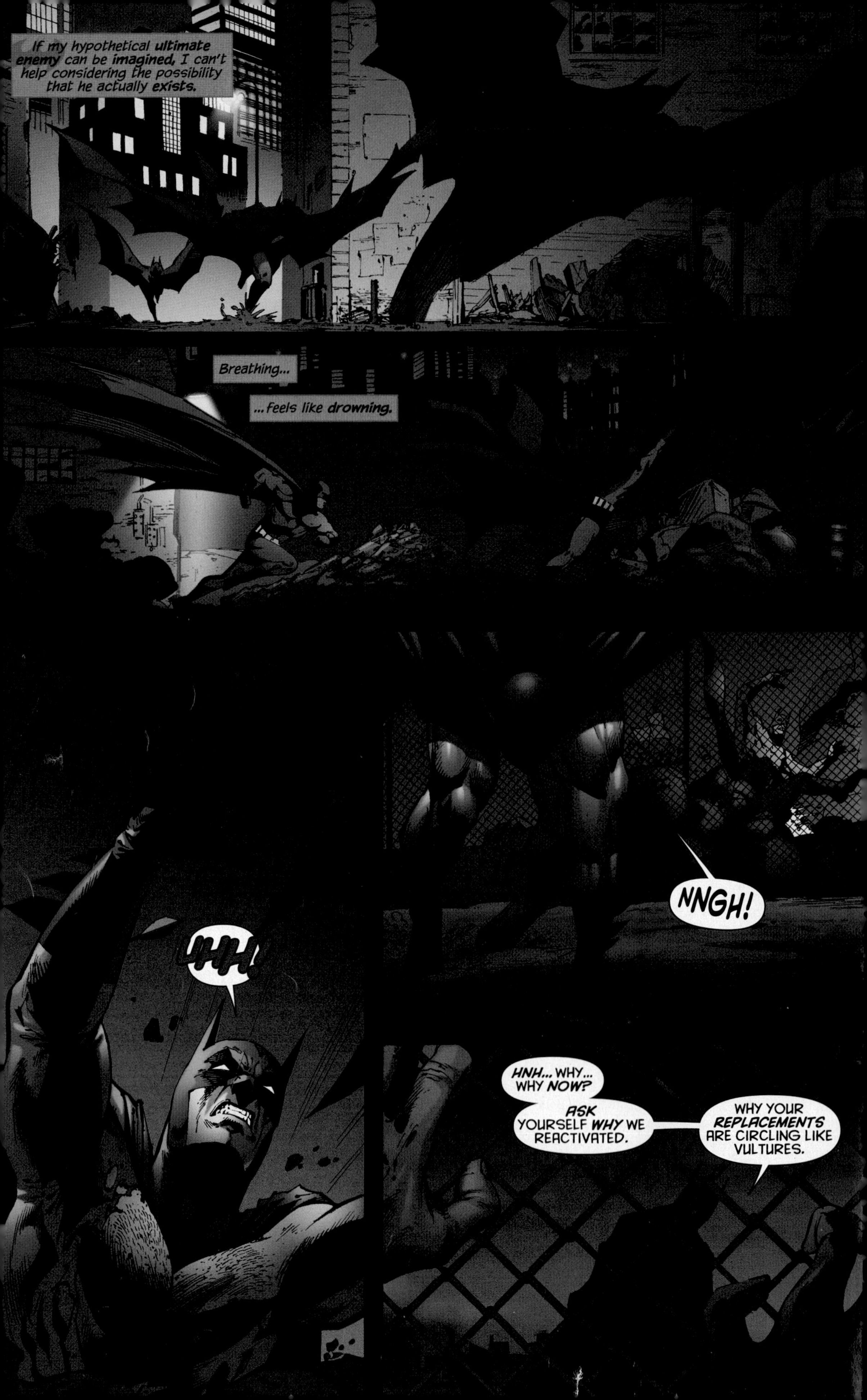
If my hypothetical ultimate enemy can be imagined, I can't help considering the possibility that he actually exists.
Breathing...
...feels like drowning.
NNGH!
HNH... WHY... WHY NOW?
ASK YOURSELF WHY WE REACTIVATED.
WHY YOUR REPLACEMENTS ARE CIRCLING LIKE VULTURES.

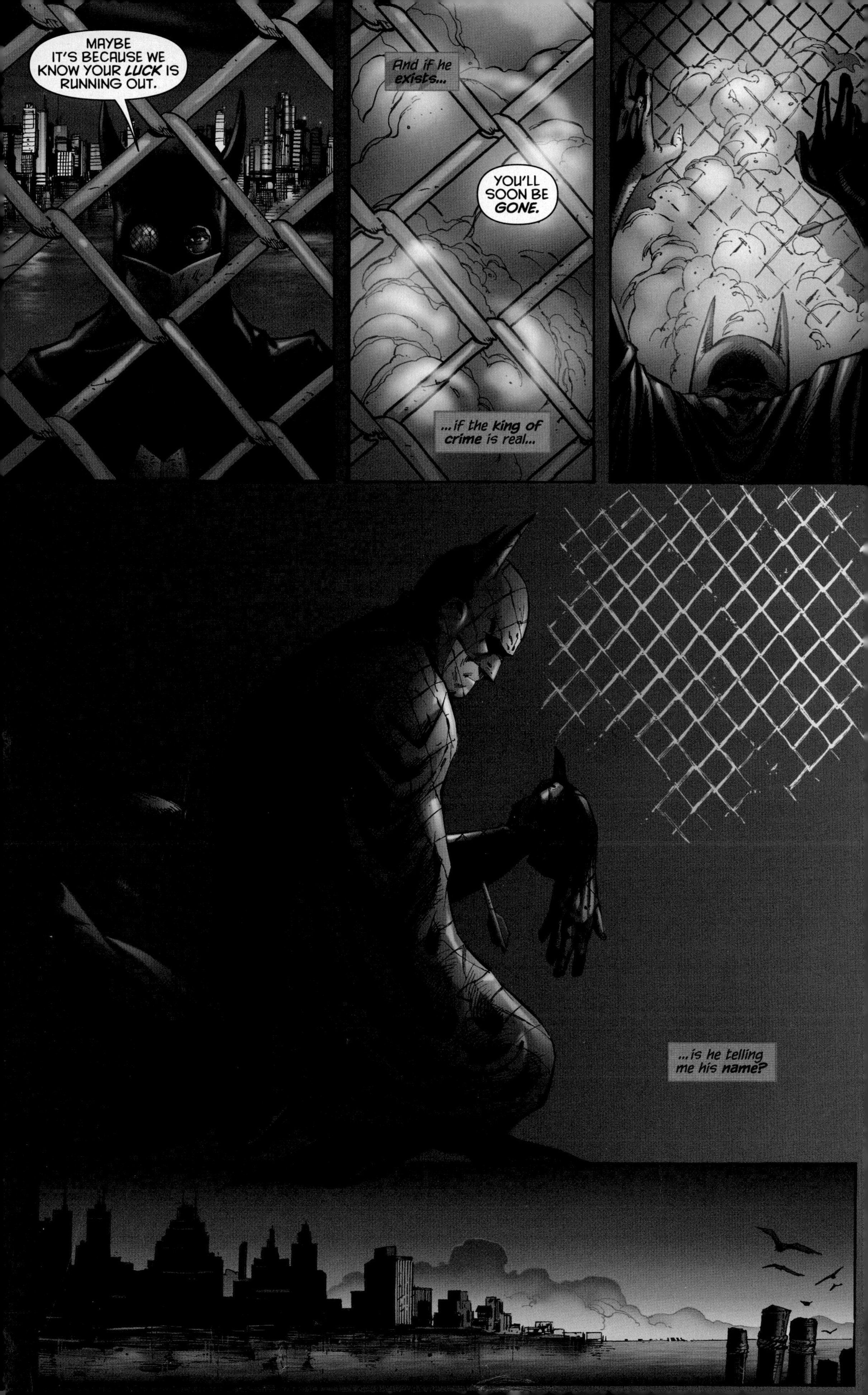
MAYBE IT'S BECAUSE WE KNOW YOUR LUCK IS RUNNING OUT.
And if he exists...
YOU'LL SOON BE GONE.
...if the king of crime is real...
...is he telling me his name?

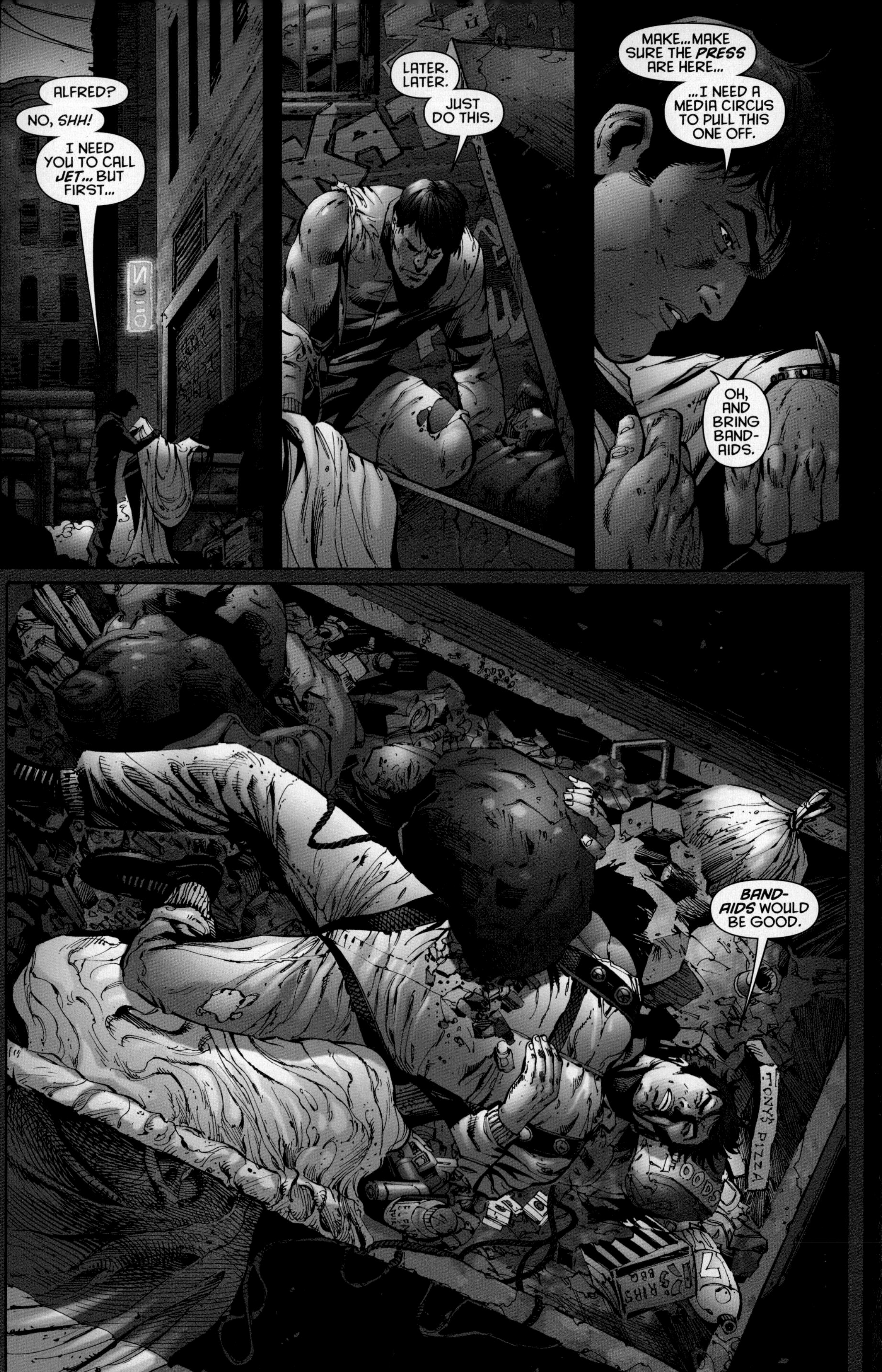
ALFRED?
NO, SHH!
I NEED YOU TO CALL JET... BUT FIRST...
LATER. LATER.
JUST DO THIS.
MAKE... MAKE SURE THE PRESS ARE HERE...
...I NEED A MEDIA CIRCUS TO PULL THIS ONE OFF.
OH, AND BRING BAND-AIDS.
BAND-AIDS WOULD BE GOOD.
TONY'S PIZZA
FOODS
D'S RIBS BBQ

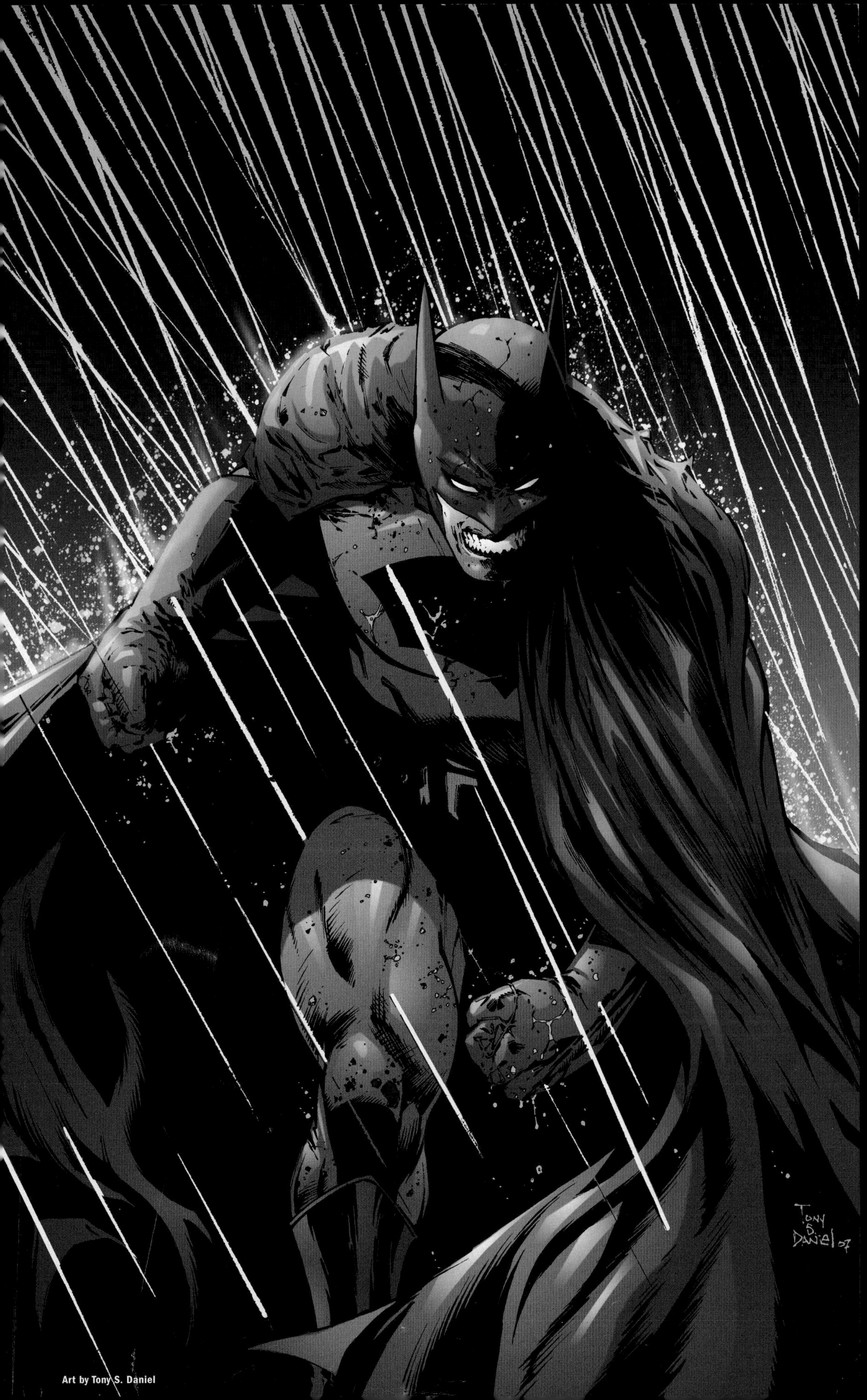
TONY S. DANIEL 07

Art by Tony S. Daniel

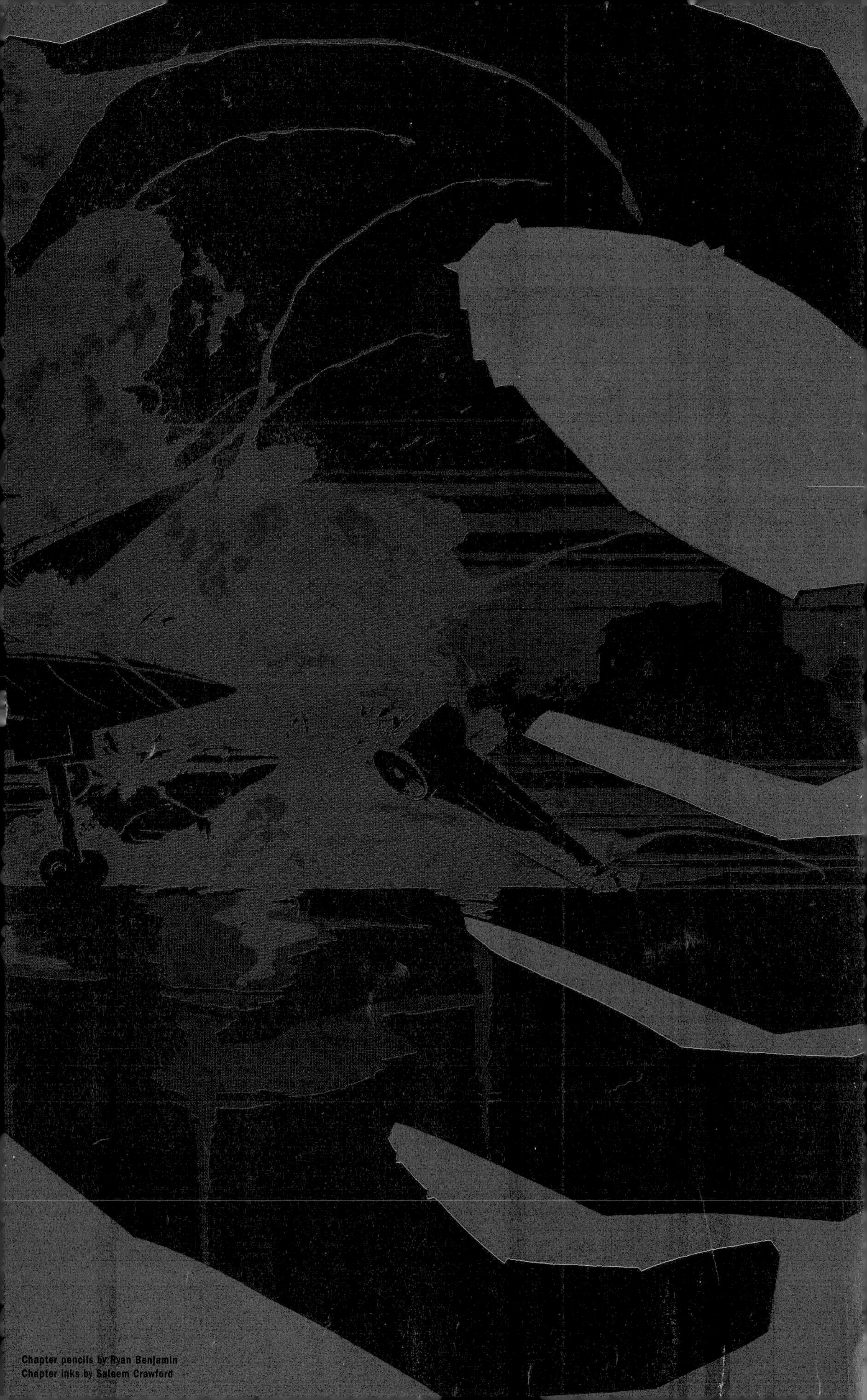

Chapter pencils by Ryan Benjamin
Chapter inks by Saleem Crawford

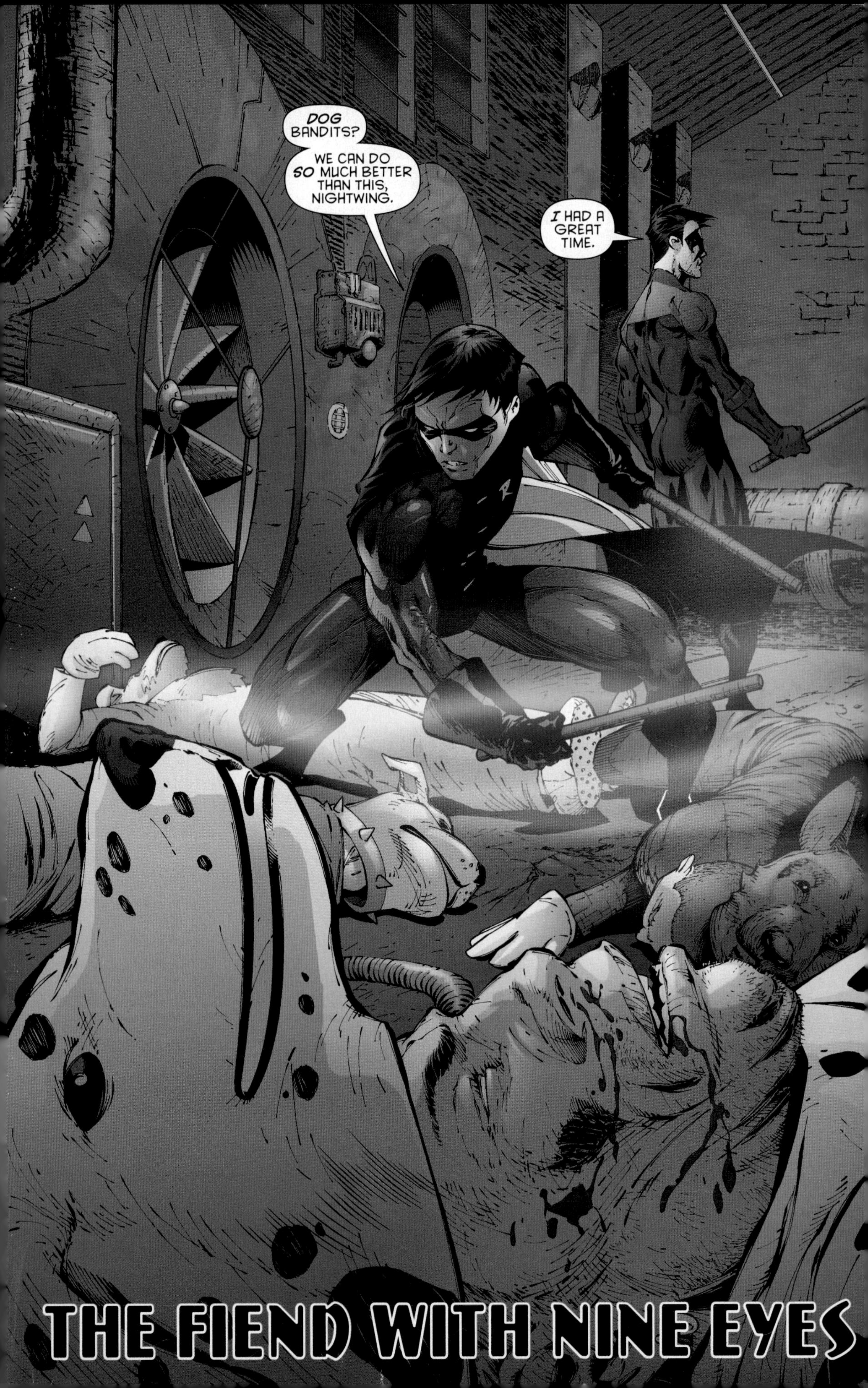
DOG BANDITS?
WE CAN DO SO MUCH BETTER THAN THIS, NIGHTWING.
I HAD A GREAT TIME.
THE FIEND WITH NINE EYES

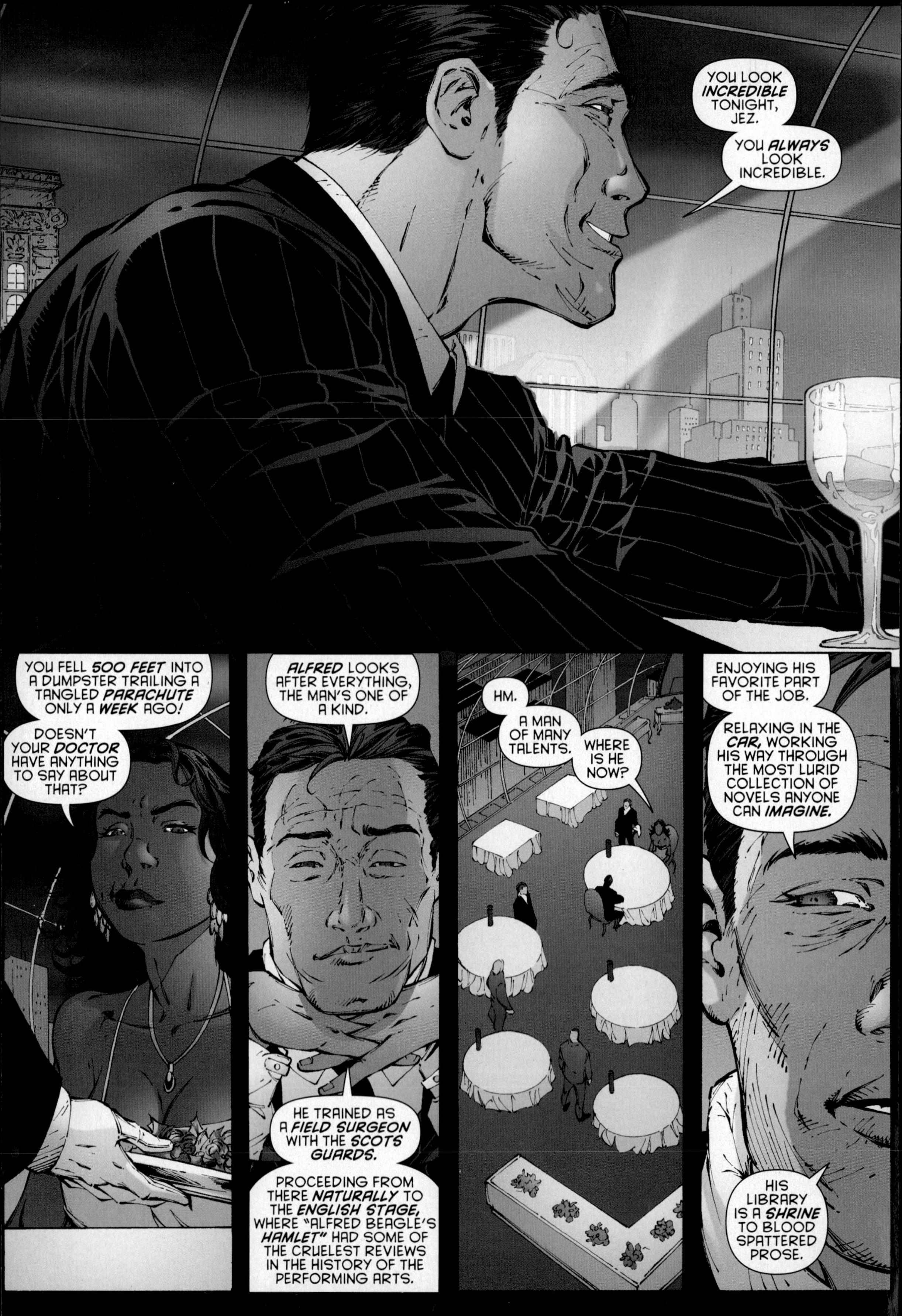
YOU LOOK INCREDIBLE TONIGHT, JEZ.
YOU ALWAYS LOOK INCREDIBLE.
YOU FELL 500 FEET INTO A DUMPSTER TRAILING A TANGLED PARACHUTE ONLY A WEEK AGO!
DOESN'T YOUR DOCTOR HAVE ANYTHING TO SAY ABOUT THAT?
ALFRED LOOKS AFTER EVERYTHING, THE MAN'S ONE OF A KIND.
HE TRAINED AS A FIELD SURGEON WITH THE SCOTS GUARDS.
PROCEEDING FROM THERE NATURALLY TO THE ENGLISH STAGE, WHERE "ALFRED BEAGLE'S HAMLET" HAD SOME OF THE CRUELEST REVIEWS IN THE HISTORY OF THE PERFORMING ARTS.
HM.
A MAN OF MANY TALENTS.
WHERE IS HE NOW?
ENJOYING HIS FAVORITE PART OF THE JOB.
RELAXING IN THE CAR, WORKING HIS WAY THROUGH THE MOST LURID COLLECTION OF NOVELS ANYONE CAN IMAGINE.
HIS LIBRARY IS A SHRINE TO BLOOD SPATTERED PROSE.

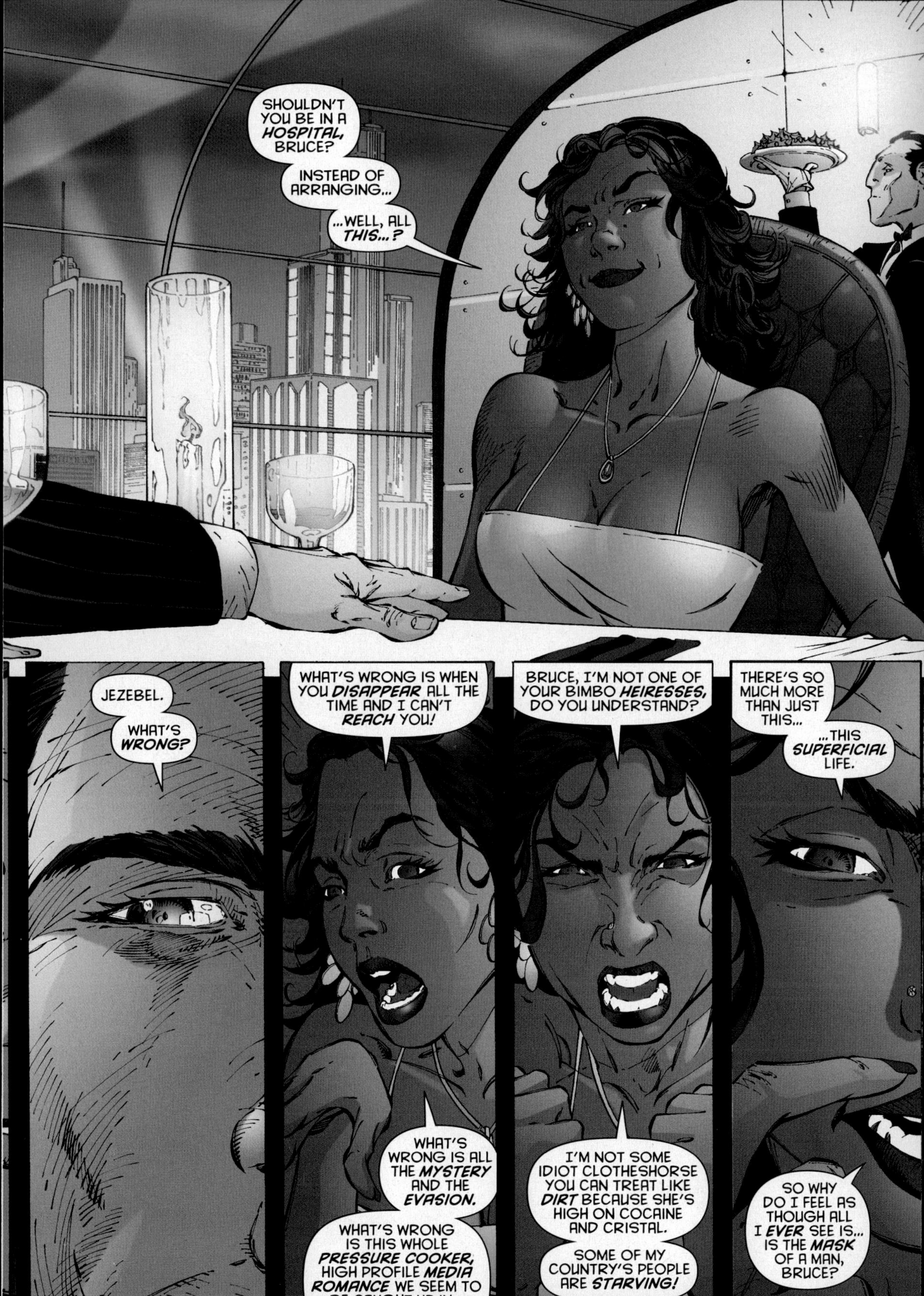
SHOULDN'T YOU BE IN A *HOSPITAL,* BRUCE?
INSTEAD OF ARRANGING...
...WELL, ALL *THIS*...?
JEZEBEL.
WHAT'S *WRONG?*
WHAT'S WRONG IS WHEN YOU *DISAPPEAR* ALL THE TIME AND I CAN'T *REACH* YOU!
WHAT'S WRONG IS ALL THE *MYSTERY* AND THE *EVASION.*
WHAT'S WRONG IS THIS WHOLE *PRESSURE COOKER,* HIGH PROFILE *MEDIA ROMANCE* WE SEEM TO BE CAUGHT UP IN...
BRUCE, I'M NOT ONE OF YOUR BIMBO *HEIRESSES,* DO YOU UNDERSTAND?
I'M NOT SOME IDIOT CLOTHESHORSE YOU CAN TREAT LIKE *DIRT* BECAUSE SHE'S HIGH ON COCAINE AND CRISTAL.
SOME OF MY COUNTRY'S PEOPLE ARE *STARVING!*
THERE'S SO MUCH MORE THAN JUST THIS...
...THIS *SUPERFICIAL* LIFE.
SO WHY DO I FEEL AS THOUGH ALL I *EVER* SEE IS... IS THE *MASK* OF A MAN, BRUCE?

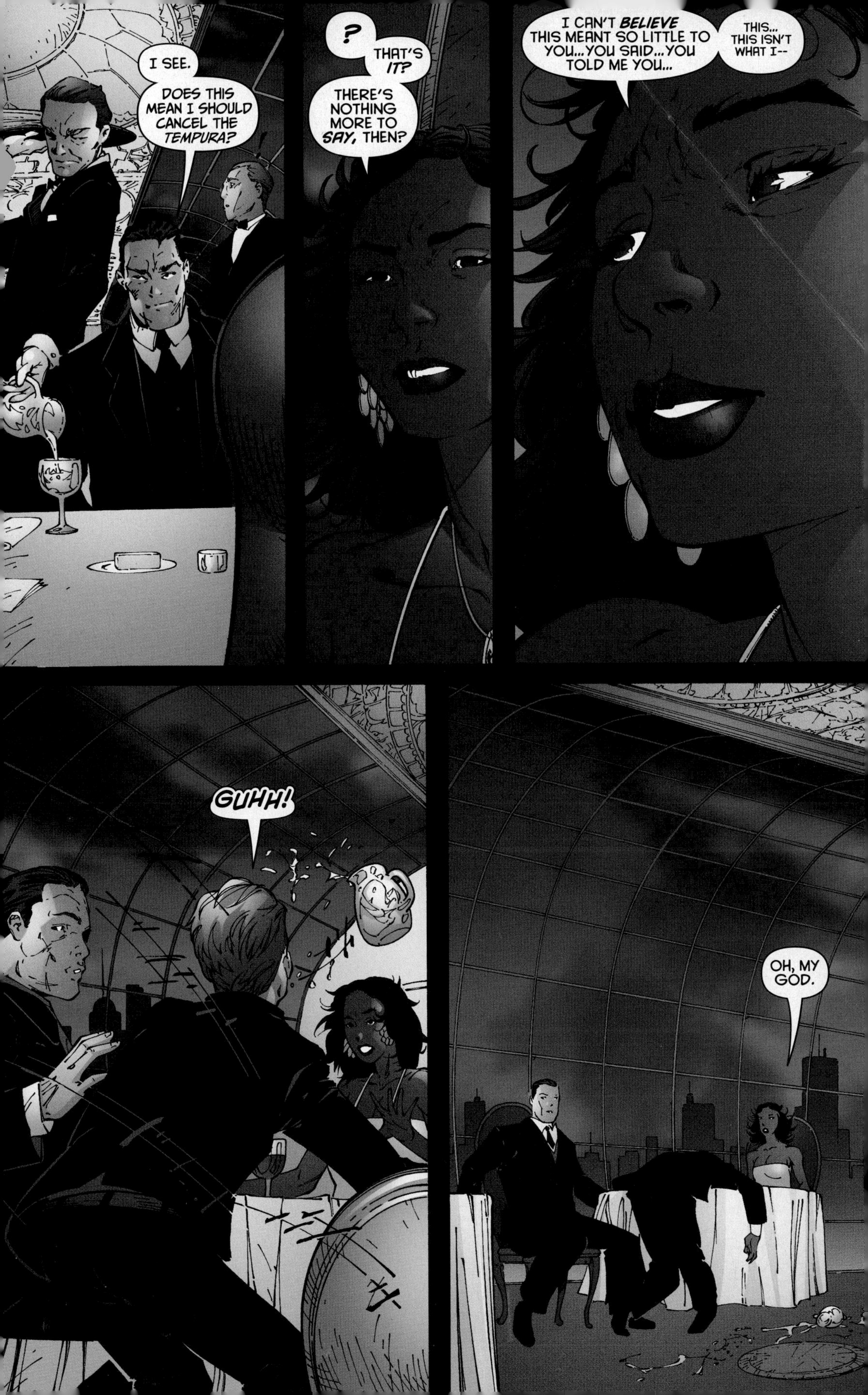
I SEE.
DOES THIS MEAN I SHOULD CANCEL THE *TEMPURA?*
?
THAT'S *IT?*
THERE'S NOTHING MORE TO *SAY,* THEN?
I CAN'T ***BELIEVE*** THIS MEANT SO LITTLE TO YOU...YOU SAID...YOU TOLD ME YOU...
THIS... THIS ISN'T WHAT I--
GUHH!
OH, MY GOD.

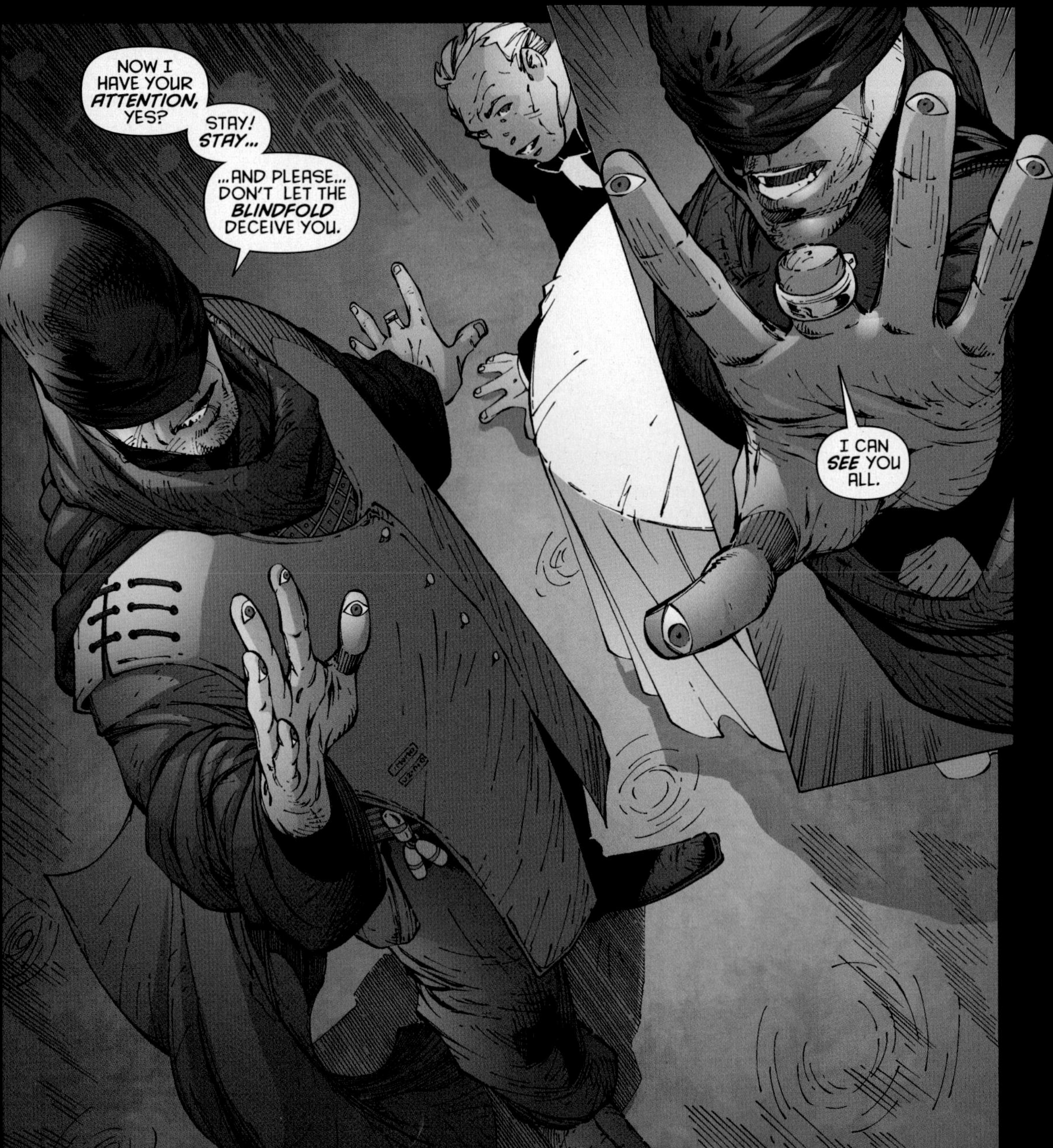
NOW I HAVE YOUR ATTENTION, YES?
STAY! STAY...
...AND PLEASE... DON'T LET THE BLINDFOLD DECEIVE YOU.
I CAN SEE YOU ALL.

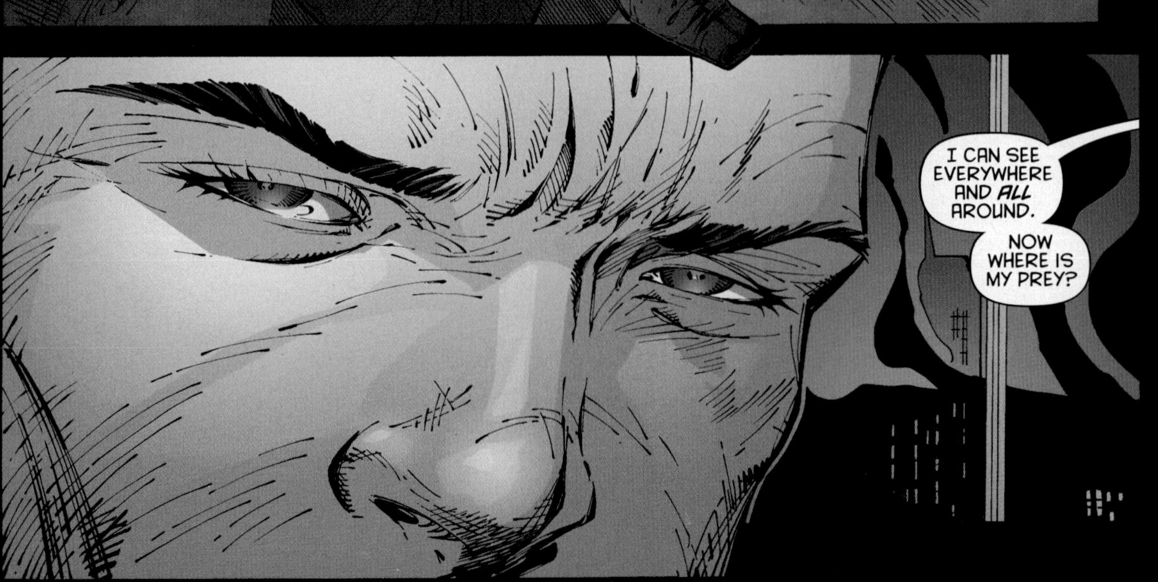
I CAN SEE EVERYWHERE AND ALL AROUND.
NOW WHERE IS MY PREY?

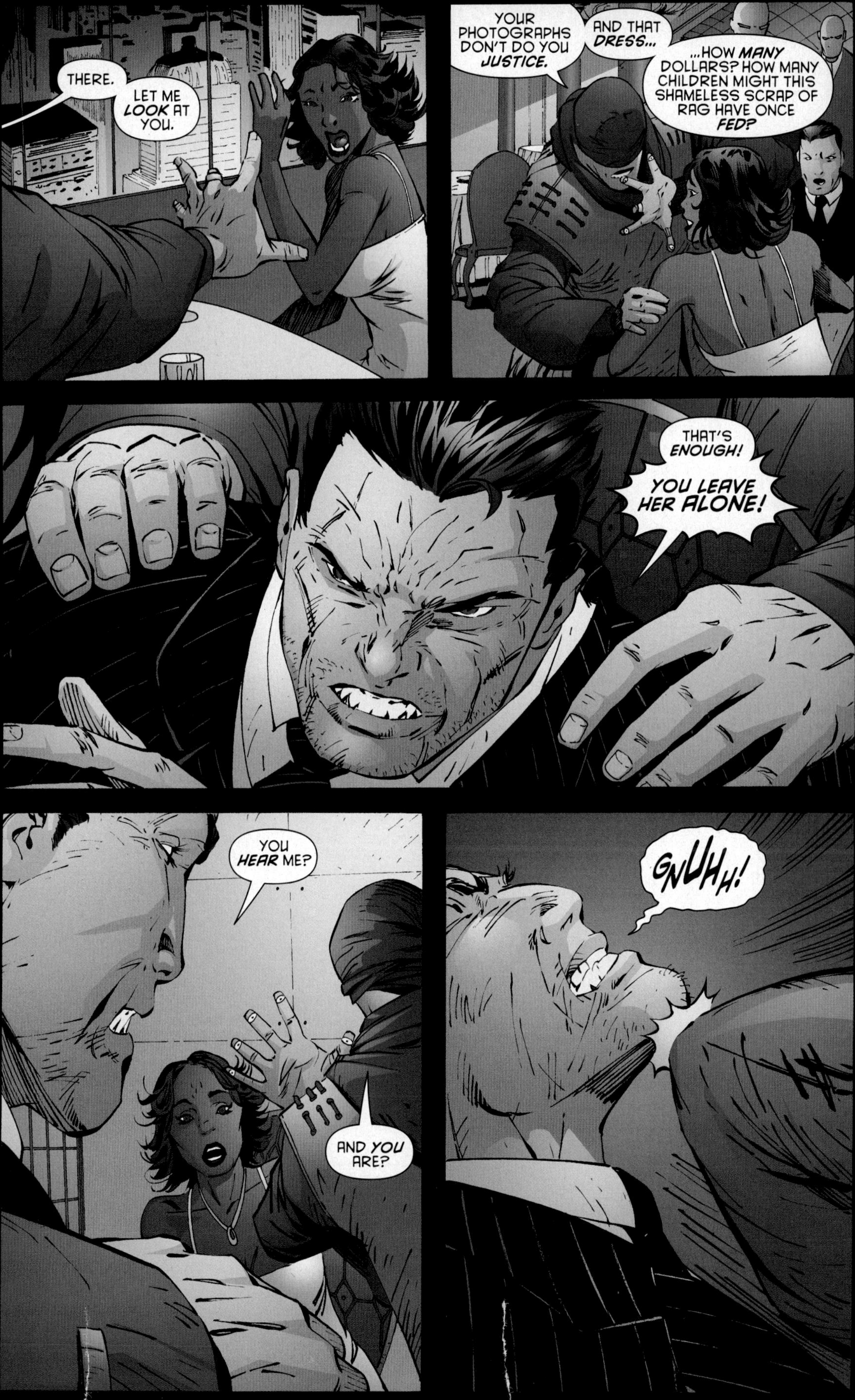
THERE.
LET ME LOOK AT YOU.
YOUR PHOTOGRAPHS DON'T DO YOU JUSTICE.
AND THAT DRESS...
...HOW MANY DOLLARS? HOW MANY CHILDREN MIGHT THIS SHAMELESS SCRAP OF RAG HAVE ONCE FED?
THAT'S ENOUGH!
YOU LEAVE HER ALONE!
YOU HEAR ME?
AND YOU ARE?
GNUHH!

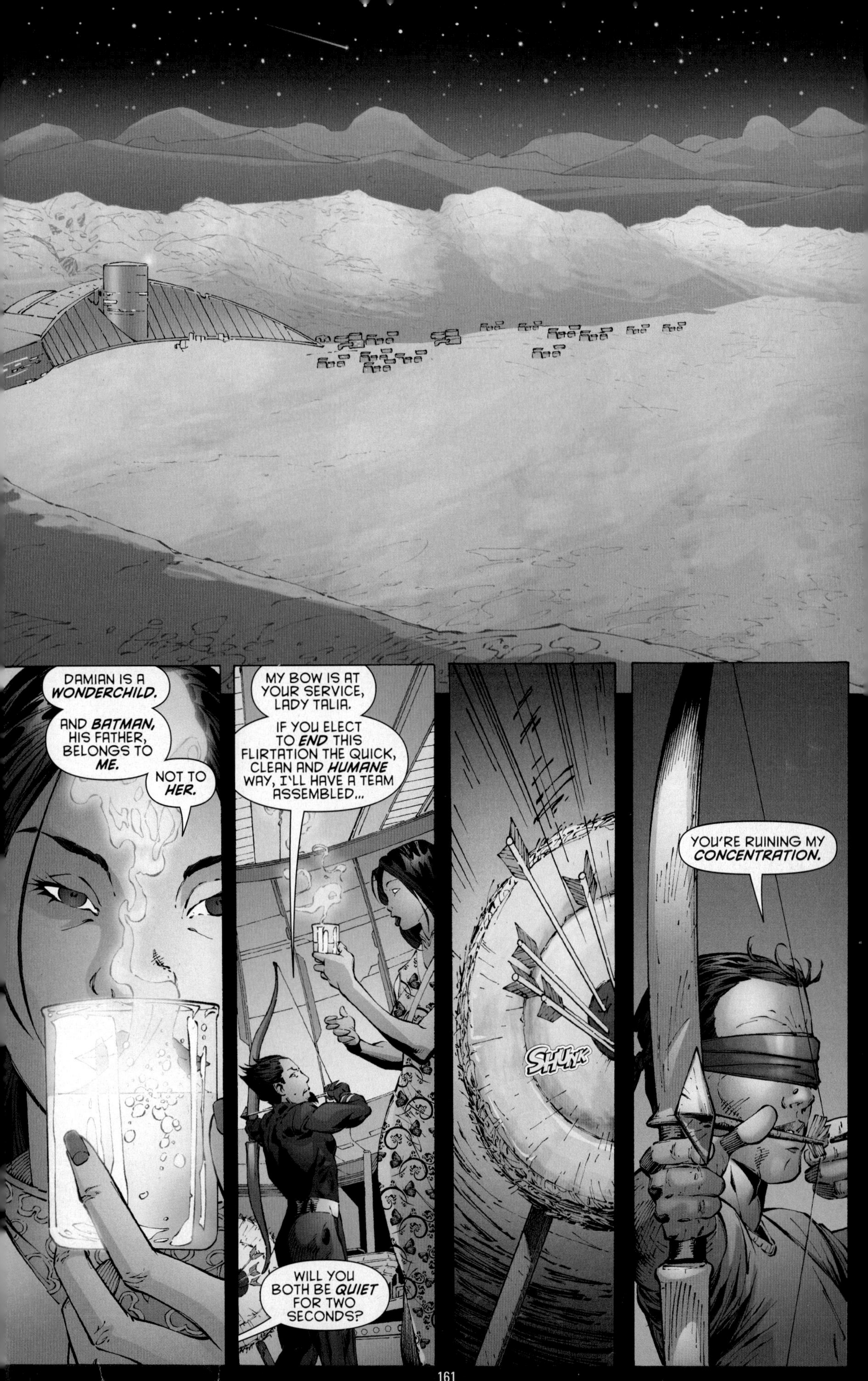
DAMIAN IS A WONDERCHILD.
AND BATMAN, HIS FATHER, BELONGS TO ME.
NOT TO HER.
MY BOW IS AT YOUR SERVICE, LADY TALIA.
IF YOU ELECT TO END THIS FLIRTATION THE QUICK, CLEAN AND HUMANE WAY, I'LL HAVE A TEAM ASSEMBLED...
WILL YOU BOTH BE QUIET FOR TWO SECONDS?
SHUNK
YOU'RE RUINING MY CONCENTRATION.

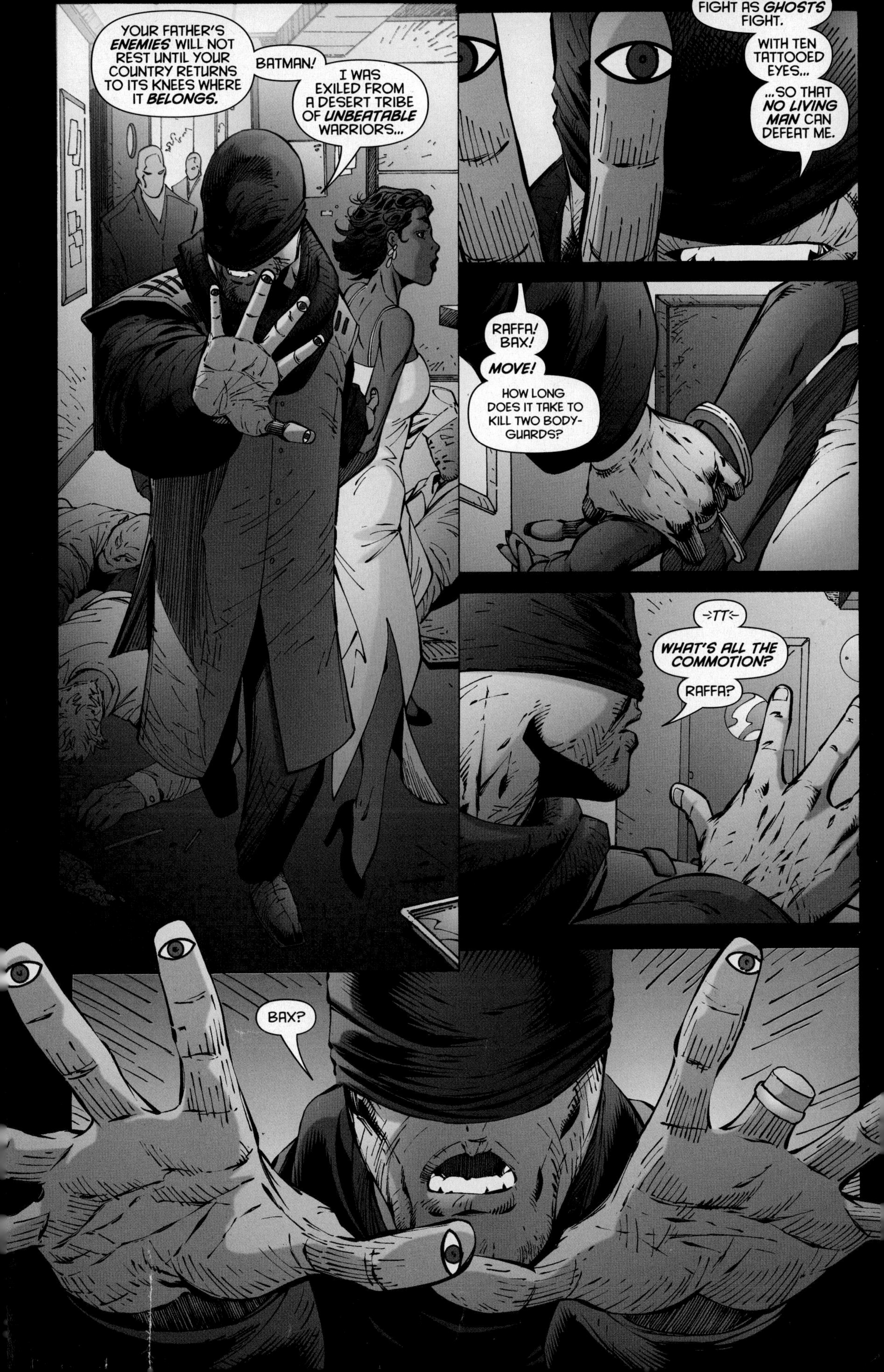
YOUR FATHER'S ENEMIES WILL NOT REST UNTIL YOUR COUNTRY RETURNS TO ITS KNEES WHERE IT BELONGS.
BATMAN!
I WAS EXILED FROM A DESERT TRIBE OF UNBEATABLE WARRIORS...
...TRAINED TO FIGHT AS GHOSTS FIGHT.
WITH TEN TATTOOED EYES...
...SO THAT NO LIVING MAN CAN DEFEAT ME.
RAFFA! BAX!
MOVE!
HOW LONG DOES IT TAKE TO KILL TWO BODY-GUARDS?
TT
WHAT'S ALL THE COMMOTION?
RAFFA?
BAX?

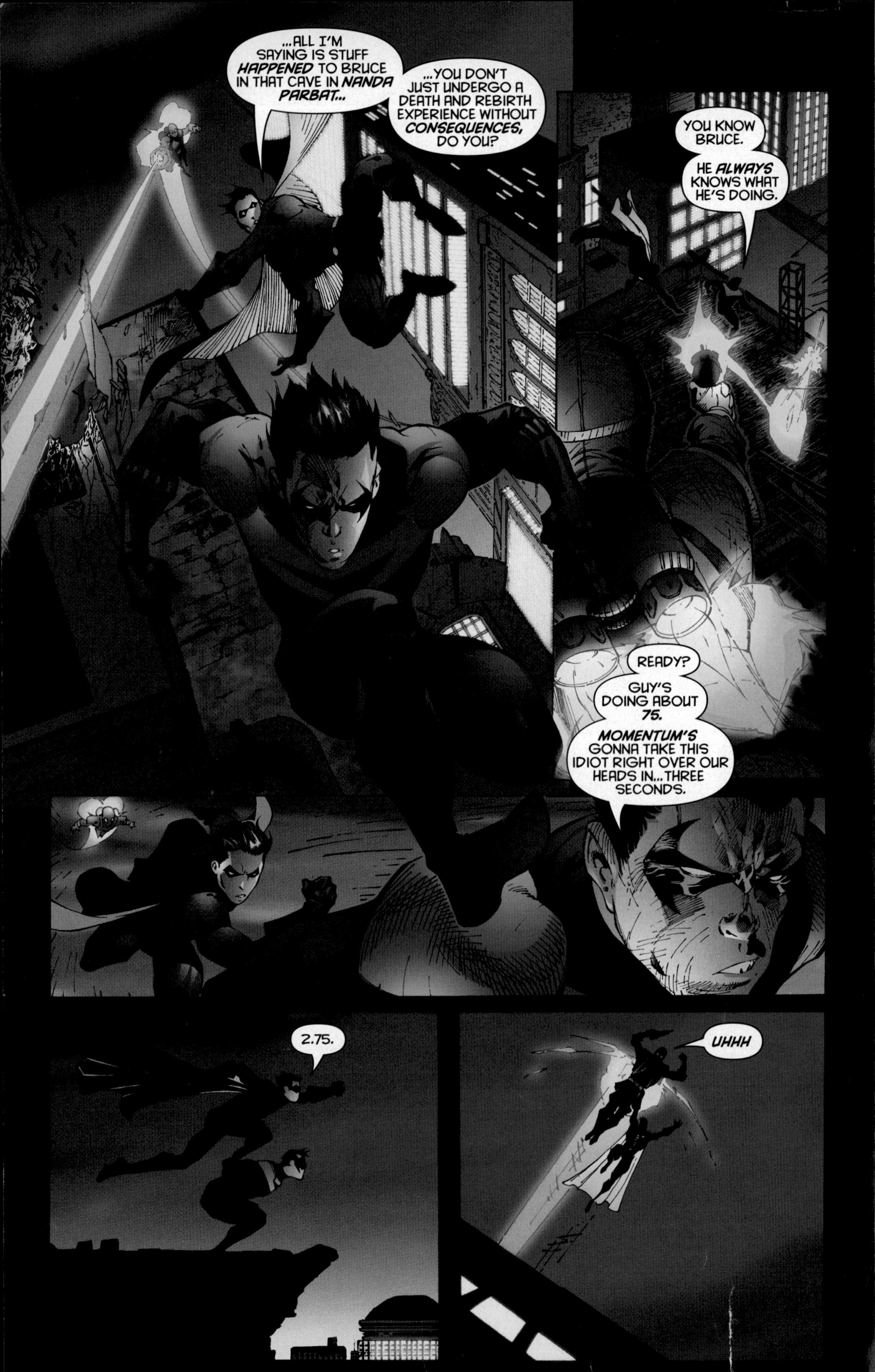
...ALL I'M SAYING IS STUFF HAPPENED TO BRUCE IN THAT CAVE IN NANDA PARBAT...
...YOU DON'T JUST UNDERGO A DEATH AND REBIRTH EXPERIENCE WITHOUT CONSEQUENCES, DO YOU?
YOU KNOW BRUCE.
HE ALWAYS KNOWS WHAT HE'S DOING.
READY?
GUY'S DOING ABOUT 75.
MOMENTUM'S GONNA TAKE THIS IDIOT RIGHT OVER OUR HEADS IN...THREE SECONDS.
2.75.
UHHH

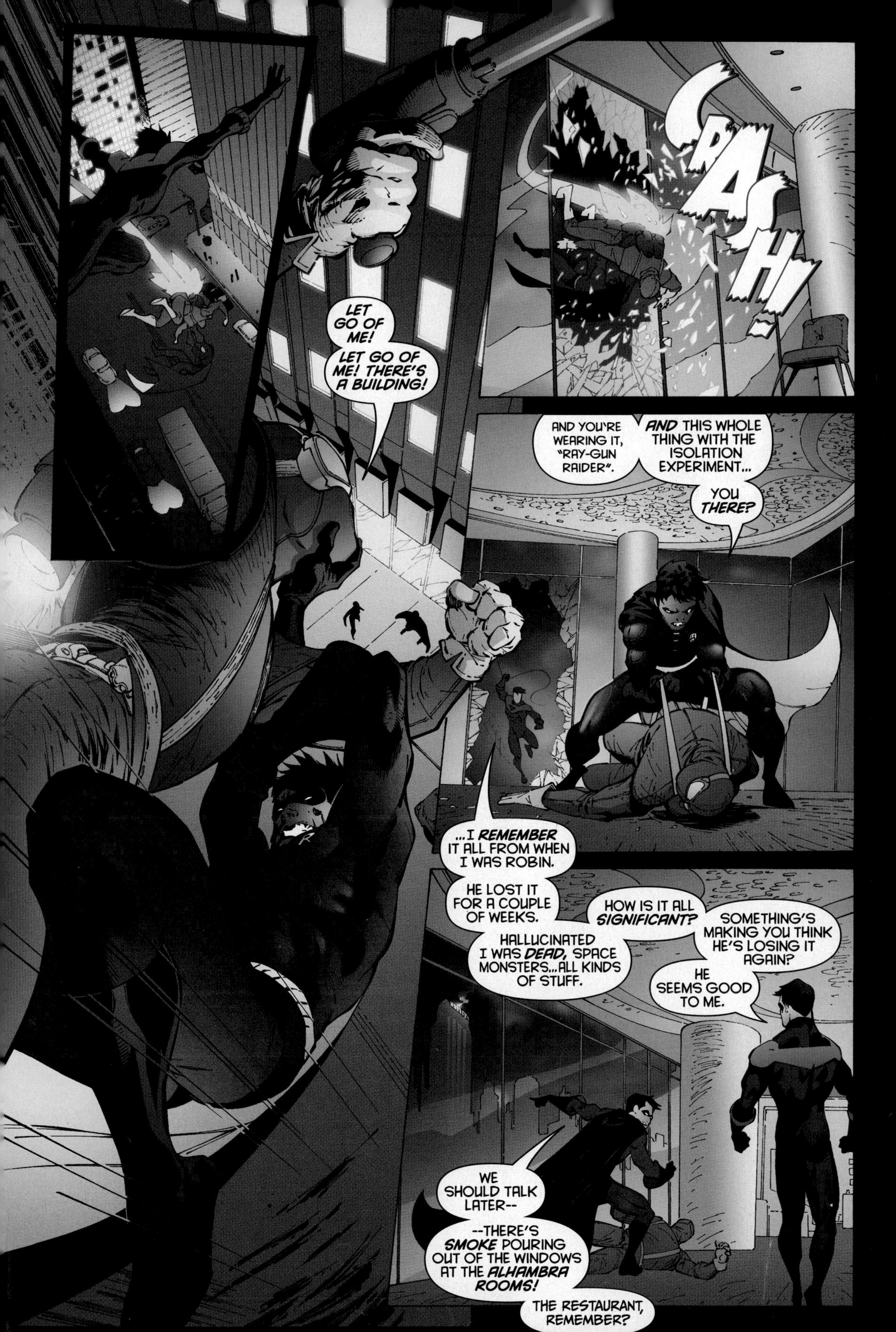
LET GO OF ME! LET GO OF ME! THERE'S A BUILDING!
CRASH!
AND YOU'RE WEARING IT, "RAY-GUN RAIDER".
AND THIS WHOLE THING WITH THE ISOLATION EXPERIMENT...
YOU THERE?
...I REMEMBER IT ALL FROM WHEN I WAS ROBIN.
HE LOST IT FOR A COUPLE OF WEEKS.
HALLUCINATED I WAS DEAD, SPACE MONSTERS...ALL KINDS OF STUFF.
HOW IS IT ALL SIGNIFICANT?
SOMETHING'S MAKING YOU THINK HE'S LOSING IT AGAIN?
HE SEEMS GOOD TO ME.
WE SHOULD TALK LATER--
--THERE'S SMOKE POURING OUT OF THE WINDOWS AT THE ALHAMBRA ROOMS!
THE RESTAURANT, REMEMBER?

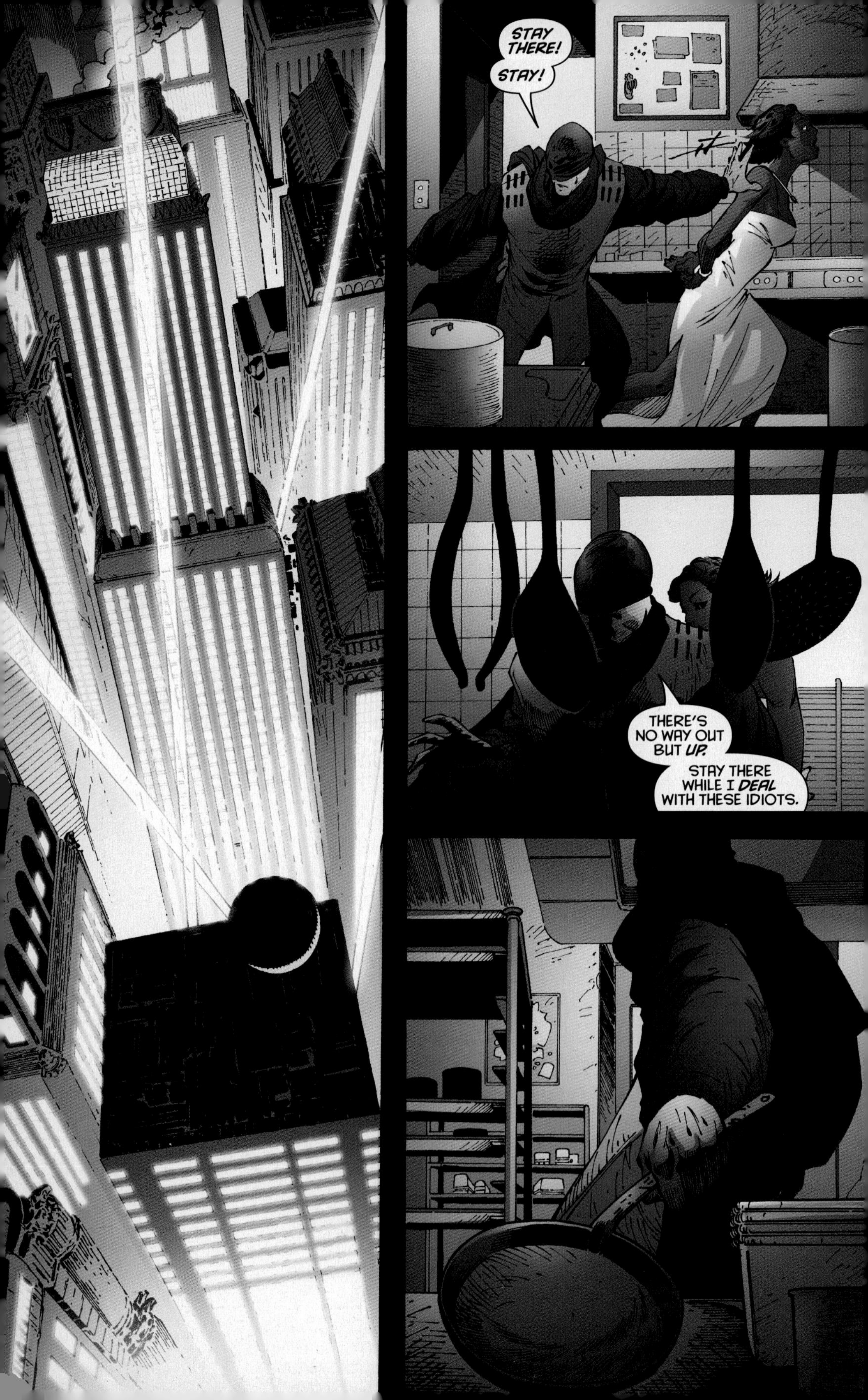
STAY THERE!
STAY!
THERE'S NO WAY OUT BUT UP.
STAY THERE WHILE I DEAL WITH THESE IDIOTS.

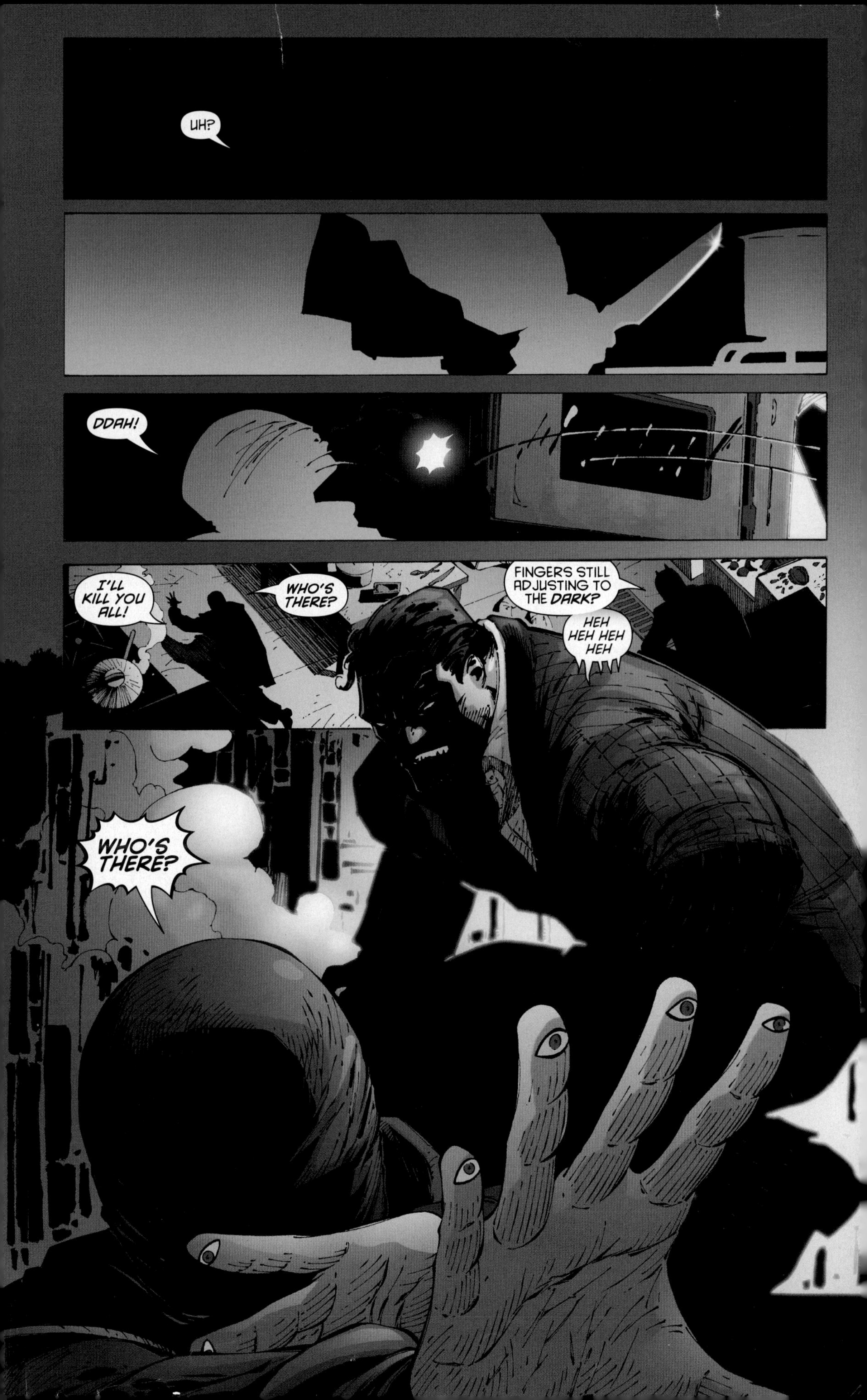
UH?
DDAH!
I'LL KILL YOU ALL!
WHO'S THERE?
FINGERS STILL ADJUSTING TO THE DARK?
HEH HEH HEH HEH
WHO'S THERE?

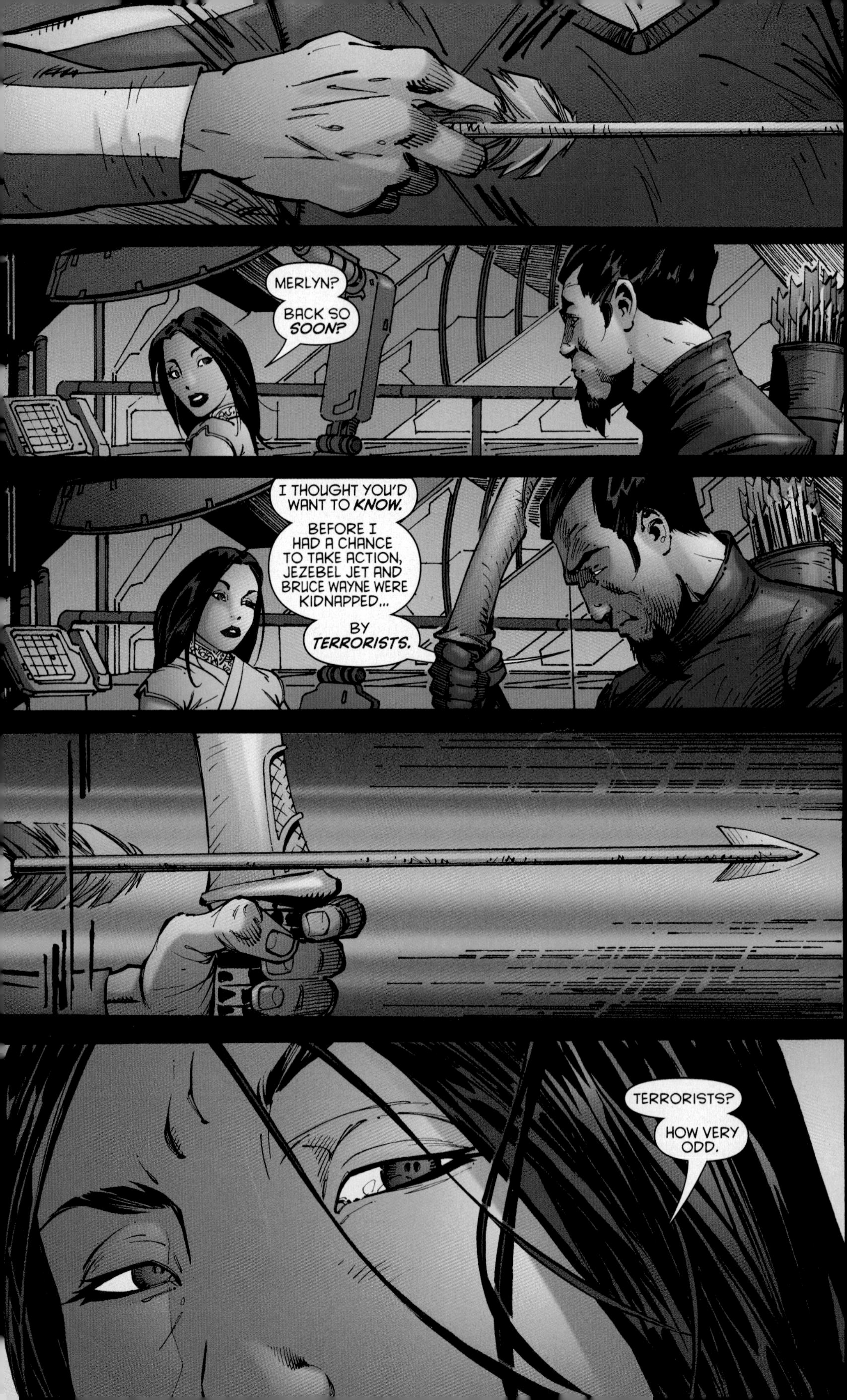
MERLYN?
BACK SO SOON?
I THOUGHT YOU'D WANT TO KNOW.
BEFORE I HAD A CHANCE TO TAKE ACTION, JEZEBEL JET AND BRUCE WAYNE WERE KIDNAPPED...
BY TERRORISTS.
TERRORISTS?
HOW VERY ODD.

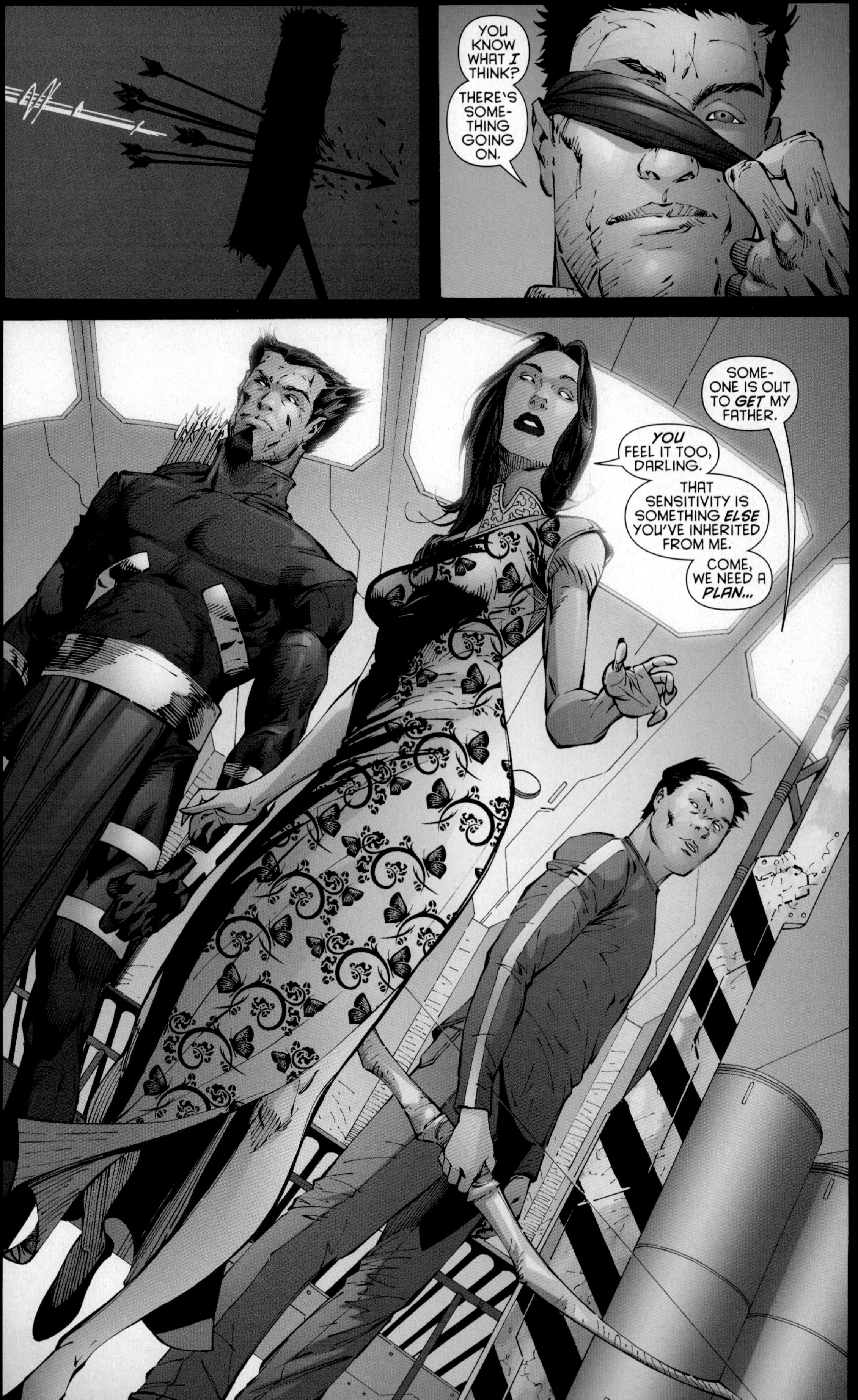
YOU KNOW WHAT I THINK?
THERE'S SOME-THING GOING ON.
SOME-ONE IS OUT TO GET MY FATHER.
YOU FEEL IT TOO, DARLING.
THAT SENSITIVITY IS SOMETHING ELSE YOU'VE INHERITED FROM ME.
COME, WE NEED A PLAN...

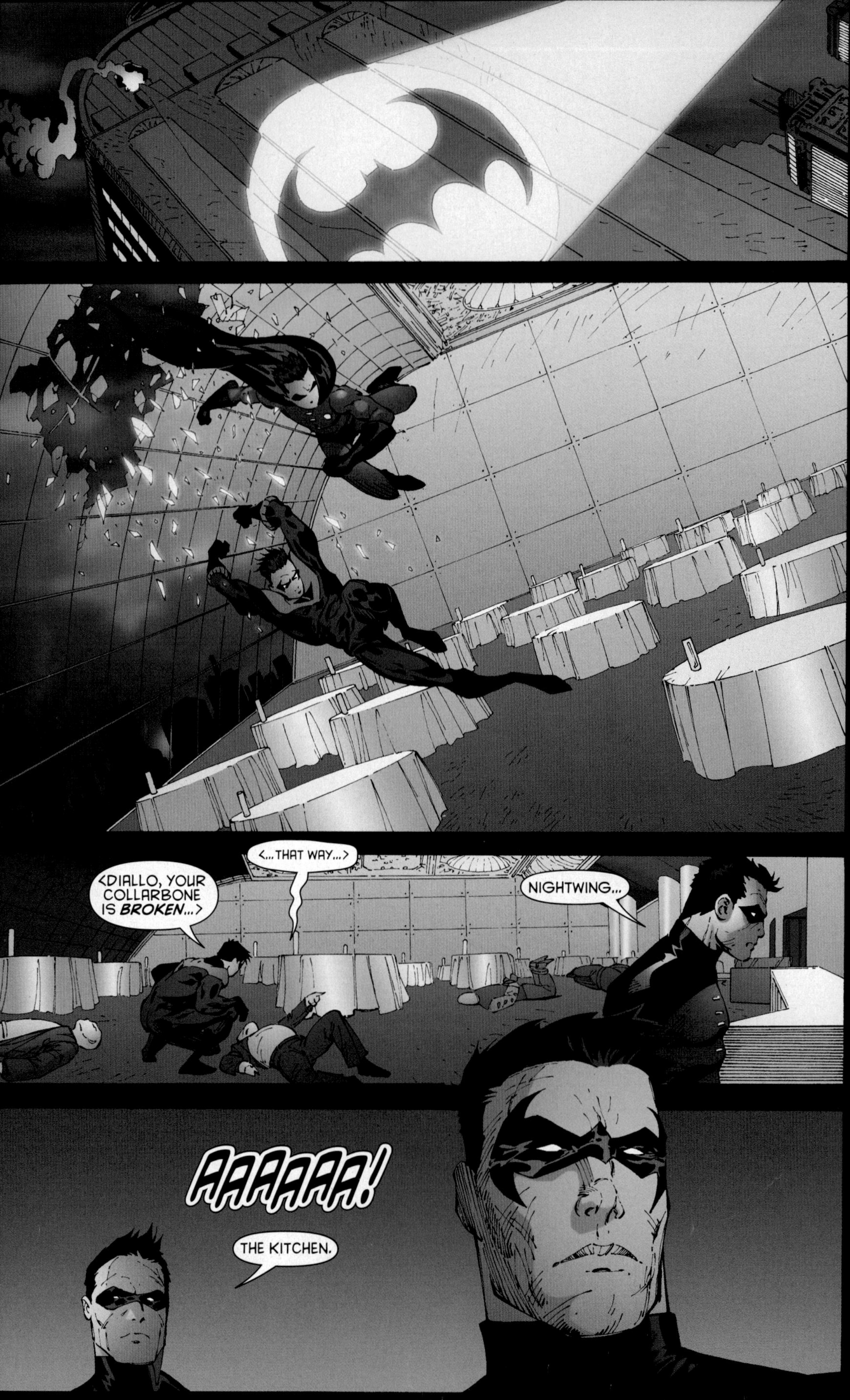

<DIALLO, YOUR COLLARBONE IS **BROKEN**...>
<...THAT WAY...>
NIGHTWING...
AAAAAA!
THE KITCHEN.

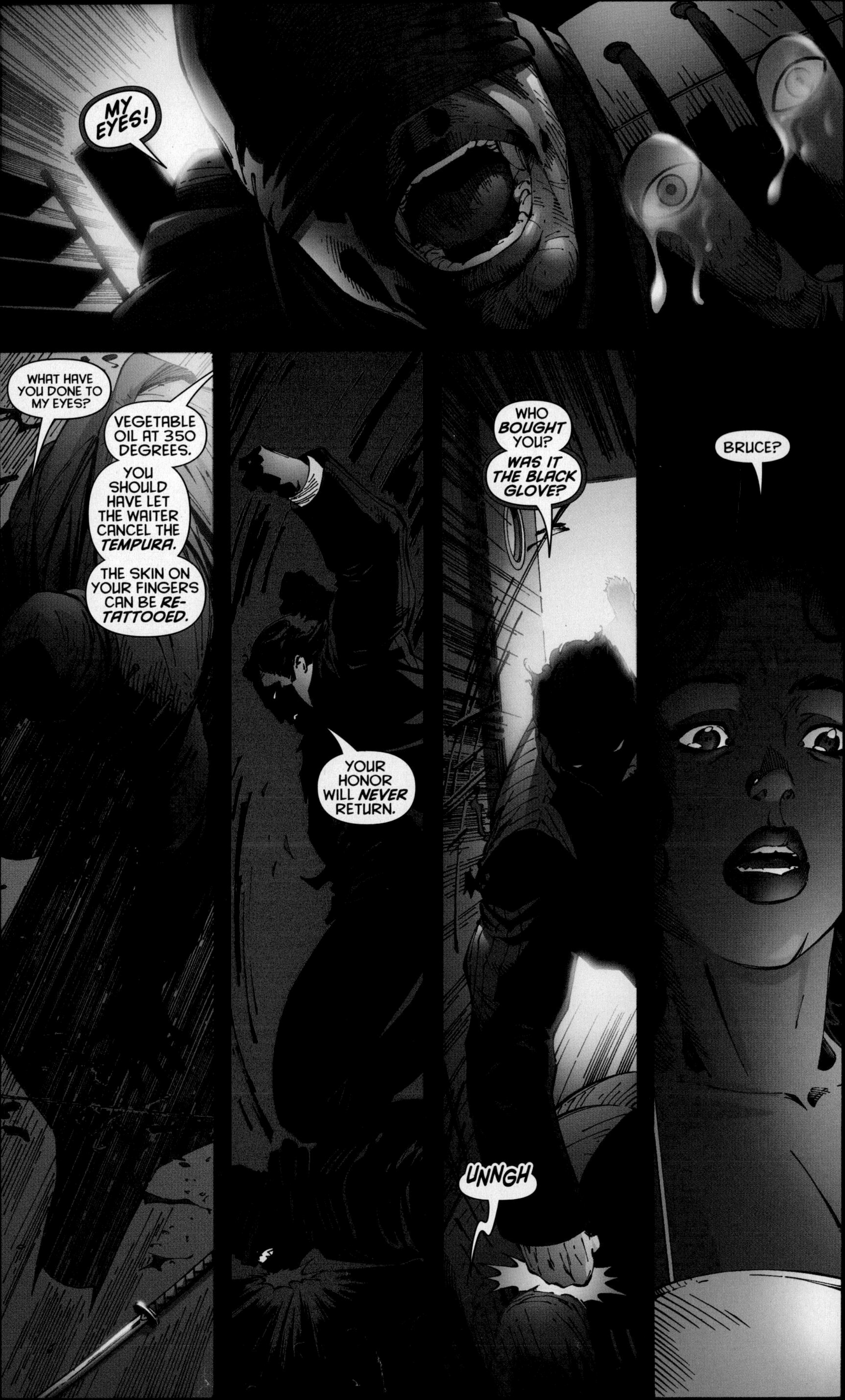
MY EYES!
WHAT HAVE YOU DONE TO MY EYES?
VEGETABLE OIL AT 350 DEGREES.
YOU SHOULD HAVE LET THE WAITER CANCEL THE *TEMPURA*.
THE SKIN ON YOUR FINGERS CAN BE *RE-TATTOOED*.
YOUR HONOR WILL *NEVER* RETURN.
WHO *BOUGHT* YOU?
WAS IT THE BLACK GLOVE?
UNNGH
BRUCE?

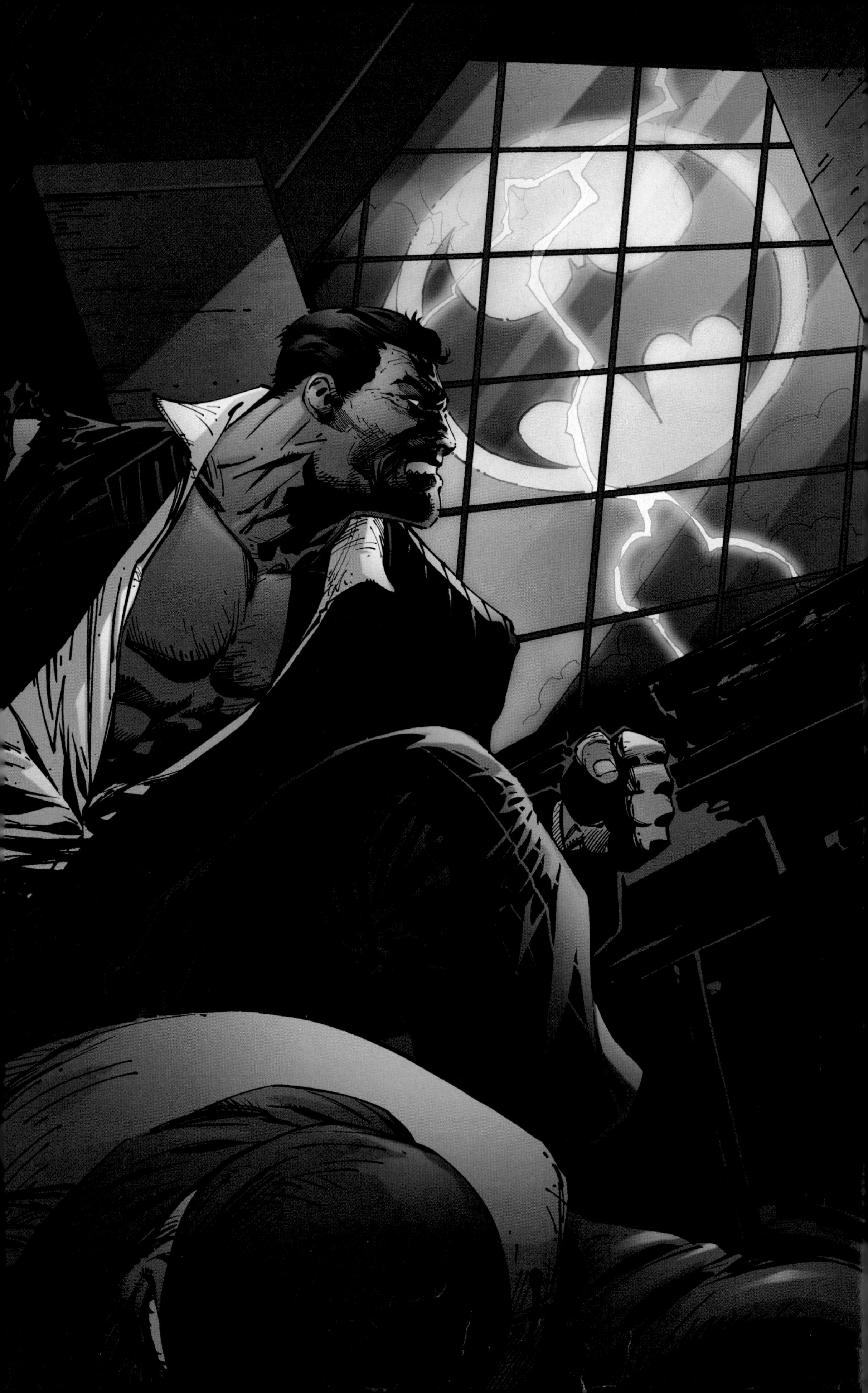

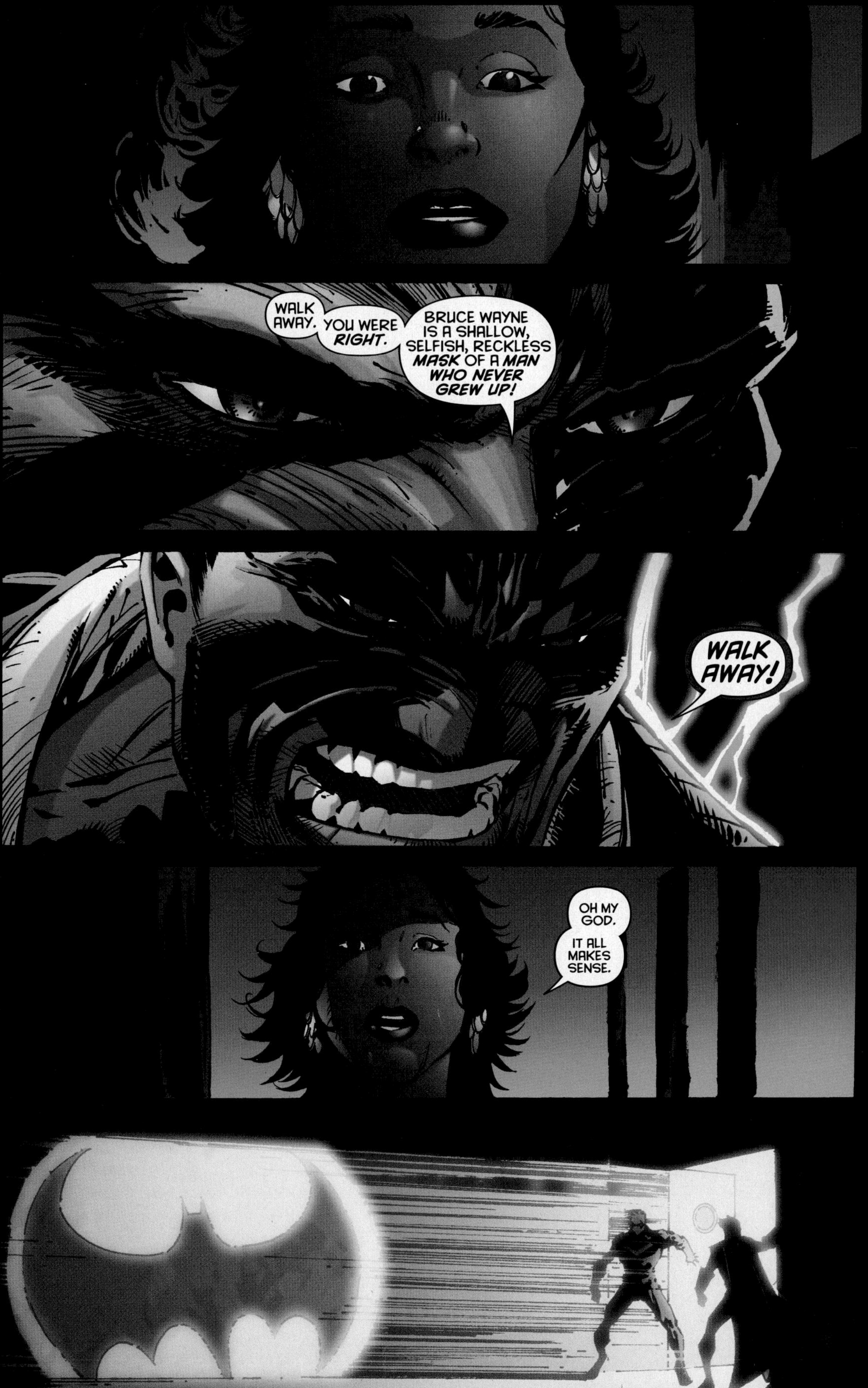
WALK AWAY.
YOU WERE RIGHT.
BRUCE WAYNE IS A SHALLOW, SELFISH, RECKLESS MASK OF A MAN WHO NEVER GREW UP!
WALK AWAY!
OH MY GOD.
IT ALL MAKES SENSE.

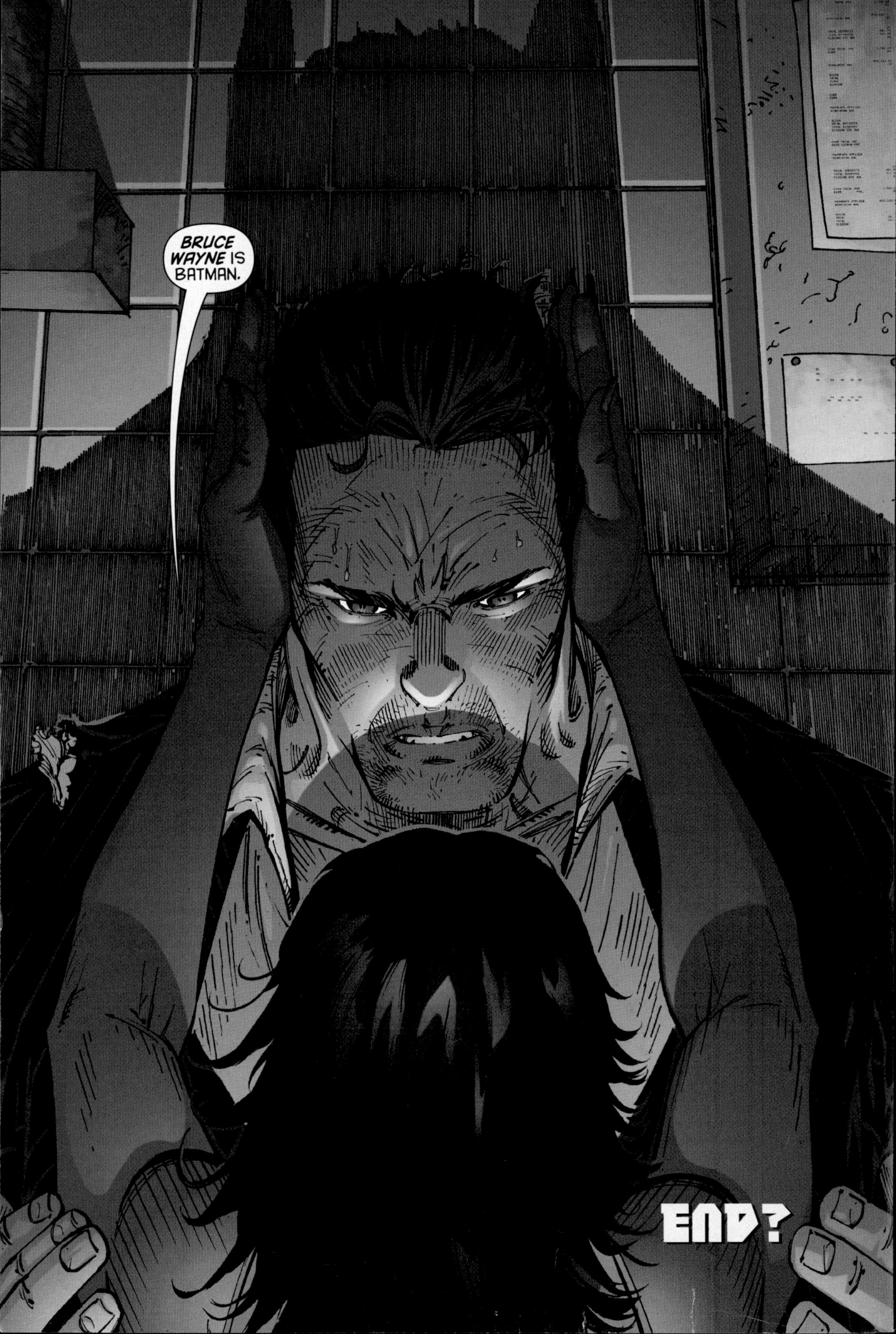
BRUCE WAYNE IS BATMAN.
END?

The story continues in

BATMAN
R.I.P.